Monatshefte Occasional Volume 13

Re-Reading Wagner

Edited by

Reinhold Grimm
and
Jost Hermand

Published for *Monatshefte*
The University of Wisconsin Press

The University of Wisconsin Press
114 North Murray Street
Madison, Wisconsin 53715

3 Henrietta Street
London WC2E 8LU, England

Copyright © 1993
The Board of Regents of the University of Wisconsin System
All rights reserved

5 4 3 2 1

Printed in the United States of America

The musical examples from *Die Meistersinger,* acts I and II, are from *The Mastersingers of Nuremberg: An Opera in Three Acts.* Arrangement by Karl Klindworth. English translation by Frederick Jameson. Copyright © 1932 G. Schirmer, Inc. (ASCAP). International Copyright Secured. All Rights Reserved. Used by Permission.

The musical example from *Die Walküre,* Act I, is from *Die Walkure.* Arrangement by Karl Klindworth. English translation by Frederick Jameson. Copyright © 1932 G. Schirmer, Inc. International Copyright Secured. All Rights Reserved. Used by Permission.

Contents

LIBRARY
ALMA COLLEGE
ALMA, MICHIGAN

Preface

A conference about Richard Wagner does not require any special justification. For more than 150 years, his works have occasioned not only worldwide enthusiasm, but also worldwide controversy – depending on the political context in which they have been placed. Only following the demise of the Third Reich, which sought to exploit his oeuvre primarily for nationalistic purposes, did it appear for a time as if the controversy about his place in the history of German culture, if not world culture, would finally subside once and for all. But fortunately, that did not happen. Wagner is still not a dead master whom one mentions in respectful but bored terms; his libretti and the accompanying theoretical writings remain rich in engaging, if frequently also irritating features.

And therefore the Twenty-First Wisconsin Workshop, held in Madison on October 12 to 14, 1990, under the title "Re-Reading Wagner," was witness to many lively discussions. The speakers who addressed problems of Wagner scholarship included Marc A. Weiner (Indiana University), Tamara S. Evans (Queens College), Peter Uwe Hohendahl (Cornell University), Edward R. Haymes (Cleveland State University), Jost Hermand (University of Wisconsin), a student collective (University of Wisconsin), Frank Trommler (University of Pennsylvania), and Hans Rudolf Vaget (Smith College). A consistent leitmotif throughout their presentations was a new, critical interrogation of Wagner's ideological orientation. Their work appears in the present volume in a revised and, in part, vastly expanded form. It is our hope that this book will contribute to keeping alive the controversy about Wagner – in its juxtaposition of progressively social and ecological as well as regressively chauvinistic and anti-Semitic elements – in order not to neglect the one Wagner in favor of the other.

The editors are above all indebted to the Anonymous Fund of the University of Wisconsin–Madison, which generously covered the travel and accommodation costs of the invited speakers, and to the Vilas Trust Fund, which made possible the publication of this volume.

Re-Reading Wagner

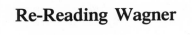

"Am Mythenstein":
Richard Wagner and Swiss Society

TAMARA S. EVANS

A Safe Haven

In 1849, Richard Wagner—composer, *Kapellmeister* to the King of Saxony and, most recently, revolutionary to boot—found himself on the run, not from his creditors, for a change, but from the police who were eager to round up members of the Dresden insurgence. En route to Paris, where both Liszt and his wife Minna wanted him to try his luck, he slipped into Switzerland and, sharing the emotions of so many other political refugees before and after him, was overcome with relief and joy. "When I drove down from Oberstraß into Zurich that evening, the last day in May, at six o'clock," he tells us in his autobiography, "and saw for the first time the Glarner Alps that encircle the lake gleaming in the sunset, I at once resolved, though without being conscious of it, to avoid everything that could prevent my settling there."[1] A colleague from his Würzburg days now living in Zurich put him up and introduced him to Johann Jakob Sulzer, Secretary of the Canton as well as President of the Committee for the Support of German Refugees, who provided Wagner—*mirabile dictu*—with a full valid federal passport right away.

Wagner traveled on to Paris but found the city as little to his liking as on his first visit. Within a week he informed Minna, who was sulking and worrying in Dresden, of his decision to settle in Switzerland: ". . . what I can offer you is a place where you can recover your health of body and mind, and that place is the splendid town of Zurich . . . There in the German-speaking part of Switzerland we shall feel at home . . ."[2] From Minna's point of view, Zurich, teeming with refugees, was too close to Germany and Austria to provide a safe haven; Wagner knew better. "As regards our residence in Switzerland, don't entertain any fear! The fugitives are nothing to me," he wrote to her in August and continued most confidently: "*I* don't rank here at all as a fugitive, for I have my full Swiss pass and permit for a year's residence, i.e., as good as for ever . . . I'm threatened with no other disagreeables, as I have sponsors and sureties enough here to enable me to be fully naturalized in the Canton . . ."[3]

Later that fall Minna arrived with bag and baggage. Although she was "ashamed of [their] stay in Zurich and [thought they] ought to make every one believe that [they were] in Paris,"[4] the Wagners settled down, and Zurich was to be their home for nearly a decade.

His years in Zurich were a productive period. As conductor, Wagner was much sought-after, and he gave Zurich's musical public his very best. He wrote a series of key essays beginning with *Art and Revolution* in 1849, soon to be followed by *The Artwork of the Future* (1850), *Judaism in Music* (1850), *Opera and Drama* (1851), *A Theater at Zurich* (1851), and *A Communication to My Friends* (1851). Exile did not stifle Wagner's poetic and musical creativity: the texts for *Die Walküre* and *Das Rheingold* were finished in 1852; in late 1853 and 1854, respectively, he had completed both scores. By 1857, while working on the *Siegfried* score and following the Wagners' move to the "Asylum" adjoining the Wesendonck estate, he diverted his energies in part to the composition of *Tristan und Isolde,* in part to the *Wesendonck Lieder* and to what was to become Zurich's *cause célèbre* of the season. Minna's jealousy of Mathilde Wesendonck and the subsequent unseemly encounters between the two women in the summer of 1858 precipitated what had been in the making for quite some time: Wagner fled, some of his belongings were confiscated, and those that were left Minna put up for sale in the local papers. Minna then paid up the debts her husband had accrued with various local merchants and left for Germany.[5]

Wagner was on the road again. When he returned to Switzerland early in 1864, pursued by his Viennese creditors, quite distraught, and begging to be put up at the home of François and Eliza Wille, he wrote to a friend that "[he] should have gone anywhere but here, where everything is so bitter and redolent of the grave."[6] His talent for exaggeration and self-pity aside, the fact remains that "the glorious country [lying] before him as if by magic"[7] — as he put it in 1849 — was now eliciting some very unpleasant remembrances.

What then were the contributing aspects that brought about what some biographers have called "the catastrophe"? The story of the rise and fall of Richard Wagner in Zurich cannot be reduced to the chronicle of an unhappy marriage and an ill-starred love affair. It is more importantly the story of an artist who went about the wrong way (at least from the point of view of the Athenians on the Limmat) when — with plans of revolutionizing, in grand style, Swiss musical and theatrical life — he also hoped to rescue the career he had jeopardized in the Dresden uprising. This is a story, furthermore, that cannot be retold in simple diachronic terms since various strands, subplots, and subtexts constitute the whole. To make sense of this confounded plot and to come to a better understanding of the ambivalent relationships between Wagner and the Swiss, I propose to take a closer look at Wagner's plans for "a theater at Zurich," at his financial situation, and at his role as a refugee on the one hand, and, on the other, at Swiss politics, economics, and cultural life during the 1840s and 1850s.

A Theater at Zurich?

As early as 1850, Wagner began to entertain lofty plans both for himself and for Zurich, a town he judged to be "devoid of all art in the public sense" and yet educable.[8] In his essay "A Theater at Zurich," Wagner outlines a radical reformation of the local theater which—caught in the vicious circle of inadequate revenues and dull adaptations of shallow foreign plays and operas—he has found in a sorry state indeed.[9] According to Wagner, the sentiment between theater and public is one of "reciprocal contempt,"[10] but the time has come for a "social humanizing of Art" (52). He suggests the following remedies: only those artworks should be produced that the artists can handle adequately, and that are easily understood by the audience "because peculiar to [their] nature" (45). Since such works are few and far between, new dramatic works will have to be created. But local demand for dramatic works having been met by Paris (with its "merely . . . brilliant technical routine"), native artists have diverted their creative energies from the theater, and thus "the German spirit has completely lost itself in an almost exclusively literary sphere of art" (49).

The Theater at Zurich, a public art institute, was, according to Wagner's prescription, to promote native dramatic art creations; it should also draw on "unknown native forces" (50) for its performers. Wagner foresaw "the gradual extinction of the player-class as a specific caste" and envisioned "its ascension into an artistic fellowship in which the whole civic society, according to aptitude and liking, would more or less take part" (51). Wagner pointed out that precedents of this common culture already existed in Zurich: there were frequent public festivals in town, and, in Wagner's view, "pictures from Folklife or from history . . . [constituted] the chief attraction of these pageants"; there were, as well, lay performances in certain country districts that bore witness to "this dramatic bent of the nation's open culture" (52). Finally, Wagner suggested the constitution of a Commission for Theatrical Affairs whose members, friends of dramatic art in Zurich, would collect voluntary contributions towards the support of the undertaking for a year. And how did Zurich respond to Wagner's essay? The leading circles remained indifferent. With the exception of the president of the local Musical Society, people agreed that these ideas "were all very grand, but unfortunately quite impracticable."[11] Gottfried Keller enjoyed reading the publication but was also skeptical regarding its consequences.[12] Besides, Keller was living in Berlin and did not count. So much, then, for a model theater in Zurich.

Simultaneously with his civic-oriented proposals for improving the Zurich theater, Wagner envisioned the future of his own career along more autocratic lines. If only he had 10,000 thalers, he wrote to Uhlig in the fall of 1850, he would arrange the following: "Here, where I happen to be, and where many a thing is far from bad—I would erect, after my own plans, in a beautiful field near the town, a rough theater of planks and beams, and merely furnish it with decorations and machinery necessary for the production of *Siegfried*." His ideas concerning the search for the cast and the musicians parallels his suggestions in "A Theater at Zurich": he would select the best singers to be found anywhere, and would try to form a chorus consisting for the most part of amateurs; the formation of the orchestra would be done the same way. "After the third performance of *Siegfried* in one week," Wagner continues, "the theater would be pulled down, and my score burnt. To those persons who had been pleased with the thing I should then say, 'Now do likewise.' But if they wanted to hear something new from me, I should say, '*You* get the money!' Well, do I seem quite mad to you? It may be so, but to attain this end is the hope of my life, the prospect which alone can tempt me to take in hand a work of art. So—get me 10,000 thalers— that's all!" [13]

In modified version, without the annihilatory flourish envisioned in his letter to Uhlig, such a happening—"the first Wagner festival," according to Martin Gregor-Dellin[14]—was brought about in 1853 on Wagner's fortieth birthday. The Zurich bigwigs and Otto Wesendonck had loosened their purse strings for the occasion.[15] The enormous success of the three concerts given on three consecutive nights under Wagner's direction together with the choral societies' torchlight serenade in his honor gave him "great hopes for accomplishing wonderful things here in the future," as he put it in a letter to Ferdinand Heine. "One day I shall certainly myself give performances here of my operas, and also of the *Nibelungen;* but naturally under quite exceptional circumstances."[16] Liszt, who visited Wagner shortly after the May concerts, shared his optimism. "[Wagner] is not abandoning his Zurich theatrical projects, and wishes to construct a new building—for which a certain number of subscribers would have to guarantee the funds," he wrote to the Princess of Sayn-Wittgenstein. "In any case he will give himself the pleasure of organizing something quite *unheard-of* as soon as he has finished the composition of his *Nibelungen,* and I willingly support him in this idea. If, as I believe, his importance continues to increase, and to become altogether predominant in Germany and Switzerland—there can be no doubt that one will succeed in finding the 100,000 francs that are necessary to realize his idea of *Bühnenfestspiel.* I imagine that in the summer of 1856 he will assemble here the company he will need to give his four dramas—and it will probably not be a bad speculation even from the pecuniary point of view—for he could easily attract several thousand foreign visitors to this place for a festival of this kind."[17]

For some years to come, Wagner stuck to his plans; he found an ideal field where the *Nibelungen* Theater could be constructed in the Zurich suburb of Hottingen.[18] The location is indeed spectacular; in later years, the city built its world-famous mental institution there, whose name, to be sure, is neither Wahnfried nor Einfried. In 1855, Wagner even considered the village of Brunnen on Lake Lucerne as festival site: lake barges, fastened together by carpenters and anchored in the bay of Brunnen, would accommodate the stage and the orchestra; the audience would be seated along the shore. The mountains of Uri would provide the most spectacular natural backdrop. Had all this come to pass—thus the speculation of Max Fehr, a Swiss Wagnerian in the 1930s—then Brunnhilde's rock would have emerged from the same waters that wash around Schiller's Rock nearby.[19] In 1859, this rock, rising about thirty feet above lake level, was dedicated to Friedrich Schiller on the occasion of his one-hundredth birthday as a token of Swiss gratitude to the author who, with his *Wilhelm Tell,* had given the Swiss founding myth its definitive form—at least from a 19th-century point of view. Its real name, however, is *Mythenstein,* named after the *Mythen,* two prominent peaks in the region.

Wagner, a frequent vacationer in the area, did not only know the Mythenstein; he also knew his Schiller. In the very first scene of *Wilhelm Tell,* the fisherman comments on the rising storm in highly dramatic language: "Der graue Talvogt kommt, dumpf brüllt der Firn, / Der Mythenstein zieht seine Haube an, / Und kalt her bläst es aus dem Wetterloch . . ."[20] When, the following summer, Wagner witnessed a storm on the lake, he took heed and eventually abandoned his plan of a floating stage. Had he achieved his plan for an open-air Nibelungen Festspiel in Brunnen, the audience would have seen not only the Mythenstein but also the Rütli—the very cradle of Swiss democracy where, according to legend, the founding fathers took their sacred oath to fight tyranny. Wagner's fascination with this site reveals the magnitude of his ambitions on several counts: the *Nibelungen* production would have taken place in the region where Schiller's operatic *Wilhelm Tell* was located, and thus helped to confirm his own position in the tradition of *German* dramatic art; relying on the Swiss collective memory, he could have encouraged the association of the Swiss myth of liberation—Nordic in origin—with the Germanic myth of the *Nibelungen.* And he would thus have been the creator of a *Gesamtmythos.* Yet nothing came of it, and all subsequent efforts to organize Swiss musical life and raise its levels to international standards failed as well. Why?

Cabin Fever

By 1856, Wagner had given up all plans for a *Bühnenfestspiel* in Switzerland. Clearly, the general lack of enthusiasm with which his daring projects were met time and again had taken its toll. As early as 1852, he occasionally signaled his profound alienation; he pleaded for amnesty, asked Liszt to intervene on his behalf, hoping to return to Germany or Austria where he would find more enlightened sponsors as well as larger devoted audiences. But year after year new "wanted" circulars were issued, and he continued to be under warrant of arrest. Switzerland was turning into a trap.

"Gradually my solitude here is becoming unbearable," he wrote to Liszt in 1852, "and if I can afford it, I shall go to Paris for the winter."[21] Two years later, he confessed to Minna: "It is a feeling I long have harbored, that *without any stimulus whatever for my art* I should be unable in time to go on here. You know how of late years I had kept nursing the hope that something might be done for music after all here: upon my side, in truth, I've spared no efforts for it. The result, however, shows there's nothing to be attempted with these people here; . . . as long as I wrote books . . ., and then poetry, it could be put up with; but for the past twelvemonth, ever since I began composing again, this utter lack of stimulus was bound to end by thoroughly depressing me."[22] From London, where Wagner was invited to give a series of concerts for the Old Philharmonic Society in early 1855, he reported to Minna that the musicians, especially the wind instruments, were far superior to the people in Zurich, and that he "had a long and very hearty welcome from the audience – much better than in Zurich! – the orchestra chimed in with loud applause."[23] One can certainly feel for Wagner who once had taken a Zurich horn player to task only to be told in no uncertain terms: "Sie, Herr Wagner, das isch de mis Horn und uf dem spiel ich so wie-n-ich will."[24]

Reflecting on his decision, taken in 1856, never to conduct a public performance in Zurich again, Wagner mentions in his autobiography that he pointed out to the members of the Musical Society "their slackness and their disregard for my urgent proposals for the establishment of a decent orchestra. The excuse I invariably received was, that although there was money enough among the musical public, yet everyone fought shy of heading the subscription list with a definite sum, because of the tiresome notoriety they would win among the townspeople. My old friend, Herr Ott-Imhof, assured me that it would not embarrass him in the least to pay ten thousand francs a year to a cause of that sort, but that from the moment every one would demand why he was spending his income in that way. It would rouse such a commotion that he might easily be brought to account about the administration of his property. This called to my mind Goethe's exclamation at the beginning of his *Erste Schweizer Briefe*. So my musical activities at Zurich ceased definitely from that time."[25] Recalling Wagner's grand yet unsuccessful plans for a production of his *Ring* near Mythenstein, hallowed site of Swiss freedom, Wagner's allusion to Goethe's comments on Switzerland reveals the depth of his own frustration: "Once upon a time," says Goethe, "[the Swiss] rid themselves of a tyrant and thought themselves free. . . . Now they continue to relate the old fable; on all sides it is drummed into one's ears *ad nauseam* – they have thrown off the yoke of the despot and have remained free. And there they are, ensconced behind their walls and imprisoned in their customs, their laws, the opinion of their neighbors . . ."[26]

Wagner felt misunderstood and victimized; he was caught in what he called "this little philistine state," and he wanted out.[27] The story of the genius among the philistines and scrooges has wound its way through a number of biographies, starting with Glasenapp's, and it usually comes in tandem with the observation – now nostalgic, now gloating – that Zurich forfeited its chances to become Wagner's Bayreuth.

Money Makes the World Go Around

But let me try a different narrative. From the inception of his exile, Wagner received privileged treatment in Switzerland. As already mentioned, Johann Jakob Sulzer provided him with a valid passport within a matter of hours. In October of 1850, Zurich issued him a residency permit which was renewed annually without further ado. Thanks to a request by the Zurich Chief of Police, who happened to love music, the Federal Government had Wagner's name crossed from the list of refugees one month later. In short, he had made all the right connections to avoid bureaucratic red tape and harassment by the authorities.

He also met the right people to bail him out of his never-ending financial problems: one was Johann Jakob Sulzer, another was Otto Wesendonck, who came to Zurich in 1851. From both men he accepted, over the years, huge sums as gifts — *à fonds perdus*. He also begged and borrowed from them without ever paying anything back. Referring to his financial situation, Wagner claimed that he lived "a life of despair and continuous enforced resignation . . ."[28] His friends, however, saw it differently. To wit, Eliza Wille in her memoirs: "Now and then I would come across remarks, quite inappropriate in my mind, that Wagner had known the deep sufferings of exile. As a refugee, respected by everybody and admired by many, he lived in the security of his own home, and he had friends who stood up for him. . . . The prolonged and bitter agony of political refugees with their hopeless search for sympathy, knocking at doors only to be refused entrance: this *Wagner* did not experience in Zurich."[29]

His financial needs were met with tact and understanding as long as it was a question of publishers paying late or in lesser amounts than anticipated, and of German theaters hesitating or outright refusing to produce his works. But word started to get around about Wagner's taste for the good life. Liszt, for example, wrote to the Princess: "[Wagner] is very well housed. He has very good rooms and has furnished them handsomely. There's a sofa or rather a *chaise longue* and small armchair in green velvet. He has the piano scores of *Rienzi, Tannhäuser,* and *Lohengrin* superbly bound. He is inclined to luxury . . . His dress is, if anything, dandified. He wears a hat of slightly pinkish white. . . . For to-day he wanted to kill the fatted calf and make a great feast. We had difficulty in moderating him on this point, and reducing the invitations to dinner to the number of 10 or 12."[30] Judging from a letter written in Aarau in late 1853, Swiss musicians in other cantons got wind and spread the gossip: "So much is certain, that in the higher circles of society they are already talking doubtfully about the frightful debts of the Flying Dutchman, and the unbecoming luxury with which he surrounds himself."[31] The author predicted the debacle of Wagner's grand plans because among the citizens of Zurich, as he put it, "the sense of money was only slightly less developed than their vanity." In the same year, a report issued by the Vienna police based on information received from spies in Zurich reached the Saxon Ministry of the Interior: "Strange reports are again circulating about Richard Wagner. In Zurich he not only lives in ostentatious luxury but also purchases the most valuable articles, such as gold watches, at enormous prices. His apartments are adorned with the finest furniture, carpets, silk curtains and chandeliers; all this creates the utmost astonishment and curiosity among the simple natives of the republic, who cannot help wondering where this man, who was so poor when he came to Zurich, gets his money from."[32] To be sure, in contradistinction to Liszt's remarks, these are the exaggerations of reactionary state employees who did not wish him well. But with "the simple natives" talking about town, it sooner or later had to dawn on his patient benefactors that they were supporting Wagner's increasingly lavish life-style while his debts kept growing.

In the summer of 1854, Sulzer and Wesendonck, who had helped with small contributions all along, decided to get him out of his financial straits once and for all. Wagner got the necessary cash on hand and promised Wesendonck the revenues from *Lohengrin* and *Tannhäuser* if he would take care of his debts and provide him with an annual allowance. Sulzer, at Wesendonck's urging, assumed the role of financial guardian, administering both his income and his expenses. The letters exchanged between Sulzer and Wesendonck at that time reveal to what extent their munificence was being tested. By midsummer, Wesendonck was already fed up: "This much is clear," he wrote Sulzer, "no money must be handed to Wagner himself. . . . I had originally thought of giving the funds to Madame Wagner, but thought it too humiliating."[33] By September, Wagner discovered debts he had forgotten about, or so he claimed; once again, he approached Sulzer in a letter that maneuvers most skillfully between contrition and blackmail: he is resigned to mollify his creditors by putting his household up for sale, but to avoid utter humiliation he would have to leave Zurich forever. And while he would be willing to expiate his carelessness, his wife would probably not survive relocation.[34] Sulzer, fond of Wagner and a gentleman besides, consulted with Wesendonck who, for the sake of friendship, was willing to help out once again. His response to Sulzer included a firm warning: "Wagner should be informed that I will no longer pay for his debts and that he would save us all the agony of having to hear about and discuss such matters in the future . . . if he causes trouble again, both for himself and for his friends, he will have to blame himself for being left in the lurch . . . It's been a nuisance for you and me, and we better get hardened."[35]

Wagner did not really change his ways. Two years later, Gottfried Keller (who had returned from Berlin in 1855) mentioned Wagner's solid lunches and the generously flowing booze in a letter addressed to Lina Duncker.[36] To Freiligrath he wrote on a whimsical note: "Richard Wagner is a very gifted man but also a bit of a hairdresser and *charlatan,* on his bric-à-brac table he has a silver hairbrush in a crystal bowl, etc., etc."[37] Still, Wagner's friends continued to come to his rescue periodically; but, as Gregor-Dellin puts it, "it would have taken more than this to plug the leaks, old and new, in Wagner's sinking ship."[38]

Otto Wesendonck, who had made a "killing" during the economic boom of 1853, nearly lost his entire fortune in the slump of 1856 caused by a crisis of the American money market.[39] He did recover alright, but, in light of these recent events that brought home to him the vulnerability of the economy, Otto Wesendonck probably considered Wagner's lofty production plans and his *music of the future* to be the junk bonds of their time. And what about his wealthy Swiss friends? In retrospect, Wagner's early assessment of his relationship with them appears like an ironic prophecy. To Uhlig he had written in early 1850 that they "agreed to leave me to my nature, and to take me, in all I undertake, just as I am and just as I do," and he took this to be the "thoroughly sound expression of the simple Swiss intelligence."[40] Given their "simple . . . intelligence," the burghers of Zurich did just this: they took him as he was and as he did—he was financially unreliable, and, with a rapidly expanding economy, they invested where they had every reason to expect better returns: in their banks, their railroads, their textile industry, and—unbelievable as it sounds—in their universities. "Philistine" high capitalism? Indeed, and smart, too: for the King who made the dream come true brought the State of Bavaria to the brink of bankruptcy.

But there is another side to this: namely, Wagner's fundamental insensitivity towards the unwritten laws of Swiss society: speculations, living beyond one's means, debts, and foreclosures are a constant theme especially in Keller's works from *Der grüne Heinrich* to *Martin Salander.* We know of the fate of Wenzel Strapinski turned Polish count; of the shame of young Heinrich who stole from his mother; of the Weidelich brother's prison sentence and of Martin Salander's harsh years in exile because he was taken in by a man he believed to be his friend. Looking beyond Keller's novels and stories to the country at large, one's financial record was, more than anything else, tied to the concept of honor and shame of its society, and Wagner, wanting to become part of it, had violated this code.

A Revolutionary

And then there is this story: Wagner entered Switzerland as a political refugee. Zurich was full of German exiles—those who had arrived in 1819 following the Karlsbad Decrees, those of the 1830s, after the Hambacher Fest and the Frankfurter Wachensturm, and those who came in 1848-1849. Many of them held influential positions as doctors, lawyers, university teachers, and publicists, and had helped to bring about what has been called Zurich's Golden Age.[41] In Wagner, they expected to meet a fellow liberal; when his royalist sympathies became known, after they had read his essay on *Judaism in Music,* many of them were appalled and kept their distance.[42] All the more ludicrous in this light, then, are the accusations leveled in a report by the Prague Police Department, and promptly sent to Dresden in 1851, that Wagner was one of the leaders of the Swiss Revolutionary Party![43] Georg Herwegh, one of his closest friends in the early 1850s, gradually drifted away from Wagner; he agreed neither with his politics nor with the company he kept. During his visit in Zurich in 1853, Liszt wrote to the Princess: "[Wagner] has by no means the democratic tone, and has assured me a score of times that, since his residence here, he has completely broken with the refugee party . . . Several of his [Swiss] friends belong to the ultra-conservative[s] . . ."[44]

One of these friends was a young lawyer by the name of Bernhard Spyri, who befriended him in the very first months of his exile, and who was the editor of the *Eidgenössische Zeitung,* Zurich's conservative daily.[45] Liberals like Gottfried Keller, acknowledging Spyri's humanitarian stance towards the refugees, labeled him nevertheless a reactionary as early as 1849.[46] Even while Spyri and Wagner drifted apart in the mid-1850s—because Spyri showed little understanding for Wagner's amorous pursuits and probably also because Spyri's bride, Johanna Spyri, author of *Heidi,* developed an immediate dislike for him—the *Eidgenössische Zeitung* regularly and enthusiastically discussed Wagner's publications and concerts from 1850 on.[47] The adulatory, propagandistic tone of Spyri's reviews even gave rise to the rumor that Wagner himself had written them as advertisements for himself.

He fared not nearly so well with the *Neue Zürcher Zeitung,* the newspaper of the Liberal Party, which held the power from 1846-1869 and received strong support by local merchants and industrialists throughout the 1850s and 1860s. From the very beginning, with the exception of a favorable preview of his first concert, Wagner was stonewalled by the *NZZ* over long stretches of time. Max Fehr has suggested in all seriousness that the liberal *NZZ* should have been more supportive of Wagner than the *Eidgenössische Zeitung,* since Wagner was a revolutionary under warrant of arrest, and noble aloofness would have been more in keeping with the latter than with the former.[48] This is of course a misunderstanding that borders on the grotesque; but one may wonder to what extent Wagner was a possible victim of conflicts that dated back to the early forties when the *NZZ* sided with the liberal Sängerverein Harmonie, and the *Eidgenössische Zeitung,* with the conservatory Stadtsängerverein;[49] another conflict erupted between the two papers in 1852 over a scandal concerning damaged insolators on telegraph poles—as a consequence of which Spyri, caught in the thick of it, was sued for libel by a prominent liberal politician. Such trivia aside, the public relations campaign for Wagner by the *Eidgenössische* and the hostility of the *NZZ* do make sense both in terms of Wagner's own development and in terms of how the public in Zurich viewed him. Hermann Köchly, Rector of the University of Zurich and a Dresden insurgent like Wagner, met him occasionally at Wesendonck's and remarked the following in a letter: "Since I don't see much of Wagner any more, I cannot tell you much about him. He formed himself a 'small community' of half a dozen people here who idolize him, who adore his insolence and silliness . . . I am used to treating people with whom I come into closer contact as my equals; I place myself neither *above* nor *beneath* them, and so I'm not cut out to take part in this swindle . . ."[50] Keller, too, felt increasingly uncomfortable in Wagner's presence. He wrote to several friends about the visit Liszt and the Princess Sayn-Wittgenstein had paid to Wagner with great pomp and circumstance in 1856. The three of them held court; on a trial basis they invited Keller a couple of times, but he evidently did not fit the part.[51] "Besides, Wagner, encouraged by Liszt in all his follies, had become once again quite eccentric and egotistical."[52] Even allowing for cognitive dissonance in some cases, gossipy tidbits like the one just quoted signal that Wagner lacked broad support. Socially, he had driven himself in a corner—politically as well as financially, he had bet on the wrong horse.

It has been said that Wagner, having withdrawn from political activism after 1849, nevertheless pursued the revolution: namely, in the field of music. As far as Zurich is concerned, Wagner's plans outlined in "A Theater in Zurich," where he proposed among other things "an artistic fellowship in which the whole civic society would more or less take part," when taken to the test proved to be not much more than democratic posturing for the sake of rescuing artistic endeavors from entrepreneurial exploitation. In fact, he showed little interest in choral societies who played a crucial role in Swiss musical life; their republicanism went past him, and he had no intention of promoting new vocal groups from any walk of life. I do not say this with accusatory intentions; indeed, the chumminess of provincial Swiss men's choirs—the butt of jokes to this day—is not in everybody's line. I merely wish to point out that, with his political past and his ideas of communal culture, he constructed his own image as *compositeur engagé.*

Those "simple natives," wont to take a spade for a spade and unaccustomed to his style of oratory, completely misunderstood his intentions and thought he really cared. In this respect, Wagner's remarks about the torchlight serenade following his May concerts of 1853, when the Zurich Choral Society awarded him an Honorary Diploma, are both revealing and, given their scornful undertone, quite embarrassing: "In my speech of acknowledgment I indicated plainly that I saw no reason why Zurich itself should not be the chosen place to give an impetus to the fulfillment of the aspirations I cherished for my artistic ideals, and that it might do so on proper civic lines. I believe this was taken to refer to a special development of the men's choral societies, and they were quite gratified at my bold forecasts."[53]

For July 1854, Wagner accepted an offer to conduct Beethoven's Seventh Symphony in Sitten (Canton of Valais), site of the Swiss Music Festival that year. Two days after his arrival, having found the orchestra inadequate and the acoustics in the small church unsuitable, he simply ran away without telling anyone, notifying the festival director of his decision in writing. *Der Bund,* a daily published in the capital, commented as follows: "Wagner's sudden departure caused a sensation only insofar as one had accredited a man like Wagner, known for his democratic orientation, with greater republican self-conquest. It was assumed that he would better be able to appreciate local conditions, and that he would understand the purpose of this festival not exclusively in its artistic or individual aspects but also in its social ones, especially as regards the *future* . . . He could have accomplished much, and with relatively little effort he would have won friendship, gratitude, and appreciation."[54]

Thus, as late as 1854, people kept clinging to the legend of Wagner the democrat without realizing that he had never been one. On his side, Wagner once again profoundly misjudged the Swiss; Spyri's reviews in the *Eidgenössische*

Zeitung were taken seriously by local Wagnerians—at most, maybe, by the conservatives in general; but the money and the real power were in the hands of the liberals. Wagner also remained ignorant of the extent to which artistic expectations and possibilities were intertwined with the political culture of his host country that had, after a fifty-year-long struggle, instituted its modern democratic constitution as recently as 1848.

A German Composer in Zurich

There is, last but not least, a story of a German among the Swiss, a story that had started near *Mythenstein* in 1291 (the year of the founding of the Old Confederacy) and whose unfolding was therefore out of Wagner's hands. Given the closed nature of Swiss society in general, and given the profound ambivalence of Switzerland—now admiring, now paranoid—especially towards its formidable neighbor to the north, the integration of Germans had always been an arduous, if not downright impossible process. Immigrants in the 1820s and 1830s had been welcomed, and their influence on Switzerland's intellectual and political life had been considerable. These same individuals, however, especially the academic, who were accustomed to the status of the professoriate back home, often behaved arrogantly and disparagingly towards the Swiss and showed little gratitude for having been granted asylum. Anti-German sentiments swept through Zurich in 1836, and a wave of extraditions spread from there into other cantons. In 1848, hatred erupted anew; the xenophobic Swiss Fatherland Society ranted against the refugees and warned of the imminent destruction of Switzerland, since Germans considered Switzerland as part of Germany. [55] The *NZZ*, too, voiced anti-German sentiments in 1848, though its position shifted the following year, when the Federal Government actually forced refugees from Baden and the Palatinate to leave the country.

Although the situation generally improved during the 1850s and 1860s, the refugees of the German colony continued to have their misgivings. The fear of deportation must have been ever present among them; a great many experienced difficulties adjusting to life in a democratic state; and most felt socially segregated. Hermann Köchly volunteered that "Swiss men and women are very unsociable domestic animals . . ." [56] Similarly, Jacob Moleschott, a well-known physiologist, commented on the fact that hospitality is not exactly the most impressive among Swiss virtues; he remembers that his Swiss university colleagues, although courteous, looked at them with suspicion, which in turn fostered German cliquishness. "[The faculty] had a Weekly Society from which the Swiss were not excluded, but the German participants were in the majority so that people generally referred to the German Society, or the German Circle." [57] Eliza Wille, at whose house the German intellectuals gathered regularly, comments on Swiss clannishness, too, and notes that the educated citizens of Zurich, even the scholars among them, continued to honor the dialect of their forefathers, which signaled to them the coziness of being among themselves. [58] The bluntest comment came from Theodor Mommsen: "If you don't kick the Confederates, they'll kick you. So the choice is easy." [59] Not just Wagner but many prominent Germans left in the late 1850s and 1860s, among them Mommsen, Hermann Köchly, Friedrich Theodor Vischer, the Herweghs, Jacob Moleschott, and Gottfried Semper. Others, like the Wesendoncks, were to follow in 1871 when German nationals, who had gathered in great numbers to celebrate the founding of the Second Reich, were insulted and beaten up by chauvinistic Swiss rowdies.

Wagner was conscious of the tensions among his Swiss and German friends whom he tried to keep apart if possible; back from Paris and Strasbourg where he had gone on a shopping spree, he writes to Liszt: "It's Sunday; I'll treat my Zurich faithfuls to lobster and oysters. You know them, don't you? In order to avoid any ill-feeling, I don't even dare to ask Herwegh over." [60] Despite such awareness, even Wagner made the mistake in "A Theater in Zurich" of using, on the one hand, the first person plural in his analysis of the local stage, thus including himself among the town's residents, and planning for and with them a theater of the future, while on the other hand referring with sweeping statements to "the peculiar inwardness . . . of the *German* spirit" and to the "*German* art-genius" (49; my emphasis) in what he intended to be a plea for the resurgence of Swiss dramatic art.

Gottfried Keller, who spent his formative years in Heidelberg and Berlin and who, upon his return in the mid-1850s, certainly did not mind the hospitality and spiritedness of many prominent Germans living in Zurich, bears witness—at times unconsciously—to the existing tensions and resentments; eventually, he broke off with the Wesendoncks and he also had a falling out with François Wille, who had become a Swiss citizen and was running for office, and whom Keller nevertheless suspected of double loyalty. [61] Even more revealing is one of his letters to Ludmilla Assing, in which he praises Wagner as a genius and a very entertaining man, very well educated and very profound. The Nibelungen text, he says, has impressed him deeply, more than anything else he has read in a long time. But then, without any transition, he seems to be changing the topic: "Besides, it's terrible, there are so many scholars and literati in Zurich, you hear more High German, French and Italian than our own Swiss German, and in the past that did not used to be the case at all. But we won't knuckle under . . ." And he continues to tell her about all the popular festivities planned for the coming summer season, of his compatriots who seize every opportunity to have parades complete with floats and wreaths wound around machine tools the minutes a new railroad line is inaugurated, and of the thousands of people congregated on such occasions. [62] Keller's letter is so interesting because of the blank between his unqualified praise of the *Nibelungen,* on the one hand, and his complaint of *Überfremdung,* on the other; he does not complain just about the presence of Germans, but it is Wagner's text, a *German* text, that triggers the complaints. And by way of association, no doubt, the mentioning of Wagner's *Nibelungen* leads into a description of Swiss folklore reminiscent of the pageantry Wagner envisioned in his "A Theater at Zurich." It is as if Keller were saying: We can do it on our own.

Am Mythenstein

In 1860, a scant two years after Wagner had left town, Gottfried Keller published his essay "Am Mythenstein." It is his final comment on Wagner; four years later, when invited by Hermann Levi to submit a contribution to a "Gedenkblatt an Richard Wagner," Keller declined and claimed he had nothing new to say. [63]

"Am Mythenstein" opens with an account of Keller's trip across Lake Lucerne to Brunnen on the occasion of the Schiller centenary which, as mentioned before, included the ceremony of renaming the famous rock in Schiller's honor. *Mythenstein,* Keller confesses wryly in an aside, is a name that has always given him a queasy feeling in the stomach. [64] He describes the scenery ahead of him as if it were a giant stage, with the mountains serving as a theater curtain. "All in all," he writes, "this was quite a set-scene!" (971). Getting off at Brunnen, Keller notices the big barges in the harbor, flagged for this festive occasion by a local politician and hotel owner, the very same man, I should add, with whom Wagner had discussed plans for a production of the *Nibelungen.* Against the stagey landscape and against Wagner's vision of an open-air stage at exactly the same site, Keller, in his imagination, begins to set up the stage—or should we say *meta-stage?*—for his very own and very Swiss *Gesamtkunstwerk* of the future. [65]

With the founding of the new state, Keller argues, the need has arisen for the creation of a new national stage (983). His criticism of the present state of the theater owes much to Wagner's essay. Like Wagner, he calls for themes that are close to the people; poets would be in unison "*with* the spirit of the people" and would receive their inspiration "*from* the spirit of the people" (986f.); and, like Wagner, he recognizes in the already existing pageants and festivals the potential for further development. Choral groups would enter into competitions; poets, too, would enter poetry contests, judged openly at these festivals, to provide texts that would lend themselves to be set to music. Keller calls for new poetry written "in pure, rhythmic language," without neglecting meaning, i.e., poetry that would bring about the perfect amalgamation of word poems and sound poems (990). He cites Wagner as an example of an artist who tried to write poetry for his own specific purpose, but who, according to Keller, did not get beyond choppy little verses, no matter how poetic and exalted his intentions and his predilection for German mythology may have been. Wagner's language, dallying with the archaic, is "not suited to render the spirit of the present, let alone the spirit of the future; it belongs to the past" (990). Keller envisions "a secular national oratorio," i.e., lay choirs engaged in an unprecedented dialogue, responding to each other with questions and answers derived from an ethics turned into music (990). In this national enterprise, Keller speaks of a "Nationalästhetik" (987). Men and women, artists and citizens would be brought together and ennobled; the laborer would be joined by the young farmer, the statesman by the merchant, the local music teacher by the conductor from the capital (991). Thus Keller is less concerned with how to educate people to make better art, than with how to provide them with an aesthetic education so they, in turn, will be a better people. "Am Mythenstein" is Keller's celebration of the democratic body politic.[66]

Let me summarize and conclude: The blithe assertion made in the 1930s, that for Wagnerians Switzerland is "hallowed soil," appears hopelessly naive.[67] Wagner's wish to settle in the German-speaking part of Switzerland did not come true, for *Geld* and *Geist* were working at cross-purposes not only on the part of the Swiss, but on Wagner's part as well. Local politics, investment patterns in a period of economic boom, as well as Swiss pride and prejudice stood in his way. With a life-style and politics that alienated even his most faithful friends and sponsors, he certainly added his share. Most importantly, his artistic aspirations, together with his predilection for mythic themes, clashed with the Swiss cultural program under the banner of a democracy on the move. Wagner, who was vowed to excellence in artistic performances, walked out on the orchestra in Sitten, whereas Keller renounced elitism for his communal artwork of the future and made a case for dilettantism as the symbolic representation of a political achievement that had been brought about by the people. As Max Frisch says a century later in his first *Sketchbook:* ". . . the German mistake — typical perhaps of the whole of the West — of imagining that because they have symphonies they also have culture could hardly happen here; the artist not as the upholder of culture but as just one link among many others; culture as a reflection of the whole people; we recognize it not only in bookcases and at the grand piano, but just as much in the way we treat those dependent on us. So long as one means culture in this sense, which seems to me its future sense, we must not be alarmed if we are occasionally treated as an anachronism . . ."[68] And thus Gottfried Keller had served the Government of Zurich for already a decade when Richard Wagner entered Bayreuth.

Notes

1 Richard Wagner, *My Life* (New York, 1936), 505. The original reads: ". . . als ich am letzten Mai abends gegen sechs Uhr, von Oberstraß hinab nach Zürich einfuhr und zum ersten Male in glänzender Sonnenbeleuchtung die den See begrenzenden Glarner Alpen glänzen sah, beschloß ich sofort, ohne dies deutlich im Bewußtsein zu fassen, allem auszuweichen, was mir hier eine Niederlassung verwehren könnte." *Mein Leben,* ed. Martin Gregor-Dellin (Munich, 1976), 429. Cf. also Wagner's letter to Minna of 29 May 1849, in *Letters of Richard Wagner,* The Burrell Collection, ed. John N. Burk (New York, 1950).
2 8 June 1849, in *Selected Letters,* trans. Stewart Spencer and Barry Millington (London, 1987), 172. "[D]agegen biete ich Dir nun einen Punkt, wo Dir Leib und Seele gesunden soll, das ist

das herrliche Zürich in der Schweiz. . . . Dort in der deutschen Schweiz sind wir wie zuhause.
. . ." Richard Wagner, *Briefe. Die Sammlung Burrell* (Frankfurt, 1953), 330.

3 From Zurich, 11 Aug. 1849, in Richard Wagner, *Letters to Minna Wagner,* trans. and ed. William Ashton Ellis (New York, 1909), 65. "Was den Aufenthalt in der *Schweiz* betrifft, habe nur ja keine Sorge! Die Flüchtlinge gehen mich gar nichts an . . . . – ich gelte hier gar nicht als Flüchtling, denn ich habe meinen vollständigen Schweizerpaß, und Aufenthaltsschein auf ein Jahr, d.h. so viel als auf immer . . . von sonstigen Unannehmlichkeiten bin ich in keiner Weise bedroht, da ich hier Bürgen und Gutseher genug habe, um mich ganz in den Canton aufnehmen lassen zu können. . . ." *Richard Wagner an Minna Wagner* (Berlin and Leipzig, 1908), 54f.

4 16 Sept. 1849 to Theodor Uhlig, in Richard Wagner, *Letters to His Dresden Friends, Theodor Uhlig, Wilhelm Fischer, and Ferdinand Heine,* trans. J. S. Shedlock (New York, 1890), 8. "Schon schämt sich meine Frau unseres Aufenthaltes in Zürich und meint, man müsse allen Leuten Glauben machen, wir seien in Paris . . ." *Richard Wagners Briefe an Theodor Uhlig, Wilhelm Fischer, Ferdinand Heine* (Leipzig, 1888), 11. Cf. also *My Life,* 518, 525f.

5 Cf. Minna's ad in *Tagblatt der Stadt Zürich,* 19 Aug. 58, in Werner G. Zimmermann (ed.) "Richard Wagner in Zürich: Materialien zu Aufenthalt und Wirken": "Zu verkaufen. *Wegen Abreise:* Ein großer eleganter Spiegel mit schöner goldener Rahme [*sic*], das Glas 4 Schuh 8 Zoll hoch und 2 Schuh 7 Zoll breit. Ein neuer nußbaumener Spieltisch mit gestochenem Fuß; ein großer runder dito. Ein dito Coulissen-Speisetisch für 14 Personen; 12 dito Stühle. Nußbaumene Bettstellen, Federmatratzen, seidene Kanapees, Fauteuils, Zimmerteppiche u.s.w. Ein Weinschrank, gut 300 Flaschen haltend, zum Verschließen, bei Frau *Wagner* auf dem Gabler in Enge, neben Herrn Wesendonk" *(Neujahrsblatt der Allgemeinen Musikgesellschaft Zürich* 172 [1988] 49).

6 To Peter Cornelius from Mariafeld, 8 April 1864, in *Selected Letters,* trans. Stewart Spencer and Barry Millington (London, 1987), 582. "Freund, die Schweiz ist mir ein Totenfeld geworden, und überallhin hätte ich gehen sollen, nur gerade nicht hierher, wo alles mir bitter und grabselig ist." *Richard Wagner an Freunde und Zeitgenossen,* ed. Erich Kloss (Berlin/Leipzig, 1909), 373.

7 From Wagner's letter to Minna of 29 May 1849, in *Letters of Richard Wagner* (New York, 1950), 150. "Höchster Wohlstand und erhabener Naturreiz liegen hier plötzlich wie durch Zauber vor mir. . . ." *Briefe: Die Sammlung Burrell,* 320.

8 *My Life,* 513. "Dies war eben das von aller öffentlichen Kunst gänzlich entblößte *Zürich.* . . ." *Mein Leben,* 435.

9 The Zurich theater received no state support. Altogether dependent on private contributions and the sales of season tickets, the *Aktientheater* could not make ends meet. See Gordon A. Craig, *Geld und Geist: Zürich im Zeitalter des Liberalismus 1830-1863* (Munich, 1988), 165.

10 Richard Wagner, "A Theater in Zurich," *Prose Works,* trans. William Ashton Ellis (London, 1893-99), 3:39. Hereafter cited in text. For the original wording see Richard Wagner, "Ein Theater in Zürich," in his *Sämtliche Schriften und Dichtungen* (Leipzig, n. d.), 5:20-52; the quotes I use are on 34, 40, 42, 44, and 47, respectively.

11 *My Life,* 595. "[W]ohl sehr schön aber leider unausführbar. . . ." *Mein Leben,* 505.

12 Gottfried Keller in a letter to Wilhelm Baumgartner in September 1851, in *Gesammelte Briefe in 4 Bänden,* ed. Carl Helbling (Bern, 1950), 1:294.

13 To Theodor Uhlig, 20 Sept. 1850, in *Letters to His Dresden Friends,* 69. "Könnte ich je über [10,000 Taler] disponieren, so würde ich Folgendes veranstalten: – hier, wo ich nun gerade bin und wo manches gar nicht so übel ist, würde ich auf einer schönen Wiese bei der Stadt von Brett und Balken ein rohes Theater nach meinem Plane herstellen und lediglich bloß mit der Ausstattung an Dekorationen und Maschinerie versehen lassen, die zu der Aufführung des Siegfried nötig sind. . . . Ist alles in gehöriger Ordnung, so lasse ich dann unter diesen Umständen drei Aufführungen des Siegfried in einer Woche stattfinden: nach der dritten wird das Theater eingerissen und meine Partitur verbrannt. Den Leuten, denen die Sache gefallen hat, sage ich dann: 'nun macht's auch so!" Wollen sie auch von mir einmal wieder etwas Neues hören, so sage ich aber: 'schießt *ihr* das Geld zusammen!' – Nun, komme ich dir gehörig verrückt vor? Möge es sein, aber ich versichere Dir, dies noch zu erreichen ist die Hoffnung meines Lebens, die Aussicht – die mich einzig reizen kann, ein Kunstwerk in Angriff zu nehmen. Also – schafft mir die 10,000 Taler – weiter nichts!" *(Briefe an Theodor Uhlig, Wilhelm Fischer, Ferdinand Heine* [Leipzig, 1888], 59f.) According to Max Fehr, 10,000 thalers were the equivalent of 37,000 Swiss francs. *Richard Wagners Schweizer Zeit* (Aarau, 1934) 1:49.

14 Martin Gregor-Dellin, *Richard Wagner: His Life, His Work, His Century* (San Diego, 1983), 244.

15 For a list of the contributors, see A. Steiner, "Richard Wagner in Zürich," *Neujahrsblatt der Allgemeinen Musikgesellschaft in Zürich* 90 (1902): 16.

16 To Ferdinand Heine, 10 June 1853, in *Letters to His Dresden Friends*, 490. "Gewiß führe ich selber noch einmal meine Opern und auch die Nibelungen hier auf: natürlich nur unter ganz ungewöhnlichen Umständen" (*Richard Wagners Briefe an Theodor Uhlig, Wilhelm Fischer, Ferdinand Heine*, 402). Similarly, on 30 May 1853 to Liszt in *Correspondence of Wagner and Liszt*, trans. Francis Hueffer (New York, 1969) 1:285. See also *My Life*, 599. The *Eidgenössische Zeitung* (19 May 1853) remarked: "Zürich wird ihm auch diese Tage nie vergessen. Dank ihm dafür; innigen, gerührten Dank." Fehr, 1:226.

17 4 July 1853, quoted in Carl F. Glasenapp, *Life of Richard Wagner*, trans. W. Ashton Ellis (London, 1904), 4:144. "Il n'abandonne pas ses projets de théâtre à Zurich, et il s'agit de construire une nouvelle salle—pour laquelle un certain nombre d'actionnaires garantiraient les fonds. En tout cas, il se donnera le plaisir d'organiser quelque chose d'inoui, alors qu'il aura terminé la composition de ses Nibelungen, et je l'entretiens volontiers dans cette idée. Si, comme je le crois, son importance continue à grandir et à devenir tout-à-fait prédominante en Allemagne et en Suisse—il n'y a pas de doute qu'on réussira à trouver les 100,000 francs qui lui sont nécessaires pour réaliser son idée de Bühnenfestspiel. Je suppose que l'été de 1856 il réunira ici le personnel qui lui sera nécessaire pour donner ses quatre drames—et probablement même la spéculation ne sera pas mauvaise sous le rapport pécuniaire—car il pourra rassembler aisément ici pour une fête de ce genre plusieurs milliers d'étrangers." Quoted in Adolf Steiner, "Richard Wagner in Zürich," *Neujahrsblatt der Allgemeinen Musikgesellschaft in Zürich* 90 (1902): 23.

18 Fehr, 1:246.

19 Fehr, 2:21. Cf. also Hans Erismann, *Richard Wagner in Zürich* (Zurich, 1987), 158.

20 "The old man of the valley's brewing up a storm. / It'll be on us sooner than we think. / The ice is rumbling and the Mythenstein / is hooded. Cold wind fills the rainy-quarter." *Wilhelm Tell*, trans. John Purdhoe (New York, 1970). 6.

21 3 Oct. 1852, in *Correspondence of Wagner and Liszt*, 225. "Nach und nach wird mir die hiesige Einöde doch unerträglich: wenn ich's erschwingen kann, gehe ich zum Winter einmal nach Paris. . . ." *Briefwechsel zwischen Wagner und Liszt* (Leipzig, 1900), 1:193.

22 Ca. 20 Oct. 1854, in *Richard Wagner to Minna Wagner*, 163. "Es ist ein lange genährtes Gefühl in mir, daß ich hier, *ohne alle* und *jede Anregung für meine Kunst*, es mit der Zeit nicht mehr durchführen können würde. Du weißt, daß ich in den letzten Jahren doch immer noch Hoffnung nährte, es würde sich hier noch einmal etwas für die Musik machen: an Anstrengungen dafür habe ich es wahrlich nicht fehlen lassen. Der Erfolg zeigt aber, daß mit diesen Leuten hier sich nichts anfangen läßt. . . . So lange ich hier Bücher schrieb und endlich dichtete, mochte es gehen: seit einem Jahre aber, wo ich nun wieder componire, muß dieser Zustand gänzlicher Anregungslosigkeit endlich aber vollkommen niederdrückend auf mich wirken" (*Richard Wagner an Minna Wagner*, 136). One year earlier, Theodor Mommsen had expressed similar fears: "So ist es in diesen kleinen Nestern. Man kommt herunter, ohne zu wissen wie" (1 June 1853 to Otto Jahn, in Craig, 153).

23 13 March 1855, in *Richard Wagner to Minna Wagner*, 172f. "Die Musiker *können* Alles machen: namentlich sind auch die Blasinstrumente sehr gut, und von einer solchen Plage, wie ich sie in Zürich mit den Leuten habe, ist natürlich gar keine Rede. . . . Ich wurde vom Publikum sehr lebhaft und lange empfangen,—viel besser als in Zürich!—Das Orchester stimmte mit lautem Applaus ein. . . ." *Richard Wagner an Minna Wagner*, 143f.

24 Quoted in Erismann, 69.

25 *My Life*, 640f. "Nur wollten die Herren [von der Musikgesellschaft] im Anfange gar nicht recht glauben, daß es mir damit Ernst sei, und es bedurfte meinerseits sehr kategorischer Erklärungen in diesem Betreff, wobei ich ihnen ihre Schlaffheit und ihre Unbeachtung meiner so angelegentlich ihnen gestellten Vorschläge zur Herstellung eines erträglichen Orchesters zu Gemüte zu führen mußte. Stets erhielt ich zur Entschuldigung, daß zwar genug Vermögen unter dem musikliebenden Publikum vorhanden sei, daß sich aber jeder scheue, mit einer bestimmten Geldzeichnung voranzugehen, weil dies eine lästige Beachtung seiner Vermögensumstände seitens seiner Mitbürger nach sich ziehen könnte. Mein alter Freund, Herr *Ott-Imhof*, erklärte mir, daß es ihn durchaus nicht beschweren würde, zu einem solchen Zwecke 10,000 Franken jährlich zu zahlen, nur würde

von diesem Augenblicke an jeder fragen, wie es denn käme, daß der Herr *Ott-Imhof* so mit seinem Vermögen verfahre? Er würde damit ein so peinliches Aufsehen erwecken, daß er leicht zur Rechenschaft über die Verwaltung seines Besitzes gezogen werden könnte. Mir fiel dabei *Goethes* Ausruf im Anfange seiner 'ersten Schweizer Briefe' ein! Doch mit dem Musikwirken hatte es von nun an in Zürich ein bestimmtes Ende." *Mein Leben,* 544f.

26 Quoted by the editor in *My Life,* 641. "[Die Schweizer] machten sich einmal von einem Tyrannen los und konnten sich in einem Augenblick frei denken; . . . nun erzählen sie das alte Märchen immer fort, man hört es bis zum Überdruß; die hätten sich einmal frei gemacht und wären frei geblieben; und nun sitzen sie hinter ihren Mauern, eingefangen von ihren Gewohnheiten und Gesetzen, ihren Fraubasereien und Philistereien. . . . " "Briefe aus der Schweiz," *Gedenkausgabe der Werke, Briefe und Gespräche* (Zürich, 1949), 9:481f.

27 *My Life,* 515; *Mein Leben,* 437. Cf. also Keller to Hermann Hettner, 18 Oct. 1856 (*Gesammelte Briefe* 1:435): "Dagegen wünscht er jedenfalls nach Deutschland zurückkehren zu können, um wieder in die Theaterluft zu gelangen und Boden unter die Kunstfüße zu bekommen."

28 28 Oct. 1852 to Robert Franz Koburg, *Selected Letters,* 271. "[A]uch ich lebe hier ein Leben der Verzweiflung und fortgesetzten, notgedrungenen Entsagung. . . ." Fehr, 1:380.

29 Eliza Wille, *Erinnerungen an Richard Wagner: Mit 15 Briefen Richard Wagners* (Zürich, 1982, letter no. 4): "Ich habe es nicht recht gefunden, wenn ich hie und da gelesen und gehört, Wagner habe in Zürich schwere Leiden des Exils gekannt. – Der Verbannte, den alle hochhielten, den viele verehrten, lebte in der Sicherheit des eigenen Herdes und hatte Freunde, die für ihn eintraten. . . . Die Lage politisch Exilierter in ihrer langen, herben Qual, mit ihrem hoffnungslosen Suchen nach Teilnahme, ihrem Anklopfen, das vielfach abgewiesen wurde, hat *er* in Zürich nicht gekannt" (51).

30 3 July 1853. This is a collage of translations from the original French taken from William Wallace, *Liszt, Wagner, and the Princess* (London, 1927), 81; and from Glasenapp, *Life of Richard Wagner* (4:137ff.). "Il est très bien logé, s'est donné de beaux meubles – entre autre un canapé ou plutôt une chaise-longue, et un petit fauteuil en velours vert – a fait superbement relier en rouge les partitions de piano de Rienzi, de Tannhäuser et de Lohengrin. Il tient à garder des airs de luxe. . . . Sa mise est plutôt élégante. Il porte un chapeau d'un blanc légèrement rosé. . . . Wagner a déclaré qu'il y aurait table ouverte chez lui du matin au soir durant mon séjour ici. Je me prends un peu de scrupule des dépenses que je lui occasionne, car il y a toujours une douzaine de personnes à table pour dîner . . . et pour souper à 9 . . ." (Steiner, 22f.). Cf. note 5.

31 The original letter by Jakob Reithard to Xaver Schnyder (16 Nov. 1853) is quoted in Fehr: "Da nun aber . . . für unsichern Erfolg Geld – viel Geld verlangt wird und . . . der Geldsinn bei den Zürichern nur ein klein wenig minder als das Organ der Eitelkeit ausgebildet ist: so möchte wohl, wenn diese einmal ernstlich zweifelt, ihre Rechnung zu finden, ein Abortus zu fürchten sein. So viel ist sicher, daß man allbereits in den obern Schichten bedenklich von fürchterlichen Schulden des fliegenden Holländers und dem ungebührlichen Luxus redet, mit der er sich umgebe" (1:397). English translation in Ernest Newman, *The Life of Richard Wagner* (New York, 1937), 2:409.

32 Newman, 2:409. "Über Richard Wagner zirkulieren wieder sonderbare Gerüchte. Er lebt in Zürich nicht nur im luxuriösesten Glanze, sondern kauft auch die wertvollsten Dinge, wie goldene Uhren etc., zu enormen Preisen. Seine Wohnung ist mit den schönsten Möbeln, Teppichen, seidenen Vorhängen und Kronleuchtern dekoriert, was die einfachen Republikaner in bedenkliches Staunen und Neugierde versetzt, so daß man sich veranlaßt gesehen, überall nachzufragen, woher dieser Mann, der so arm nach Zürich kam, es nehme." Woldemar Lippert, *Richard Wagners Verbannung und Rückkehr* (Dresden, 1927), 45.

33 26 June 1854; in Gregor-Dellin, 253. "Soviel ist klar: ihm selber darf kein Geld in die Hand gegeben werden. . . . Von Anfang an hatte ich schon vor, die fonds an Madame Wagner zu geben, es scheint mir aber so demütigend. . . ." Fehr, 1:298.

34 14 Sept. 1854; in Fehr, 1:310.

35 13 and 14 Oct. 1854. "Ich glaube aber auch, daß es nicht unzweckmäßig ist, ihn wissen zu lassen, daß ich für die Zukunft für seine Schulden nicht mehr aufkommen will und daß ich hoffe, uns allen wird die Pein erspart, ferner über dergleichen Sachen sprechen zu hören und sprechen zu müssen . . . wenn W. sich und seinen Freunden . . . abermals Not verschafft, so hat er es sich selbst zuzuschreiben, wenn man ihn stecken läßt. . . . Der Ärgers ist genug gewesen für Sie und mich und endlich muß man abgehärtet werden." Fehr, 1:406f.

36 13 January 1856 to Lina Duncker; *Gesammelte Briefe,* 2:147.

37 30 April 1857 to Ferdinand Freiligrath. "Dann ist auch Richard Wagner ein sehr begabter Mensch, aber auch etwas Friseur und *Charlatan*. Er unterhält einen Nipptisch, worauf eine silberne Haarbürste in kristallener Schale zu sehen ist etc. etc." *Gesammelte Briefe* 1:262.

38 Gregor-Dellin, 255.

39 *My Life*, 670.

40 Feb. 1850 to Uhlig, in *Richard Wagner's Letters to His Dresden Friends*, 32. "[S]ie waren so vollkommen darin einverstanden, mich ganz nach meiner Natur gewähren zu lassen, und mich mit Allem, was ich thue, so zu nehmen wie ich bin und wie ich es thue, daß diese ganz gesunde Äußerung des einfachen Schweizerverstandes meiner Freunde nicht wenig dazu beitrug, gerade bei ihnen. . . . mich am wenigsten allein zu fühlen." *Briefe an Theodor Uhlig*, 31.

41 Craig, 279.

42 *Judaism in Music* was critically received by Friedrich Theodor Vischer as well as by Otto Wesendonck. Wagner's anti-Semitism did far more damage to his reputation in German circles than in Swiss ones. On anti-Semitism in Switzerland, see Craig, 156.

43 Fehr, 1:93.

44 3 and 4 July 1853, in Glasenapp 4:137f., 142. "[Wagner] n'a nullement les allures démocratiques—et m'a assuré à vingt reprises que depuis son séjour ici il avait complètement rompu avec le parti des réfugiés et s'était même fait voir et bien venir auprès des gros bonnets de la bourgeoisie et de l'aristocratie du canton." Steiner, 23.

45 Wagner called him "open-hearted, very receptive, enthusiastic, devoted . . ." (to Uhlig, Feb. 50, in *Richard Wagner's Letters to His Dresden Friends*, 132). He changed his tune somewhat in later years when he described Spyri as "a singularly good-tempered man, but not overburdened with intellect" (*My Life*, 557).

46 14 June 1849 to Baumgartner; *Gesammelte Briefe* 1:281.

47 For a representative selection, see Zimmermann, *Neujahrsblatt der Allgemeinen Musikgesellschaft Zürich* 170 (1986) and 172 (1988). Spyri refers to Wagner repeatedly as "*unser* Richard Wagner."

48 Fehr, 1:22.

49 Hans Erismann, *Richard Wagner in Zürich* (Zurich, 1987), 66ff.; cf. also Zimmermann, *Neujahrsblatt* 172 (1988): 55.

50 On 6 April 55 to his friend Schwender. "Auch mit Richard Wagner habe ich den Verkehr abgebrochen, kann Dir dabei bei ihm nicht dienen. Er hat sich hier eine 'kleine Gemeinde' von einem Halbdutzend Menschen gebildet, die mit ihm Kultus betreiben . . . [= die seine Insolenzen und Albernheiten—die ich *entre nous* mehr für studiert als für naiv halte—vergöttern und (was sehr praktisch ist) gelegentlich seine Schulden bezahlen.] Ich bin gewohnt, jeden, mit dem ich näher umgehe, als einen Gleichberechtigten zu behandeln, mich nicht *über*, aber auch nicht *unter* ihn zu stellen, tauge daher zu solchem Schwindel nicht. . . ." Ernst Böckel, *Hermann Köchly* (Heidelberg, 1904), 173. The passage in brackets is censored in Böckel's biography and can be found in Gysi, 22.

51 9 May 1856 to Ludmilla Assing. "Vorigen Herbst war die Liszt-Wittgensteinsche Familie in Zürich, manche Woche, um bei Wagner zu sein, und da wurden alle Kapazitäten Zürichs herbeigezogen, einen Hof zu bilden. Ich wurde versuchsweise auch ein paarmal zitiert, aber schleunigst wieder freigegeben." *Gesammelte Briefe* 2:54.

52 8 March 1857 to Lina Duncker. "Richard Wagner ist durch die Anwesenheit Liszts, der seinetwegen kam, wieder sehr rappelköpfisch und eigensüchtig geworden. . . ." *Gesammelte Briefe* 2:166.

53 *My Life*, 599. "[I]n meiner Antwortsrede deutete ich unverhohlen an, daß ich nicht einsähe, warum nicht gerade Zürich doch vielleicht berufen sein sollte, auf biederer bürgerlicher Grundlage der Erfüllung meiner höchsten Wünsche im Betreff des mir vorschwebenden Kunstideales einen fördernden Vorschub zu leisten. Ich glaube, man bezog dies auf ein besonderes Erblühen der Männer-Gesangvereine und war mit meinen kühnen Verheißungen erträglich zufrieden." *Mein Leben*, 509.

54 "Seine plötzliche Abreise erregte nur insoweit Sensation, als man einem Mann wie Wagner, mit seiner demokratischen Richtung mehr republikanische Selbstüberwindung zugetraut hatte, voraussetzend, daß er die dortigen Verhältnisse besser würdigen und den Zweck des Festes nicht allein vom rein künstlerischen oder individuellen, sondern auch vom sozialen Standpunkte aus, namentlich im Hinblick auf die *Zukunft*, erfassen würde. . . . Er hätte viel wirken, und sich Freundschaft, Dank und Anerkennung mit geringer Mühe erwerben können." Quoted in A. Steiner, *Neujahrsblatt* 90 (1902): 28. Compare Spyri's apologetic comments in the *Eidgenössische Zeitung*

of 13 July 1854; in Zimmermann, *Neujahrsblatt der Allgemeinen Musikgesellschaft Zürich* 172 (1988): 7.

55 Klaus Urner, 198f.

56 Ernst Gagliardi et al., *Die Universität Zürich 1833-1933 und ihre Vorläufer: Festschrift zur Jahrhundertfeier* (Zürich, 1938), 466: "Die Schweizer und Schweizerinnen sind überhaupt ganz ungesellige Haustiere . . ."

57 Jacob Moleschott, *Für meine Freunde: Lebens-Erinnerungen:* "Es bestand in Zürich eine Wochengesellschaft, von welcher zwar die Schweizer nicht ausgeschlossen waren, in welcher aber doch die deutschen Teilnehmer so sehr die Überhand hatten, daß im Handel und Wandel immer von der deutschen Gesellschaft, vom deutschen Kränzchen die Rede war." Moleschott added: "Obgleich unter seinen Mitgliedern viele anziehende Persönlichkeiten und Männer ersten Ranges sich fanden, hielt ich mich von dem geschlossenen Kreise fern, weil ich mich immer zu dem Grundsatz bekannt habe, daß, wer eine öffentliche Anstellung, und noch dazu eine auszeichnende, im Auslande gefunden, es vermeiden soll, bei den dort seßhaften Landsleuten den Schwerpunkt seines gesellschaftlichen Verkehrs zu suchen" (Gießen, 1894), 280f.

58 Eliza Wille, 49.

59 3 April 1853 to Otto Jahn: "Tritt man die Eidgenossen nicht, so treten sie einen, und da ist die Wahl nicht schwer" (Craig, 154).

60 30 Oct. 1853. "Auch einen Hummer und Austern hatten wir mit, heute ist Sonntag, da werden meine Züricher Treuen damit traktiert; Du kennst Sie? Um keine Verstimmung zu verursachen, darf ich nicht einmal Herwegh dazu einladen." In Fehr, 1:260.

61 Keller, *Gesammelte Briefe* 4:103-9.

62 24 April 1856. "Außerdem ist es schrecklich, wie es in Zürich von Gelehrten und Literaten wimmelt, und man hört fast mehr Hochdeutsch, Französisch und Italienisch sprechen als unser altes Schweizerdeutsch, was früher gar nicht so gewesen ist. Doch lassen wir uns nicht unterkriegen. . . ." *Gesammelte Briefe* 2:43f.

63 26 May 1884; *Gesammelte Brief* 4:283.

64 Gottfried Keller, "Am Mythenstein," *Sämtliche Werke und ausgewählte Briefe* (Munich, 1958) 3:968-94. "Am Mythenstein" is not available in English; the translations are mine. All subsequent page numbers in parentheses refer to this edition.

65 Compare Keller's questions concerning Wagner's idea of a *Gesamtkunstwerk* in his letter to Wilhelm Baumgartner, dated Sept. 1851 (*Gesammelte Briefe* 1:294).

66 Cf. Adolf Muschg, *Gottfried Keller* (Munich, 1977), 280f.

67 "Die Schweiz ist—nach dem schönen, 1934 von Professor Wolfgang Golther in Zürich geprägten Worte—für den Wagnerfreund 'geweihter Boden' " (Fehr, 1:v).

68 Max Frisch, *Sketchbook 1946-1949,* trans. Geoffrey Skelton (New York, 1977), 109f. "[D]er deutsche und vielleicht abendländische Irrtum, daß wir Kultur haben, wenn wir Sinfonien haben, ist hierzulande kaum möglich; der Künstler nicht als Statthalter der Kultur; er ist nur ein Glied unter anderen; eine solche Sache des ganzen Volkes; wir erkennen sie nicht allein auf dem Bücherschrank und am Flügel, sondern ebensosehr in der Art, wie man seine Untergebenen behandelt. Sofern man Kultur in diesem Sinne meint, der mir der zukünftige scheint, müßten wir in keiner Weise erschrecken, wenn sie uns gelegentlich einen Anachronismus nennen. . . ." *Tagebuch 1946-1949* (Frankfurt, 1950), 169f.

Richard Wagner and the *Altgermanisten:*
Die Wibelungen and Franz Joseph Mone

EDWARD R. HAYMES

Let us begin with a few quotes from a treatise on the relationship between heroic legend and history:

> Der sagenhafte Gibicho ist zu Anfang des 7. Jahrhunderts aus Burgund an den Oberrhein gekommen, von jener Zeit schreiben sich die Gibichungen her, ihre Verwechslung mit den Nibelungen wird in der Mitte des 12ten Jahrh. bezeugt und hundert Jahre später ihre Beziehung auf Kobold. Die Häufigkeit der Form Gobelo im Rheinland hat in der Sage der Nibelungen ihren Grund, die im Rheinland heimatlich war. Daher findet man in andern Ländern wenige Zeugnisse dieses Namens, weil sie auch die Sage nicht hatten, warauf derselbe beruht. Bemerkenswerth ist die Gleichzeitigkeit der Gobelinen am Rhein und der Gibelinen in Italien, und die rheinischen Gibelinen beweisen, daß diese Partei keinen schwäbischen, sondern burgundisch-fränkischen Ursprung hatte.[1]

A second passage from the same text:

> Gibelin ist ein burgundischer Name und in Burgund dreihundert Jahre älter als in Italien, wohin er aus Burgund gekommen.[2]

And finally:

> Nach dieser Darstellung ist es nicht zu wundern, wenn der Namen Nibelung im politischen Sinne verhaßt war; vielleicht ist er aber in dieser Beziehung nicht gebraucht worden und schon im 11ten Jahrhundert durch Gibeling ersetzt worden. Da die fränkischen Kaiser und die Hohenstaufen . . . durch Heiraten mit dem burgundischen Geschlechte verwandt waren, so konte [*sic*] man diese Verbindung der Nibelungen und Gibichungen am passendsten mit Gibelungen ausdrücken, weil dieser Namen ein Mischen jener beiden ist.[3]

Connoisseurs of Wagner's more obscure prose writings will doubtless recognize the tone and argumentation of the composer's essay "Die Wibelungen: Weltgeschichte aus der Sage," a prime example of the kind of mixed-up reasoning that led to the grand pastiche of medieval motifs we find in *Der Ring des Nibelungen* and elsewhere. The quotes are not from Wagner, however, but from a sometime professor of history in Heidelberg named Franz Joseph Mone. Mone's *Untersuchungen zur Geschichte der teutschen Heldensage,* from which these quotes are taken, was published in Quedlinburg in 1836 and had an important place in Wagner's personal library in Dresden. In a letter to King Ludwig in 1869, he mentions it along with Wilhelm Grimm's *Deutsche Heldensage* as a source for the Siegfried legend.[4] In a letter to Franz Müller dated 1856, he listed the sources of the *Ring* and marked the Mone book as "sehr wichtig."[5] Curt von Westernhagen, who wrote an otherwise very perceptive survey of Wagner's personal library, found this indication of importance puzzling. "Es mag an einer für uns nicht mehr greifbaren Assoziation gelegen haben."[6] The associations are quite "greifbar," as we shall see.

Franz Joseph Mone was in many ways typical of the self-made first generation of *Altgermanisten*. He was born in Mingolsheim near Bruchsal in 1796. He studied history and worked most of his life as a historian, but his great love was the study of Germanic heroic legend. He published studies on the *Nibelungenlied* and *Otnit*[7] very early in his career, along with an essentially unedited printing of one of the *Otnit* manuscripts (1821). Later, he turned his attention to the Celtic past with such enthusiasm that his biographer in the *Allgemeine Deutsche Biographie* of 1885 refers disapprovingly to his *Keltomanie*.

When Wagner set about in Dresden in 1843 to assemble a definitive personal library, academic Germanistics was only a little over three decades old. These first three decades had been dominated by the exploration of the field, the publication of many texts, and a protracted debate on the relative merits of mythological and historical explanations of heroic legend. Mone was solidly in the mythological camp. In the lengthy introduction to his *Otnit* edition of 1821, he stoutly defends the mythological view against the historical, as represented for him by the Brothers Grimm, who—as we shall presently see—did not hold the views Mone attributed to them:

> Die drei Sagenkreise, des Heldenbuchs, Rolands und des Grals, enthalten keine Geschichte, sondern die älteste Religion der west- und nordeuropäischen Völker in geschichtlicher Umstaltung [sic].[8]

Wolfdietrich is for Mone an "altdeutscher Herakles" interpreted according to the Zodiac:

> Ich bemerke dabei, daß damit auch die Übereinstimmung des westfränkischen oder Rolandischen Sagenkreises mit dem des Heldenbuchs immer deutlicher hervortritt. Das Rolandslied habe ich schon einmal als das westfränkische Nibelungenlied angegeben. Flos ist der rolandische hörnen Sigfrit, Ogier ist Wolfdietrich, Karl im Rolandsliede ist der nämliche Mann, wie Etzel im Heldenbuch, u.s.w. Wer diese Forschungen weiter verfolgt, wird gewiß zu merkwürdigen Aufschlüssen gelangen.[9]

I think we can agree with his concluding sentence, although in a somewhat different sense of the word "merkwürdig" from that in which he meant it.

We can recognize in the young Mone a disciple of the mythological syncretism associated with Friedrich Creuzer. In fact, Mone wrote the Germanic sections of Creuzer's *Symbolik und Mythologie der alten Völker,* published between 1819-1823.[10] Mone's contribution formed the fifth and sixth volumes of the larger work and was published under the separate title of *Geschichte des Heidenthums im nördlichen Europa.* Creuzer managed to alienate both the Romantic forebears of his view of myth and the newer, more scholarly critics by his insistence on the primacy of symbols over myth. He argued that the Greek myths were merely attempts by monotheistic missionaries from India at making the truths about the one god palatable to the primitive ancestors of the Greeks. Many Romantics were willing to trace Greek and Germanic mythology back to Indian sources, but few of them were willing to admit Creuzer's insistence on the primacy of symbols. Wagner mentions having read Creuzer during his school years, but he did not include his work in his personal library in Dresden.

Perhaps the main excess of this school from our perspective was the tendency to equate everything with everything, as we can see in the quotes from Mone above. In his introduction to *Otnit,* Mone carried this method even further in his discussion by equating Otnit with Odin, Adonis, and Attis, and by equating Siegfried with Baldur and Thor.[11] He is, in spite of Creuzer's aberration, clearly a Romantic mythographer.

The term "romantic" is no longer pejorative when applied to literature, but it seems to be so when applied to philology and mythology. The sober textual criticism of Karl Lachmann, with his thorough grounding in classical philology and his natural proclivity for careful and methodical study, is what we remember today from the decades of the 1820s, 1830s and 1840s. Lachmann, however, was more of an exception than the rule.[12] We tend today to ignore the fact that most work done in the field of Germanic philology in that generation was carried out by people who thought more like Mone than like Lachmann. Even the dominant figures of the period, Jacob and Wilhelm Grimm, are guilty of distinctly "romantic" notions about their work.[13] Jacob's wide-ranging studies were informed by the unifying notion of an underlying Germanic mythology and language. His differences with Mone seem to us today to be more of emphasis than of substance. Mone felt that heroic legend had picked up historical names and references in passing as it moved from its truly mythological function in the distant past to its being written down in the Middle Ages. Both Jacob and Wilhelm Grimm also felt that myth was the older level, but allowed for a somewhat greater role of history in forming or reforming the stories. For Mone, this allowed history too great a role. The Grimms were also far less ready to project mythological structures into the pre-Germanic past or to reconstruct pre-Germanic myths from traces found in historical documents. Yet for us, much of Jacob Grimm's work on German mythology is almost as speculative as Mone's.[14]

Both Jacob Grimm (b. 1785) and his brother Wilhelm (b. 1786) were, like Mone, self-taught Germanists. Both had studied law, but only Wilhelm completed his degree. Wilhelm Grimm's compendious *Deutsche Heldensage,*[15] published in 1829, is mentioned several times by Wagner as an important source for his work. The major part of this book is a collection of quotations from medieval poetic and documentary sources referring to figures and events of heroic legend.

This is followed by an attempt at bringing some order into the chaotic world of the various heroic legends by sorting out the different story lines. Wilhelm Grimm concludes his discussion with some general remarks about *Heldensage*. Here he raises again the question of the mythical background of heroic legend:

> Ich nehme die schon am Eingange berührte Frage, ob der Ursprung der Sage mythisch oder historisch sey, hier wieder auf. Nach dem, was darüber vorgebracht ist, darf ich als ausgemacht betrachten, daß die geschichtlichen Beziehungen, welche die Sage jetzt zeigt, erst später eingetreten sind, mithin die Behauptung, daß jene Ereignisse die Grundlage geliefert, aller Stützen beraubt ist. . . .
>
> Wer einen mythischen Ursprung annimmt, hegt folgende Vorstellung. Die Helden, welche die Dichtung in geschichtlichem Schein auftreten läßt, waren früherhin Götter, verkörperte, sinnbildlich aufgefaßte Ideen über Erschaffung und Fortdauer der Welt. Als sich das Verständniß dieser Ideen verlor, bildete sich das Epos, in welchem die Götter zu menschlichen Helden, ihre Thaten zu geschichtlichen Begebenheiten herabsanken.[16]

One gets the feeling, finally, that Wilhelm Grimm was not totally at ease with either side of the question. From our distance, the differences between Jacob and Wilhelm Grimm on the one side and Mone on the other regarding the question of myth and *Heldensage* seem small. Both saw myth as the parent of heroic legend.

The successes of Jacob Grimm's work on the history of the German and Germanic languages led him to believe he could carry out similar studies on myth. Jacob tended to restrict his study of myth to the area of Germanic and specifically German religion. The speculative mythology of Mone and Creuzer went much further into the prehistoric past than Grimm was willing to go in his own work. His magnum opus in this area, the *Deutsche Mythologie* of 1835, is an attempt at recovering what could be known of German heathen religion with as little reference as possible to the richer Norse tradition of the *Eddas*. To do this he refers to a vast collection of items from folklore, folk song, and early literature.

Jacob Grimm vigorously rejected attempts by other scholars to derive German mythology from foreign models. The following quote displays the nationalistic tone we can sometimes hear in his writing, as well as his astute use of linguistic arguments to justify his methods in myth study:

> Unsere gelehrsamkeit, dem vaterland abspenstig, an pracht und ausbildung der fremde gewöhnt, mit auswärtiger sprache und wissenschaft beladen, in der heimischen armselig, war bereit die mythen unsrer vorzeit griechischen und römischen, als höheren, stärkeren unterzuordnen und die selbständigkeit deutscher poesie und sage zu verkennen, gleich als dürfe auch in der grammatik das deutsche ist geleitet werden aus est und esti [*in Greek Letters*], statt die ansprüche dieser drei formen völlig gleichzustellen.[17]

Grimm has little to say about possible pre-Germanic stages of the mythology. He had grown more careful in his methods since his early study on *Irmensäulen* (published in 1815), which Denecke calls an "abschreckendes Beispiel."[18]

Mone and the Brothers Grimm were very strict in their distinction between history, *Heldensage,* and myth. Wagner, for his part, was not as careful, and much of what he refers to under the term *Sage* in his writings would have been considered "myth" by his unwitting mentors. He is equally careless about using the term "myth" to refer to what Mone and the Grimms would certainly have called *Sage.* Most careful usage at that time would have required the presence of gods or other supernatural beings before speaking of myth. Wagner tended to blend the mythological with the heroic to produce the kind of mixture we find in the *Ring,* a mixture that, to be sure, owes as much to Greek drama and epic as it does to any surviving Germanic models. The interaction between gods and men in the *Ring* has clear antecedents both in Homer and in Greek drama, while such interaction is nonexistent in the German texts and rare in the Norse.

Both Mone and Wagner tended to see heroic stories as degenerations of original mythic patterns. Mone equates the Nibelungen *Sage* with both the Roland story and the Grail legend. Wagner provides a similar exercise in the following passage from the "Epilogischer Bericht" accompanying the published texts of the *Ring* poems:

> Der große Zusammenhang aller echten Mythen, wie er mir durch meine Studien aufgegangen war, hatte mich namentlich für die wundervollen Variationen hellsichtig gemacht, welche in diesem aufgedeckten Zusammenhange hervortreten. Eine solche trat mir mit entzückender Unverkennbarkeit in dem Verhältnisse Tristans zu Isolde, zusammengehalten mit dem Siegfrieds zu Brünnhilde, entgegen. Wie in den Sprachen durch Lautverschiebung aus demselben Worte zwei oft ganz verschieden dünkende Worte sich bilden, so waren auch, durch eine ähnliche Verschiebung oder Umstellung der Zeitmotive, aus diesem einen mythischen Verhältnisse zwei anscheinend verschiedenartige Verhältnisse entstanden. Die völlige Gleichheit dieser besteht aber darin, daß Tristan wie Siegfried das ihm nach dem Urgesetze bestimmte Weib, im Zwange einer Täuschung, welche diese seine Tat zu einer unfreien macht, für einen Anderen freit, und aus dem hieraus entstehenden Mißverhältnisse seinen Untergang findet.[19]

I don't think I am pushing the evidence too far if I find an anticipation of modern archetypal criticism in this passage, along with the Mone-like rush to see connections and similarities everywhere.

When Wagner settled in Dresden in 1843, he assembled a personal library that was intended to serve him the rest of his life. When he left Dresden hurriedly in 1849 in the wake of the uprising, he placed the library in the keeping of his brothers-in-law, who were members of the publishing family of Brockhaus. The library was kept as security for loans the composer had made and eventually, when Wagner was unable to repay these debts, was stored in the deepest vaults of the publishing house where it survived even the bombing of World War II. It was removed intact to Wiesbaden when the publisher moved there, and it is now kept there. Its contents are described in the Westernhagen survey mentioned above.

The library contained much material that would eventually find its way into Wagner's work. In particular, we can see a collection of books designed to educate our autodidact on a wide variety of subjects having to do with Germanic myth and heroic legend. The study of these materials led to an explosion of writing in 1848-49. The fruits of this explosion are not as well known as his musical works, or even as his unsavory essay "Das Judentum in der Musik" published in 1850, but they are central to the intellectual process involved in the production of the *Ring* text in the early 1850s and in the planning of the works that were to occupy the remainder of Wagner's life.

During this burst of activity, Wagner drafted prose résumés for three operas, one on Wieland the Smith, one on Friedrich Barbarossa, and one on Siegfried's death. He also wrote an extended description of the Nibelung legend as background to the Siegfried opera. This description contains almost all of the story of the *Ring* as it was to be worked out later. Finally, he wrote a strange essay which he published as a pamphlet, entitled "Die Wibelungen, Weltgeschichte aus der Sage."[20] This essay represents the link between Wagner's historical interest in Germany's past and the career of Barbarossa, on the one hand, and the Nibelung legend on the other. It also develops the intellectual justification for turning his back on history and for turning his entire attention to myth.

This essay is dizzying. In the first place, Wagner's prose style is deservedly infamous. My first impression was that Wagner wrote the way he did out of fear that someone might understand what he was actually saying, but later I decided that he wrote in what he perceived to be a lofty style without the discipline necessary to make such a style work. I admit in advance that there are several passages in the essay that I was simply unable to make sense of; they seem to lack a clarifying main clause. For these reasons, the essay is very difficult to summarize, but I'll give it a try.

When the peoples of Europe left their original home in Asia, they brought with them the idea of a primeval kingship related to a single royal family. Wagner equates this with the royal family of the Franks and sees the successes of the Franks in uniting the German tribes as the effect of the general reverence for the ruling family maintained by the people through ancient heroic legend. The legend is that of the Nibelungs, which consists in this essay mainly of Siegfried's killing of the dragon and winning of the treasure, followed by his murder by his closest family. The treasure is the symbol for the royal power, for the claim to *Weltherrschaft* characterized the Frankish kingship. In spite of the decline of the ruling family in the later period of Merovingian rule, the family was able to renew itself by shifting to another, equally royal branch, called "Pipingen" or "Karlingen" by Wagner. Charlemagne was the greatest representative of this royal power, both because of his ability to use the innate reverence of the German peoples for his royal line and because he was able, through his adoption of the Roman imperial title and his alliance with the Church, to combine the long-separated powers of king and priest.

After Charlemagne, Wagner argues, things went downhill again until a distant descendant of the Frank royal line, Friedrich Barbarossa, was able to bring it to flower again. The imperial power at this time was called by a variant of the ancient Nibelung name. This name was Wibelung. The forces of the German peoples who had been conquered by the Franks were known as Welfs. These names in their Italian variants Ghibelini and Guelphi eventually came to designate warring factions in Italian politics during the last part of the 13th century.

Siegfried is equated on the one side with the Sun god, as the slayer of the dragon of darkness and winter, and on the other with Christ. He is for Wagner the archetypal dying and returning god. His successors have to regain the hoard by avenging his death again and again. When the hoard becomes nothing more than property and its owners no longer have to carry out great deeds to win it, the hoard loses its ideal meaning. Medieval Germany was ready to transfer the ideal meaning of the hoard to the Holy Grail and to return the Grail to the eastern lands from which the primeval hoard had come. Barbarossa's crusade was actually a journey to the east to recover the Grail. His death on the journey recapitulates Siegfried's death. The political power attached to the hoard degenerated to pure hereditary ownership of property, and the nobles of Wagner's time were merely recipients of unearned wealth and status.

I have not been able to describe all the fine points of Wagner's argument, but this is the main thrust. After establishing a legitimacy going back beyond history for the royal family of the Franks, Wagner goes out of his way to show them in decline. His real hero seems to be the German *Volk,* which understands the mystical importance of both the royal family and the Nibelung myth that accompanies them. He uses the imagined perceptions of the *Volk* to refute statements made by medieval historians. I shall quote an example of this later.

Wagner collects ideas and materials from many different sources and combines them to produce or support his own deductions from them. In many ways, the process that produced the Wibelungen essay was quite similar to the process that produced the complex structure of the *Ring.* The most important difference was that Wagner was mainly combining what we would call secondary materials in the Wibelungen essay, while most of the *Ring* was constructed from stories and motifs derived directly from primary sources. Synthesis of this sort, however, was not restricted to self-taught dilettantes like Wagner. Let us compare some of Wagner's syntheses with those of the scholars he drew on.

Jacob Grimm's work on mythology includes a vast amount of materials collected from all kinds of sources. For modern tastes he is too ready to postulate relationships on the most tenuous of evidence, but he relies on the mass of material to make his point. One or another of his items might be open to question, might even be completely wrong, but the sheer bulk of his argument should carry the day.

We should, however, try to put ourselves in the position of the layman Richard Wagner as we read passages from Grimm's *Mythologie* like the following:

> Die höchste und oberste gottheit, wie man annehmen darf, allgemein unter allen deutschen stämmen verehrt, würde in gothischer mundart geheißen haben Vodans; sie hieß ahd. Wuotan, und diese benennung erscheint noch, wenn gleich selten, als eigenname: . . . Langobarden schrieben Wodan oder Guodan, Altsachsen Wuodan, Wodan, wiederum in Westfalen, mit dem vortritt des G, Guodan, Gudan, Angelsachsen

Voden, Friesen Weda, nach der neigung ihres dialects auslautendes N wegzuwerfen, und o auch ohne folgendes i umzulauten. die nord. form ist Odinn, bei Saxo Othinus, faeröisch Ouvin (gen. Ouvans, acc. Ouvan).[21]

This passage is not at all atypical. Grimm can hop from dialect to dialect and from form to form because of his sovereign mastery of the linguistic materials, but one can imagine the layman seeing something very much like the linguistically impossible combinations Wagner comes up with in his ruminations. Consider the following passage from the Wibelungen essay, which echoes both Mone and Grimm:

> Daß dieser Name nicht nur die Hohenstaufen in Italien, sondern in Deutschland schon deren Vorgänger, die fränkischen Kaiser, bezeichnete, ist durch Otto von Freisingen historisch bezeugt: die zu seiner Zeit in Oberdeutschland geläufige Form dieses Namens war "Wibelingen" oder "Wibelungen." Diese Benennung träfe nun vollständig mit dem Namen der Haupthelden der urfränkischen Stammsage, sowie mit dem bei den Franken nachweislich häufigen Familiennamen: Nibeling, überein, wenn die Veränderung des Anfangsbuchstabens N in W erklärt würde. Die linguistische Schwierigkeit dieser Erklärung löst sich mit Leichtigkeit, sobald wir eben den Ursprung jener Buchstabenverwechselung richtig erwägen; dieser lag im Volksmunde, welcher sich die Namen der beiden streitenden Parteien der Welfen und Nibelungen nach der der deutschen Sprache inwohnenden Neigung zum Stabreim geläufig machte. . . . "Welfen und Wibelungen" wird das Volk lange gekannt und genannt haben, ehe gelehrten Chronisten es beikam, sich mit der Erklärung dieser ihnen unbegreiflich gewordenen populären Benennungen zu befassen.[22]

It would be difficult to differentiate this passage from many similar ones in Mone's *Untersuchungen*. The reference to "gelehrte Chronisten" refers to Otto von Freising, who explained the battle cry of the Ghibelines by reference to the Swabian village of Waiblingen, an explanation still quoted in virtually every medieval history book. Both the logic and the tone of the passage are perfectly consonant with the writings of Mone and even some of the more rhapsodic passages in Jacob Grimm. All that is lacking is the depth of erudition in language and history Grimm could draw on. Grimm would often presuppose the linguistic argumentation behind his proof, something that the lay reader — even one as eager to grasp everything as Wagner — could easily overlook. It is perhaps characteristic of Wagner that the eventual form of the name for "die höchste und oberste gottheit" he chose, namely *Wotan,* is one that exists neither in the sources nor in Grimm's reconstructions.

Wagner can scarcely be faulted for building his Germanistic speculations on the work of Jacob Grimm, the most distinguished Germanist of his time, and the man celebrated in later generations as the *Vater der Germanistik.* That he made equally uncritical use of less reliable scholars such as Mone can perhaps be attributed to his isolation from academia. Wagner's recent biographers cannot be excused quite so easily. Martin Gregor-Dellin, for example, speaks correctly of "Die Wibelungen" as a "tollkühne essayistische Phantasie." Then he refers to the Nibelung-Ghibelin connection as an "etymologisches Hochseil-Kunststück

sonderbarster Art" (245).[23] Like Westernhagen, he seems unaware of the fact
that Wagner derived this etymological combination wholesale from Mone's
Untersuchungen, as the passages quoted at the beginning of this paper clearly
demonstrate. Mone provides pages of examples to show the spread of names he
can derive from Nibelung, as well as a demonstration that the name Nibelung
is closely associated with Franks and Burgundians.

The notion was not even original with Mone. In 1816, Carl Wilhelm Göttling
published a monograph with the title *Nibelungen und Gibelinen,* which was politely
but thoroughly dismantled by Wilhelm Grimm.[24] We may find it difficult to
imagine, but Wagner was occasionally less daring than his models. Mone felt
that the name Nibelung had continued even into his own time:

> Da wir die Napoleon in Verbindung mit den Gibellinen antreffen . . ., so fragt sich,
> ob das zufällig oder absichtlich war? Napoleon ist der ältere Namen, welcher der
> richtigen Form mehr entspricht; ich weiß keinen Grund anzugeben, wie er nach Italien
> kam, als durch die fränkische Eroberung des Langobardischen Reiches. Nur habe
> ich dafür bis jetzt kein altes Zeugnis gefunden.[25]

Wagner did include this notion in one draft of his essay, where he speaks of a
resurrected Nibelung army battling once again against the Welfs. He points out
that Napoleon's final defeat took place near the earliest places associated with
the Franks and the Nibelung legend in the Netherlands. Wagner deleted this
passage from the published version.[26] It seems that some of Mone's notions were
too extreme even for Wagner.

Many details of the Wibelungen essay, however, can be traced back to Mone.
Mone points out that the *Völkerwanderung* was only a stage in the development
of heroic legend. "Auf diese Art geht der Ursprung der Heldensage periodisch
rückwärts bis auf den Auszug unsers Volkes aus Indien und Persien."[27] The one
basic idea of all heroic legend can be recognized in the stories of many peoples.
This idea is "der Mord eines guten Verwandten und die Blutrache am ganzen
Geschlecht der Mörder."[28] He sees this pattern in Persian epic, in Homer, and
in the Nibelungen legend. Mone may not be the actual source of Wagner's concept
of the life of the legend among the *Volk,* but his statement of this point is concise
and must have supported Wagner's own inclination in this area. Mone writes:

> Diese Consequenz und die lange Dauer der Heldensage beweisen, daß der
> ursprüngliche Mythus sich sehr stark und tief dem Geist unsers Volkes eingeprägt
> haben muß, und nur daraus ist begreiflich, daß er sich in der geschichtlichen
> Umgestaltung der Heldensage so oft erneuert und seine Wirkung so lang angehalten
> hat. Der Ursprung des Mythus und Epos geht in die Urzeit unseres Volkes zurück,
> für die wir fast keine Erkenntnisquelle mehr haben, als eben die Heldensage.[29]

Neither Mone nor Wagner was afraid to use the slightest bits of evidence to peer
far into the past.

Mone expends many pages on a discussion of the *Nibelungenhort.* Wagner
follows him in his division of the hoard's meaning into idealistic and materialistic

facets. Mone stresses that the hoard was originally intended to be used to pay mercenaries in order to gain power. For Wagner, this intermediate step was unnecessary. He recognized that the hoard was power itself.

There are many other sources for the Wibelung essay, but it seems clear that Franz Joseph Mone was the major inspiration and authority for the most outrageous notions in it. Mone's interpretation of his evidence on the Nibelung-Gibelin name is carried almost verbatim into Wagner's text. Mone's concepts of myth and *Sage* lose some of their precision in Wagner's adaptation, but they gain in imaginative scope. Echoes of Jacob and Wilhelm Grimm are also present, but Wagner seems to know that the stricter scholars would not provide much that could be put through his mill. He was at some point made aware of the questionable scholarly value of Mone's work, but it does not seem to have bothered him much. In *Mein Leben* he wrote:

> Indem ich mich nun namentlich der deutschen Heldensage gründlicher zu bemächtigen suchte, als dies früher nur durch die Lektüre der *Nibelungen* und des *Heldenbuches* möglich gewesen war, fesselten mich endlich ganz vorzüglich die ungemein reichen, obwohl ihrer Kühnheit wegen von strengeren Fachgelehrten mit Bedenken angesehenen "Untersuchungen" Mones über die Heldensage. . . . Von entscheidendem Einfluß auf die bald in mir sich gestaltende Behandlung dieses Stoffes war an der Hand der *Mone*schen "Untersuchungen" die Lektüre der Wälsungensaga [*sic*].[30]

It is clear from this that Wagner was more interested in writings that fired his imagination than in scholarly rigor.

I have been concerned here to show, however, that Wagner did not make up such phantasmagoria as the Wibelung essay out of whole cloth. There were respected voices that provided much of the material, and Wagner did little more than combine them. The Wibelung essay is at once Wagner's self-administered M.A. thesis in mythological history and a bridge to the *Ring* itself. Unfortunately, it is a bridge as foggy and insubstantial as the rainbow provided for the gods in most productions of *Das Rheingold,* so we need to watch our footing as we try to cross it. The essay shows that Wagner did not look upon the Nibelung legend simply as interesting old stories that would make good theater, but as the very fabric of the German peoples' understanding of themselves, in other words, as functioning myth. After passing through the studies that led to this essay and the sketch for the Nibelung drama, Wagner was convinced that these works would speak to German audiences as the Greek dramas had spoken to the Greeks, as articulations of their mythical identity.

Critics standing outside this pattern of thought, ranging from Eduard Devrient in 1848[31] to Anna Russell in our own time, have recognized that the *Ring* is made up of stories alien to most opera-goers' experience. There is doubtless a great deal of self-delusion in Wagner's belief that he could reawaken the mythical power of these stories to dramatic life for the German *Volk,* and it is perhaps ironic that Wagner's myths have turned out to be far more universal than his theory would have them be. Certainly, this is because they speak to universal human mythical patterns rather than specifically German ones.

Wagner learned many things from the *Germanistik* of his day; not all of it was solid scholarship and some of it was downright goofy. There can be no doubt that the study of some of this material strengthened his nationalistic, anti-French, and anti-Semitic biases. The attack on Meyerbeer which he published as "Das Judentum in der Musik" appeared only one year after the Wibelungen essay, and both works often breathe the same air. The concept of *Volk* Wagner and others derived from the Romantics would grow and fester and become one of the roots of racist propaganda from Houston Stewart Chamberlain to Hitler. This development has been thoroughly explored elsewhere,[32] and I would like to conclude with a slightly different perspective.

In the 13th century, three Icelanders set about preserving the Germanic myths that were still somehow available to them in oral tradition in the form of mythological and heroic poetry. One of them simply collected the poems and wrote very brief prose bridges to connect them where necessary. His might be called the scholarly approach, and for this reason his product, the *Poetic Edda,*[33] has been of greatest interest to scholars in the last two hundred years. His personal contribution was probably minimal, and we admire the poems he collected and edited for themselves rather than the contribution of the collector. The *Poetic Edda* consists of about thirty poems including the majestic *Völuspa,* the poem that tells about the origin of the world and the end of the gods. It was Wagner's main source for both the figure of Erda in *Das Rheingold* and *Siegfried* and the Norn scene in *Götterdämmerung.* The collection also contains several poems in which the gods and giants engage in a battle of words. These poems were the source for the Wanderer's riddling contest with Mime in the first act of *Siegfried.* The collection concludes with poems about the heroes Sigurd (the Norse Siegfried), Helgi the Slayer of Hunding, and Sinfjötli, Sigurd's half-brother.

The *Poetic Edda* is the equivalent in many respects of the editions of medieval poems produced during the early part of the 19th century. Editors like Mone, Friedrich Heinrich von der Hagen, and even Jacob and Wilhelm Grimm produced editions that were more or less accurate reproductions of single medieval manuscripts. They, like the collector of the *Poetic Edda,* were mainly interested in preserving and disseminating relics of a past that might otherwise be lost.

The second of the three Icelanders is also nameless. He retold the stories preserved in the poems of the *Poetic Edda* in the form of a traditional prose saga. This work, the *Völsungasaga,*[34] became a major source for Wagner in his work on the *Ring.* It is a relatively artless retelling of the stories; so much so that some scholars have felt that they could reconstruct almost verbatim some of the lost poems on which it was based. Perhaps the closest parallel to this achievement in the 19th century can be found in the retelling of myth and heroic legend by popularizers like Bullfinch and Schwab.

The third man was Snorri Sturluson, a major figure in 13th-century Icelandic politics and literature, who lived from 1179 to 1241. His work, which was actually the earliest to bear the title *Edda,* is now generally called the *Prose Edda*[35] to distinguish it from the *Poetic Edda.* It is no accident that an individual author's name is associated with this work, since it is clearly a new and individual work of art. Snorri's materials were essentially the same as those used by the other two authors/collectors, but his approach was that of a sovereign artist rather than an obsequious servant of the tradition.

Snorri's work was conceived as an instruction book for skalds, Icelandic court poets who were much in demand in the courts of the kings and earls in Norway and Denmark. The first main section of the work, entitled "Gylfaginning" or "The Deluding of Gylfi," is a narrated dialogue between a King of Sweden named Gylfi and the god Odin in which Odin's responses to Gangleri's questions take the form of stories about the gods. This dialogue brings together the cosmology and mythology of the Germanic heathens, completely reshaped to fit into this new artistic form. Bridges and motivations lacking in the source poems are filled in without commentary and the past and future history of the gods of Asgard is presented in a style that is cogent and entertaining, as in the story of the building of Valhalla. I often wish Wagner had transferred this incident a little more literally to *Das Rheingold*. It would have made Loki/Loge an even more equivocal character and provided interesting challenges for the stage directors and makeup artists. In the story, the gods had contracted with a giant for the construction of Valhalla, for which he was to receive not only Freya, but also the sun and the moon as payment. In order for the giant to receive his wages the work had to be finished before the first day of summer. The work proceeds more rapidly than the gods had expected because of the giant's helper, a stallion named Svathilfari. The gods call on Loki to help them. In Snorri's words:

> Loki swore oaths that, no matter what it cost him, he would arrange things so that the builder should forfeit his wages. The same evening, when the builder was driving out after stones with his stallion Svathilfari, a mare ran out of a wood up to the horse and whinnied to him. And when the stallion knew what kind of horse that was, it became frantic and broke its traces asunder and ran after the mare, but she took to the wood with the builder after her.[36]

The gods see that the giant will not be able to finish his job anymore and Thor kills him. "Loki, however, had had such dealings with Svathilfari that some time later he bore a foal. It was grey and had eight legs, and amongst gods and men that horse is the best."[37] This horse is Odin's famous steed Sleipnir.

The second section of the book, "Poetic Diction," abandons the narrative framework to answer a sort of catechism of questions about poetic symbols or kennings. Many stories are told here, including the Nibelung story, but the emphasis is on the use of these stories to explain the use of such kennings as "otter's ransom" for gold. The story told here is the source of the ransom of Freia in *Das Rheingold*. The gods Odin and Loki have to steal the gold of the dwarf Andwari to pay *wergeld* for the killing of an otter (actually a man who had assumed the shape of an otter). Part of this treasure was a ring. Snorri tells us that the "dwarf begged [Loki] not to take it from him, saying that if only he were allowed to keep it he could by its means become wealthy again. Loki said that he was to be left without a single penny and, taking the ring from him, was going away, when the dwarf declared that the ring would destroy everyone who owned it."[38] The curse was as effective as Alberich's in the *Ring*.

The final section of Snorri's *Edda* is called "Poetic Metres" and consists of a virtually untranslatable collection of poems designed to demonstrate different metric and strophic forms.

Snorri introduced his work with an intriguing foreword. It begins with an almost literal translation of the first verses of Genesis. After the Flood, men again forget God and begin to explain the earth in terms derived from the observation of living bodies, i.e., the earth is seen as flesh, rocks and stones as bones, and underground water as blood. This section prepares the reader for the creation of the earth from the body of the giant Ymir described later in the "Deluding of Gylfi."

The history of postdiluvian humanity then focuses on Troy, "the most famous of all palaces and halls." The grandson of Priam is identified as Thor and a further descendant as Odin. These men took their families with them to the North where they were known as Aesir, because they had come from Asia. The most important families of the North—including the Volsungs—are descended from Odin. Snorri does not mention that they were revered as gods. In fact, he explains their ability to change shape and appear to Gylfi in many different forms in the "Deluding of Gylfi" as simple trickery, thus the title of the section. The gods are made harmless by being represented as mere human magicians. Their stories are presented with no commentary on their veracity.

The foreword allows Snorri to place his stories of the Norse gods within a larger Christian context. The gods are not really gods, but merely heroes of the past. The foreword draws upon several notions about history and place of the pagan gods that were known in the Middle Ages, but Snorri is remarkable for his ingenuity in placing the heathen lore in a context that would not be objectionable to his Christian contemporaries.

What is remarkable to me is the similarity of Snorri's achievement to Wagner's. Snorri retold traditional stories in a way that explained away their inconsistencies and produced a unified whole. He wrote a separate essay that, like Wagner's Wibelungen essay, is usually ignored in favor of the more artistic main dish. Snorri's foreword serves as a bridge between the Christian thinking of his contemporaries and the mythical stories that were still known, but were no longer believed. Wagner's Wibelungen essay bridged the distance between the historical nationalism of Wagner's earlier plans to write an opera on Friedrich Barbarossa and the mythical nationalism of the eventual plan for the *Ring*.

We should keep these parallels in mind when we look both at Wagner's accomplishments and his misdemeanors. R. G. Finch, who is a distinguished medievalist, recently published an extensive litany of Wagner's sins against medieval literature.[39] He concluded that we should follow Erda's advice in *Das Rheingold*, when she says to Wotan "dir rath' ich, meide den Ring." Finch does admit that he is condemning the *Ring* only in its role as a source of information about Norse and German mythology. It is my impression that Finch, like most modern critics, does not realize how much Richard Wagner worked like the best of medieval poets. Like Snorri Sturluson and the anonymous poet of the Middle High German *Nibelungenlied,* Wagner took the older materials available to him and transformed them into a new whole, one that made sense to him and one he felt was valid for his own time. The fact that we are still discussing it today indicates that, in some important ways, he succeeded.

Notes

1 "The legendary Gibicho came to the Upper Rhine from Burgundy at the beginning of the 7th century; the Gibichungs claim to originate at that time; their confusion with the Nibelungs is recorded in the middle of the 12th century, as is, a hundred years later, their relationship to Kobold. The frequency of the form Gobelo in the Rhineland has its basis in the legend of the Nibelungs, which was native to the Rhineland. For this reason, one finds few references for this name in other regions because they did not have the legend on which the same was based. Noteworthy is the simultaneity of the Gobelins on the Rhine and the Ghibelines in Italy, and the Rhenish Ghibelines prove that this party did not have a Swabian origin, but rather a Burgundian-Frankish one." Franz Joseph Mone, *Untersuchungen zur Geschichte der teutschen Heldensage* (Quedlinburg, 1836), 15. All translations except that in note 19 are mine.

2 "Ghibeline is a Burgundian name and three hundred years older in Burgundy than in Italy, where it migrated from Burgundy." Ibid.

3 "After this presentation we should not be amazed that the name Nibelung was hated in its political sense; perhaps it was not even used in this connection and had been already replaced in the 11th century by Gibeling. Since the Frankish emperors and the Hohenstaufen . . . were related through marriage to the Burgundian dynasty, one could most fittingly express this connection between the Nibelungs and the Gibichungs with Gibelungen, since this name is a mixture of the other two." Ibid., 26.

4 *Selected Letters of Richard Wagner,* tr. and ed. Stewart Spencer and Barry Millington (London, 1987), 745.

5 Richard Wagner, *Dokumente zur Entstehungsgeschichte des Bühnenfestspiels* Der Ring des Nibelungen, ed. Werner Breig and Hartmut Fladt = Richard Wagner, *Sämtliche Werke* vol. 29, 1 (Mainz, 1976), 19.

6 Curt von Westernhagen, *Wagners Dresdener Bibliothek* (Wiesbaden, 1966), 35.

7 *Otnit,* ed. Franz Joseph Mone (Berlin, 1821). The name is spelled both "Ortnit" and "Otnit" in the medieval manuscripts. Most later scholars have adopted the former spelling. Mone, however, uses "Otnit" throughout.

8 "The three legendary cycles, the *Heldenbuch,* Roland, and the Grail, contain no history, but rather the oldest religion of the west and north European peoples in historical guise." Mone, *Otnit,* x. The *Heldenbuch* is a term derived from late medieval collections of heroic stories. The content varies from manuscript to manuscript. Writers of Mone's generation were used to referring to the narratives usually contained in such collections as if they formed a coherent body of texts.

9 "I note in addition, that the agreement of the West Frankish or Rolandish legendary cycle with the Heldenbuch also becomes clearer and clearer. I have already referred to *The Song of Roland* as the West Frankish *Nibelungenlied.* Flos is the Rolandish *Horned Sigfrit,* Ogier is Wolfdietrich, and Charles [Charlemagne] is the same man as Etzel in the *Heldenbuch,* etc. Whoever pursues this research further will certainly come to remarkable results." Mone, *Otnit,* viii.

10 Georg Friedrich Creuzer, *Symbolik und Mythologie der alten Völker, Besonders der Griechen* (Leipzig, 1819–23).

11 Mone, *Otnit,* 40ff.

12 For an overview of the early history of Germanic philology, see Rudolf von Raumer, *Geschichte der Germanischen Philologie vorzugsweise in Deutschland* (Munich, 1870); Josef Körner, *Nibelungenforschungen der deutschen Romantik* (Darmstadt, 1968); and Johannes Janota, *Eine Wissenschaft etabliert sich: Wissenschaftsgeschichte der Germanistik* 3 (Tübingen, 1980).

13 For an overview of the work of both brothers, see Ludwig Denecke, *Jacob Grimm und sein Bruder Wilhelm* (Stuttgart, 1971), and the histories cited in note 12 above.

14 Jacob Grimm, *Deutsche Mythologie* (Berlin, 1875).

15 Wilhelm Grimm, *Die deutsche Heldensage* (Darmstadt, 1957).

16 "I take up here again the question touched on at the beginning of this study whether the origin of heroic legend is historical. After that which has been presented I can consider it demonstrated that the historical connections which the legend now shows have entered only later, especially since the claim that those events had provided the basis is now robbed of all foundation. . . .

   Anyone who assumes a mythical origin cherishes the following notion: the heroes, whom legend portrays in a historical guise, were earlier gods, were incarnate, figuratively conceptualized ideas about the creation and continuation of the world. When the understanding of these ideas got lost, epic was formed, in which the gods sank down to the stature of human heroes and their deeds to historical events." Ibid., 397–98.

17 "Our scholarship–hostile to the fatherland, used to the magnificence and development of the foreign, laden with alien language and scholarship, impoverished in things of its own land–was prepared to subordinate the myths of our antiquity to the Greek and Roman, finding them stronger and higher. It was prepared to deny the independence of German poetry and legend, just as if in grammar it would have to derive *ist* from *est* and *esti,* instead of recognizing the claims of all three forms as completely equal." Jacob Grimm, *Deutsche Mythologie* 2:xx.

18 "Horrifying example." Ibid., 112.

19 "The great interconnection of all genuine myths, which had become clear to me through my studies, had made me sensitive in particular to the wonderful variations which come forward in this freshly discovered connection. Such a connection appeared with delightful clarity in the relationship between Tristan and Isolde and Siegfried with Brünnhilde. As in the case of languages where two often completely different words are developed through sound shifts, a similar shifting or rearrangement of the temporal motifs can bring out of one mythical relationship two apparently different relationships. The complete identity of these consists in the fact that Tristan, like Siegfried, wins for another the woman the ancient laws had reserved for him while under the influence of a delusion that makes his act unfree, and eventually meets his downfall as a result of the resulting false relationship." *Dokumente,* 131.

20 Richard Wagner, *Gesammelte Schriften und Dichtungen in zehn Bänden,* ed. Wolfgang Golther (Berlin, n. d.) 2:115–55. The pamphlet originally appeared in 1849.

21 Grimm, *Mythologie,* 1:120. "The highest, the supreme divinity, universally honoured, as we have a right to assume, among all Teutonic races, would in the Gothic dialect have been called *Vôdans;* he was called in OHG *Wuotan,* a word which also appears, though rarely as the name of a man. . . . the Longobards spelt it *Wôdan* or *Guôdan,* the Old Saxons *Wuodan, Wôdan,* but in Westphalia again with the *g* prefixed, *Guôdan, Gudan,* the Anglo-Saxons *Wôden,* the Frisians *Weda* from the propensity of their dialect to drop a final *n,* and to modify *ô* even when not followed by an *i.* The Norse form is Odhinn, in Saxo Othinus, in the Faröe isles Ouvin, gen. Ouvans, acc. Ouvan." Translation from Jacob Grimm, *Teutonic Mythology,* tr. James Steven Stallybrass (1883; repr. New York, 1966) 1:131.

22 "The fact that this name refers not only to the Hohenstaufen in Italy, but in Germany referred also to their predecessors, the Frankish emperors, is historically demonstrated by Otto of Freising. The form of the name that was common in Upper Germany was 'Wibelingen' or 'Wibelungen.' This name would coincide completely with the name of the main heroes of the original Frankish tribal legend, as well as with the demonstrably common Frankish name Nibeling, if the change of the first letter from *N* to *W* could be explained. The linguistic difficulty of this explanation can be solved easily as soon as we consider the origin of this confusion of letters correctly. This origin lay in the speech of the people, which adopted the names of the two warring parties Welf and Nibelung according to the native tendency of the German language to alliteration. . . . 'Welfs and Wibelungs' were probably well known to the people before it occurred to learned chronicle writers to concern themselves with these popular designations, which had become incomprehensible to them." *Gesammelte Werke* 2:162–63.

23 "A daring essayistic fantasy," and an "etymological high-wire trick of the most bizarre kind." Martin Gregor-Dellin, *Richard Wagner: Sein Leben, sein Werk, sein Jahrhundert* (Mainz, 1983), 245.

24 Wilhelm Grimm, *Kleinere Schriften* (Berlin, 1882) 2:161–75. Mone refers to Göttling in his *Untersuchungen*, so Wagner may have looked it up; but he did not have the book in his Dresden library nor does he refer to it in any of the writings I have explained. The idea of an association between the Nibelungs and the Gibelins was still being discussed at the same time Wagner was working on these questions. Albert Schott published an essay entitled "Welfen und Gibelinge" in Schmidt's *Zeitschrift für Geschichte* 5 (1846): 317ff. Jacob Grimm demolished his arguments in the same volume of this journal, pp. 453–60. I have not seen Schott's original article.

25 "Since we find the Napoleons in association with the Ghibellines . . . it must be asked whether this was accidental or deliberate. Napoleon is the older name and it matches the correct form better; I can give no reason why it came to Italy, unless it was through the Frankish conquest of the Lombard kingdom. Unfortunately, I have not been able to find any old documentation for this up to now." Mone, *Untersuchungen*, 12.

26 The deleted passage is quoted in Helmut Pfotenhauer, "'Der große Zusammenhang aller echten Mythen': Zu Richard Wagners mythologischer Arbeit am 'Ring'," in *Germanistik in Erlangen: Hundert Jahre nach der Gründung des Deutschen Seminars* (Erlangen, 1983), 313–14.

27 "In this way the origin of heroic legend goes step-by-step backwards to the exodus of our people from India and Persia." *Untersuchungen*, 3.

28 "The murder of a good relative and the blood vengeance on the whole race of the murderers." Ibid., 5.

29 "This consistency and the longevity of heroic legend prove that the original myth must have impressed itself very deeply in the mind of our people, and only that can explain why it has renewed itself so often in the historical form of heroic legend and why its effect has survived so long. The origin of the myth and epic goes back to the primeval times of our people for which we have almost no sources except for the heroic legend itself." Ibid., 4.

30 "As I sought to gain a command of German heroic legend more thoroughly than had been possible earlier with the reading of only the *Nibelungen* and the *Heldenbuch*, I was entranced by the exceptionally rich *Investigations* on heroic legend by Mone, even though these are criticized by stricter scholars because of their boldness. . . . Of decisive importance for the treatment of this material that was forming in me was, along with the Mone *Investigations*, my reading of the Volsung Saga." *Dokumente*, 17.

31 Ibid., 29.

32 David C. Large provides an overview in his "Wagner's Bayreuth Disciples," in *Wagnerism in European Culture and Politics* (Ithaca, 1984), 72–33. For a critical examination of the connection between Wagner and the National Socialists, see L. J. Rather, *The Dream of Self-Destruction: Wagner's Ring and the Modern World* (Baton Rouge, 1979), esp. 167–72.

33 Ed. Hans Kuhn (Heidelberg, 1962). An English translation is available in *Poems of the Vikings: The Elder Edda*, trans. Patricia Terry (Indianapolis, 1969).

34 A facing page translation is available in the edition by R. G. Finch, *The Saga of the Volsungs* (London, 1965). Somewhat more accessible is *The Saga of the Volsungs: The Norse Epic of Sigurd the Dragon Slayer*, trans. Jesse L. Byock (Berkeley, 1990).

35 The narrative portions are in Snorri Sturluson, *Edda: Gylfaginning og Prosafortellingene af Skáldskaparmál*, ed. Anne Holtsmark (Copenhagen, n.d.). A translation of these portions is contained in Snorri Sturluson, *The Prose Edda: Tales from Norse Mythology*, trans. Jean I. Young (Cambridge, 1954).

36 Ibid., 67.

37 Ibid., 67–68.

38 Ibid., 111.

39 R. G. Finch, "The Icelandic and German Sources of Wagner's Ring of the Nibelung," *Leeds Studies in English* 17 (1986): 1–23.

Reworking History:
Wagner's German Myth of Nuremberg

Peter Uwe Hohendahl

When Hitler's army surrendered to the Allies in the spring of 1945, the city of Nuremberg, like so many other German cities, was little more than a pile of rubble.[1] Many of the houses, churches, fountains, and statues that had stood as manifestations of the German culture of the 15th and 16th centuries had ceased to exist. The end of the Third Reich in 1945 seemed to be also the end of German history as it had been conceived by 19th-century German historians, critics, and artists, Richard Wagner among them. *Die Meistersinger von Nürnberg,* with its representation and glorification of 16th-century German culture, was undoubtedly among the artworks that had played a very prominent part in the appropriation of the Bayreuth Festival by the National Socialists.[2] The fascist claim that the yearning for a truly German culture, as it was expressed in Wagner's opera, found its fulfillment in the Third Reich, overshadowed this work. It was of course not accidental that the trials against the most prominent leaders of the Third Reich took place in Nuremberg. The choice of the Nuremberg location was clearly a moral and political response to the *Parteitage,* the highly dramatic national rallies of the Nazis.

Clearly, the image of the organized masses at the party rallies had compromised what seemed to be Wagner's vision of a German folk culture. In 1945 it must have been very difficult, to say the least, to imagine a rebirth of the Bayreuth Festivals, since they had been part of the official state culture between 1933 and 1945. Yet the Bayreuth Festivals were revived, and *Die Meistersinger* was among the early productions. In 1951, Rudolf Hartmann staged *Die Meistersinger,* using numerous elements of Heinz Tietjen's 1943 production.[3] The old Nuremberg, which had been completely destroyed in 1944, reappeared on stage. Especially in the third act, in which the citizens of Nuremberg gather at the *Festwiese,* Hartmann pretty much copied the 1943 production, as if the German defeat had never occurred. The critical reaction to this would come only five years later. It was Wieland Wagner in his 1956 production of *Die Meistersinger* who, by focusing on the discrepancy between historical and aesthetic reality, challenged the Bayreuth tradition. In order to rescue the opera he dropped the realistic style which the audience was used to associate with *Die Meistersinger,* and replaced it with abstract forms and images.[4] "In the second act nothing reminds us any more of *Butzenscheiben* romanticism. Blue-violet light fills the

1. The Kugel pharmacy and Town Hall of Nuremberg, 2 January 1945. From *Der Luftkrieg in Nürnberg: Quellen des Stadtarchivs zum 2. Januar 1945.* Printed by the Town Council of Nuremberg (Nuremberg, 1945), p. 52.

almost empty stage. Above the kidney-shaped open space of the stage, which shows a stylized pattern of pavement, hangs a huge elder ball with lilac leaves and white blossoms. The stage is filled only with two filigree benches, a small elder tree on the right side and, as symbol of the intoxicating midsummer night, a small statue of cupid."[5] Similarly, the *Festwiese* of the third act, which had been an essential element of traditional productions since it provided the space for the celebration of the unity of Hans Sachs and the *Volk,* was replaced by an abstract, geometrical space in the shape of an amphitheater.[6] What Wieland Wagner attempted was, in the words of Hans Mayer, a complete "Entrümpelung" of the opera.[7] By radically changing the style of the production, he wanted to remove *Die Meistersinger* from its historical environment—most importantly, of course, from its appropriation by the Nazis. The fusion of *Festwiese* and the Nazi party rallies, the blending of Wagner's vision of German art with fascist culture, was dissolved in a modernist production. Instead of a national myth, Wieland Wagner wanted to present an artful and complex comedy.

But could this strategy succeed? Can we separate nationalist and pre-fascist ideology and the celebration of the aesthetic? In 1964, Marcel Reich-Ranicki, responding to Wieland Wagner's 1963 production, argued that this attempt was doomed from the very beginning because Wagner's opera, written in the 1860s, contained the very nationalism that his grandchild wanted to eliminate. "Wieland Wagner's plan did not work out; it could not work out, for *Die Meistersinger* cannot be staged against the full score, nor can it be de-Germanized—and this is precisely what his forced attempts at de-romanticizing the opera were meant to accomplish. One may regret and deplore this impossibility, but one cannot change it: the Germanomania and the national pathos are intrinsic parts of the work."[8] It is obvious that Reich-Ranicki rejected the style of the 1963 production, but it is not quite clear how he expected Wieland Wagner to deal with Wagner's synthesis of art and nation. Both Adorno,[9] whom Reich-Ranicki attacked in his essay, and Hans Mayer, who responded to his polemic, equally emphasized the intrinsic nature of the national myth which could not simply be removed from the work (its text and music) through technical stage devices: for instance, an abstract design. Adorno and Mayer underlined the historical origin of the Nuremberg myth, pointing to its romantic and Young German antecedents as well as to Wagner's recasting of its elements. It was a difference in their readings of this tradition, then, that divided the critics of the 1963 production. While Reich-Ranicki kept his distance from the new Bayreuth, Mayer clearly welcomed the transformation of the tradition as it was reflected in the new productions of *Die Meistersinger.*

The debate of 1964, for the first time, pointed to a rather complex problem which Wagner criticism had rarely approached because it was either assumed—by 19th-century critics of Wagner, for instance—that Wagner's representation of Hans Sachs and Nuremberg and the real Nuremberg of the 16th century were more or less identical, or it was assumed – for example, by postwar critics – that Wagner's text was part of the history of modern German ideology and had little or nothing to do with the historical configuration of Meistersinger culture. Yet this opposition divides what was one for Richard Wagner. Wagner had seen the old Nuremberg, its Gothic and Renaissance buildings; he was familiar with the atmosphere of a largely intact medieval town. He was also familiar with the reappropriation of Nuremberg's history in the early 19th century when he began to work on the material in 1845.[10] Not only did Wagner's response, as it took shape in a number of sketches and drafts between 1845 and the completion of the opera in 1868, incorporate and modify earlier appropriations, but it also compared them with his own experience of contemporary German culture and politics. With the transformation of the historical environment – 1848, 1862, 1866 – the reading of the Sachs material was likely to change as well, as Wagner's drafts and programmatic statements about *Die Meistersinger* make quite clear.[11] Hence the above-mentioned complexity is this: we are dealing with an intricate dialectic between layers of historical representations and constructions in which the meaning of the individual element is always determined by all other elements.

I wish to distinguish three visions of Nuremberg that were current during the 1840s when Wagner conceived his *Meistersinger* project: the romantic vision in Wackenroder's *Herzensergießungen* and E. T. A. Hoffmann's novella *Meister Martin,* the liberal vision as it was articulated in Gervinus's history of German literature (1835-42), and the Biedermeier vision which we find in Albert Lortzing's 1840 opera *Hans Sachs.* Wagner was familiar with this opera, as he was acquainted with Gervinus's treatment of Hans Sachs and the German Meistersinger. Finally, he had also read Hoffmann's novella, and he had seen the numerous pictorial representations of Nuremberg by 16th-century artists.[12] It is not enough, however, to mention these materials as potential or actual influences on Richard Wagner, as if *Die Meistersinger* were a composite of elements taken from various traditions. Rather, the point of my reconstruction is to position Wagner within the development of the Nuremberg myth, which found its final articulation in the *Parteitage* of the 1930s.

What the three early 19th-century visions of Nuremberg have in common is the contrast between 16th-century German culture and its contemporary counterpart. Wackenroder explicitly invokes, in the letter of a young German painter (who lives in Rome) to his friend in Nuremberg, the old artisan tradition found in the paintings of Albrecht Dürer.[13] The praise of the Nuremberg masters, especially of Albrecht Dürer, assumes that there is a major difference between the premodern world of Renaissance Nuremberg and the age of the author. The narrator invokes the Nuremberg of the past in order to glorify an authentic, organic culture in which the artist, unlike his modern counterpart, was still part of the social community. In this context, the much-quoted and much-maligned *Butzenscheiben* of Renaissance houses serve as an appropriate filter for the light that falls on the old *Folianten* containing the works of Hans Sachs.

The contrast between the old Germany and the present articulates a cultural difference, but not a national program. The concept of Germany in the *Herzensergießungen* is pre-Napoleonic: it emphasizes the yearning for a lost culture rather than national rivalry or ideas of national hegemony. Wackenroder's Nuremberg suggests a lost *Heimat* that possibly never existed. It would be highly inappropriate to search for historical factuality in this vision. For Wackenroder, the essence of Nuremberg is expressed in Dürer's paintings, not in the facts of social history.

In Gervinus's *Geschichte der deutschen Nationalliteratur* (1835-42), the social and political components have become much stronger and much more explicit. In its overall design, Gervinus's literary history attempted to present the development of German literature, from its beginnings to the end of the 18th century, as the articulation of Germany's national identity. According to Gervinus, the formation of this cultural identity culminated around 1800 in the synthesis of Weimar. After a decline during Romanticism, it could be transcended only by transforming the cultural energy into political energy. In other words, the cultural identity of the Germans prepared the way for their political identity that should be achieved in the near future. Gervinus's teleological conception of literary history, while insisting on a strictly historical treatment of the material, encouraged contemporary appropriations, since the idea of a process of identity formation allowed the retrieval of older authors as prefigurations of the present. This is especially true because Gervinus also stressed certain constant elements which recur in changing configurations. One of them is the popular/erudite opposition, which is particularly important for his presentation of the 16th and 17th centuries. These centuries, according to Gervinus, were characterized by strong tensions between popular vernacular literature and the neo-Latin humanism of the university-trained literati. In other words, high culture was not necessarily German culture. For this reason, Opitz's reform of German literature at the beginning of the 17th century was extremely important since it overcame, at least partially, the popular/erudite dichotomy. In this context, the poet and playwright Hans Sachs, whom Gervinus treats at the end of the second volume of his literary history, serves as a transitional figure between the popular tradition of the Middle Ages and modern German literature. "He stands in the middle between old and new art; in his works, he points to the older elements which the nation had produced and he lays the foundations for those elements which the nation would create later."[14] More importantly, Sachs, together with Luther and Hutten, is for Gervinus one of the founding fathers of the German nation, a "Reformator in der Poesie."[15] Dividing the vernacular tradition into an aristocratic and a plebeian branch, Gervinus stresses the popular element in Hans Sachs's work, both in terms of its background and its intention. For it is true that the emphasis on the popular character of Hans Sachs contains an explicit political element. Gervinus argues that Sachs, like Hutten, was a committed Protestant, but, unlike Hutten, not a radical, and that it was his moderate political stance that served the German nation long after Hutten's strident voice had fallen silent.

What Wagner could learn from Gervinus's treatment was the solid patriotism of Hans Sachs. The poet comes across as social critic and upright citizen. The mastersinger Hans Sachs, however, is hardly mentioned; yet it was precisely Sachs's position within the development of *Meistersang* that became crucial for Wagner's opera. In his chapter on the *Meistergesang,* Gervinus appropriately stressed its grounding in the culture of medieval towns. Again, it is the transitional nature of this highly formalized and rigidly institutionalized poetry which interested Gervinus. Contrasting court and town, he observes: "Until then, poetry had to live by begging at the courts and had not been able to get rid of a parasitic tone vis-à-vis its patrons and supporters, but mastersong (*Meistergesang*) is the basis of our more recent, independent poetry also in the sense that it taught the poets how an emphatic practice of this beautiful tradition contains happiness — even when the success is only modest — which does not need remuneration."[16] The argument that in the schools of *Meistersang* art emancipated itself from patronage balances the argument that *Meistersang* was unoriginal and rigid. In short, Gervinus offered two conflicting views of *Meistersang.* On the one hand, it transcended the limitations of courtly medieval poetry; on the other hand, its form and poetic theory remained within the parameters of the medieval world.[17]

Gervinus's vision of Hans Sachs and Nuremberg culture is closely connected with the liberal discourse on popular culture of the 1830s and 1840s. Both the Young Germans and the Young Hegelians of the 1840s (Robert Prutz, for example) promoted a revival of popular culture — not, however, as pure entertainment but as a democratic cultural experience that transcended narrower notions of aesthetic culture. Such a desire for a cultural revolution did not inspire Albert Lortzing when he composed his opera *Hans Sachs,* based on a libretto by Philipp Reger (who used Deinhardstein's 1827 play). The solution of the dramatic conflict at the end of the third act depends very much on the figure of Emperor Maximilian, who rescues Hans Sachs from exile and enables him to marry Kunigunde, the daughter of Meister Steffen, the rich and powerful goldsmith. The triumph of the poet and Meistersinger Hans Sachs over his rival, the patrician Eoban Hesse, confirms, first of all, the social and cultural order, and, secondly, the subservience of art (*Meistersang*) to the larger political order represented by the Emperor. The Emperor's personal interest in Hans Sachs and his decision to intervene in favor of the poet suggest a relationship of patronage in which the artist enjoys the protection of the prince when narrow concerns blind the local authorities. The *Schlußchor* underlines this conservative idea of state and art when the major figures (including Hans Sachs) and the choir sing in unison: "We shout with joy, hail Max! Germany's sun! You are the people's joy and bliss, you are its delight!"[18] If the opera can be read as a plea for popular art, it is a popular art which does not undermine or threaten existing hierarchies.

While it is obvious that Wagner used Reger's libretto for his own work — the basic plot is very similar — it would be misleading to assume that Wagner also

2. The house of Hans Sachs in the Spitalgasse. Etching by Johann Adam Klein (1792–1845). From *Hans Sachs und die Meistersinger in ihrer Zeit.* Germanisches Nationalmuseum (Nuremberg, 1981), p. 158.

took over the rather conservative vision of Nuremberg we find in Lortzing's opera. Wagner's own vision, as he sketched it out in 1845,[19] is much closer to that of Gervinus. Especially modeled on Gervinus's narrative is the tension between the rigid formality of *Meistersang* and the desire of the "young man" (Walther in the final version) to become a true poet. Already in the first draft, Wagner introduced the figure of the *Merker* as the principal opponent who competes with the young poet for fame as well as for the hand of the young woman. *Merker* clearly represents the poetic conventions of the school which the young man fails to understand. Wagner leaves no doubt that the *Meistersang* tradition is coming to a close. In the third act, his Hans Sachs, following Gervinus rather closely, reflects on the decline of art. Sachs sees himself as the last practitioner of a long tradition and advises the young poet, in the spirit of Gervinus's liberal program,

LEONARDVS KETNERVS LECTORI.

Qualia vel Naso romana voce, Maroq́;
Carmina disparibus cōpoluere modis.
Talia compoluit maiori laude Ioannes
Carmina, germana voce legenda tamen.
Iam pia de summo cōscribens carmina Christo,
Iam rerumq́; vices, tempora, fata, canens.

Plurima, quæ cecinit, monumēta leguntur vbiq́;
Sed quia nota vigent, nil recitasse iuuat.
Fœlix, quæ talem peperit sibi fœmina natum,
Cuius ob ingenium patria floret humus.
Qui patriam multis virtutibus ornat & auget,
Quem colit æterno nomine posteritas.

Quod si Musarū didicisset sacra, vel Artes,
Iam tua laus maior, Noricaberga, foret.
Tanti igitur vultus hos noueris esse Poetæ,
Quos tibi ceu viuos picta Tabella refert.

M. D. XLVI.

1545 : HANS . SACHSN . ALTER · 5 I · IAR.

Johann Betz.

Ih Abcōterfactur/
sagt Hanns Sachs von Nüremberg an/
Schōmachern/der vil schōn gedicht/
D 10 weiß Sprüch/har zůgericht/
Nach aber der ic vlen Poetrey/
Ju Deudscher sprach/lustig vnd frey/

Auch durch Maister gesang mit fleiß/
Auff gaistlich vnd weltliche weiß/
Wölche dann gůte mittel sind/
Dardurch gmainer Man vnd seine Kind/
M gn Schrifft vnd Weißheit auch erfarn/
Togenlich darnach zugebarn/

Got zu ehr/vnd dem nechsten zunn/
Damit man Tag-t erhall im schwn.
Wölche alles ist gnnglam bewoffn/
Darumb bleybt sein Lob auff gewisist.
Jm 1 5 4 6. Jar/
Gedruckt durch Hanns Guldenmundt.

3. Woodcut, self-portrait of Hans Sachs at the age of 51. From *Hans Sachs und die Meistersinger in ihrer Zeit*. Germanisches Nationalmuseum (Nuremberg, 1981), p. 149.

to give up poetry in favor of political intervention. Not Sachs, but Hutten should be his model. In other words, the young poet is destined to become a revolutionary. By the same token, *Merker,* the guardian of conventions, is described as fearful of the people because they do not understand the rules. The logic of the plot, as it unfolds at the beginning of Act III, points to an act of radical subversion: the young poet would defy the *Meistersinger* and become a leader of the masses (who, historically speaking, had many reasons to be dissatisfied with the town government). Yet this radical project is not carried out. Instead, at the end, Hans Sachs defends the art of *Meistersang* (though somewhat ironically), and the citizens of Nuremberg praise him as their greatest poet. This resolution of the tensions between the old and the new owes more to Lortzing's and Reger's treatment of the material than to Gervinus.

The 1845 draft is rather ambivalent about the relationship between art and German history. In the figure of Hans Sachs they coincide, with the young poet, presumably the representative of the future, being finally reduced to the conventional role of the young man who wins the bride. The solution Wagner develops in the final version of the opera (1861) is certainly more complex than the sketch of 1845, but it retains some of the earlier tensions and internal contradictions.[20] While the plot line does not undergo major changes, its emphasis with regard to the interpretation of Hans Sachs and the culture of Nuremberg has shifted.

4. View of Nuremberg. Colored pen-and-ink drawing from the so-called *Hallerbuch* (1533). Based on a woodcut of 1493, a Gothic perception of Nuremberg. From *Geschichte Nürnbergs in Bilddokumenten,* ed. Gerhard Pfeiffer (Munich, 1970), picture no. 32.

The ending of the 1868 version underscores the national rather than the revolutionary element. As several critics have pointed out, the praise of German art does take on new meaning after the Prussian victory over Austria. Still, it does not suffice to stress Wagner's affirmative patriotism, since it is not Nuremberg or the German Empire that is praised; rather, the homage to Hans Sachs focuses on German art. Significantly, the Emperor, who figures so prominently at the end of Lortzing's opera, is absent from Wagner's text. In fact, one might argue that Hans Sachs takes his place. The final words are:

> Hail! Sachs! Hans Sachs!
> Nuremberg's poet Sachs![21]

The later reception of the Bayreuth production of *Die Meistersinger* tended to interpret the ending as an affirmation of the Second Empire. During the 1920s, it became even popular to include the audience: the spectators would rise and sing the German national anthem. After the lost war, they could find themselves represented in a work of art which anticipates the end of the German Empire. Between 1933 and 1945, as might be expected, this reading received official sanction. In a radio speech of 1933 (the occasion was the broadcast of the Bayreuth production), Goebbels claimed *Die Meistersinger* for the "German Revolution" of the National Socialists. Stressing the popular element of the opera, he noted: "An art that does not emerge from the people ultimately does not find its way back to the people. Through more and more refined forms, it attempts to reach a balance with the tart and sometimes coarser but more popular forms produced by an art which is rooted in the people and which recognizes the popular as the ground of all creative forces."[22] Obviously, in this reading the myth of Nuremberg serves as a prefiguration of Nazi art. The logical extension of this claim was the 1935 Nuremberg production in which the stage setting for Act III looks like the Nuremberg Party Rally.[23] When we compare this setting with the design of the 1868 production, the radical metamorphosis of the myth becomes apparent.[24] Artificial construction has replaced nature; the romantic element which Wagner wanted to present as the background for his apotheosis of German art has vanished. Hitler's Nuremberg, exemplified by the party rallies, was a strictly modern design where the human masses have become the material for the architecture.

It is relatively easy to label the fascist interpretation of *Die Meistersinger* as misuse; one can, for instance, point to Wagner's own statements to demonstrate the difference. Yet authorial intention and the history of the work are never identical. Hence the legitimacy of Goebbels' claims is not automatically refuted by referring to Wagner's statements. In fact, Goebbels' eulogy of Wagner and *Die Meistersinger* does address the crucial problem: namely, the role of art in the social community. Goebbels, however, does this by simply extending the fascist conception of folk culture to the opera. It is an act of incorporation which strips *Die Meistersinger* of its individual features by repressing the work's tensions and

5. Nazi Party rally, 1934. From *Geschichte Nürnbergs in Bilddokumenten*, ed. Gerhard Pfeiffer (Munich, 1970), picture no. 337.

contradictions. To put it differently, Goebbels' appropriation, in spite of its reference to German history, denies the opera's own historicity. It denies the historical locus of Wagner's "Phantasmagorie," to use Adorno's term.[25] The fascist ideology cannot accept the liberal components of the national myth of the 16th century.

There is little doubt that Wagner's Nuremberg does not reproduce the historical conditions of the 16th century.[26] The town was anything but a harmonious community in which its citizens simply enjoyed work and art. It was a town ruled by a small elite of patrician families, without participation of the craftsmen and small businessmen (not to mention the lower classes). The censorship of the *Rat* could be severe, as the historical Hans Sachs found out when he addressed political issues in his writings.[27] In the highly stratified society of Nuremberg, the *Meistersinger* clearly did not play the significant role that Wagner assigns them. Their poetic practices were much more confined to their own social group. Had Wagner been more familiar with the historical conditions, he would not have chosen the Nuremberg setting for his opera, for the strength of 16th-century Nuremberg was an advanced, highly diversified capitalist economy, one that resulted in social differentiation rather than in unity. Only through a strong misreading could the historical Nuremberg become appropriate material for Wagner's cultural myth. Of course, as we have seen, Wagner's sources and models (with the exception of Wagenseil's 17th-century work on *Meistersang*)[28] were already part of the re-writing of Nuremberg culture in the 19th century.

The search for a national identity that preoccupied German intellectuals during the 19th century made use of the past by transforming it into narratives of teleological development or into momentary images in which this identity was completely embodied. As Thomas Nipperdey pointed out in a recent essay, nationalism is not a mythic structure, but it has an inclination towards mythical thought.[29] There is a need for a narrative of origin and for symbolic figures which define the national essence. The mythical transformation of the past is in evidence among liberals and democrats as well as conservatives. Clearly, the French Revolution provided the most striking examples of such *Mythisierung*. And again, in 1848, the energy of the revolution in Germany draws on mythical models. Wagner's ecstatic praise of the revolution in 1848 combined the myth of the rebirth of the world with the allegory of the goddess of the revolution. "Indeed, we recognize: the old world goes to pieces, from it a new one will rise, for the noble goddess of the revolution is flying, carried by the wings of the storms, her majestic head radiant with lightning flashes, holding the sword in her right hand and the torch in her left."[30] The 1845 draft of *Die Meistersinger* is closely related to the revolutionary mythology; it marks the shift from the old to the new, from rules to freedom. After 1850, when adjustments had to be made, Wagner rewrote the narrative several times until he organized the opposition of old and new in such a way that the old reveals itself as the new, the rules of *Meistersang*

6. The *Hauptmarkt* of Nuremberg around 1600. Pen-and-ink drawing by Wolf Jakob Stromer. From *Geschichte Nürnbergs in Bilddokumenten*, ed. Gerhard Pfeiffer (Munich, 1970), picture no. 250.

as the firm ground on which the community should be based, and Hans Sachs as the symbolic center of the ideal community.

The libretto of *Die Meistersinger* is organized around a number of overlapping oppositions which cannot easily be synthesized. Social, generational, and aesthetic differences motivate the two strands of the narrative, the love story of Walther von Stolzing and Eva Pogner and the rivalry within the school of the *Meistersinger*. In the figure of Walther, these two strands come together, since the lover is at the same time the aspiring *Meistersinger* whom the members of the school, notably Beckmesser, the rival in the competition for Eva's hand, do not want to admit. A third motif needs also be mentioned, although it is not unfolded in a complete narrative: the presentation of the community as a whole in the brawl of Act II and in the final festival scene of Act III. These scenes are connected with the major strands primarily through the figure of Hans Sachs and, in a less obvious way, through the figure of Eva, who is both the object of the desire and, at the same time, the final judge in the poetic competition.

The most apparent opposition is that between rule-dominated *Meistersang* and unrestricted poetic song. This opposition is paralleled by a social distinction between the *Meistersinger* (who are without exception *Bürger*) and Walther, the aristocratic outsider. The second opposition is slanted in favor of the citizens while

7. Bayreuth Festival, 1956. Stage design by Wieland Wagner. From Oswald Georg Bauer, *Richard Wagner* (New York, 1983), p. 175.

8. The Festival Meadow in Act III as a Nazi Party rally, authorized by Hitler. German Opera House, Berlin, November 17, 1935. From Oswald Georg Bauer, *Richard Wagner* (New York, 1983), p. 171.

the first is resolved in favor of free poetic song. Combined, this means that Walther, the winner in the poetic competition, is also, socially speaking, representing the inferior side of the opposition: namely, the declining feudal nobility, an older social formation that has been superseded by the free and self-governed town. To add to this complexity is the matter of the age difference. Following conventional comedy structure, the young lovers Walther and Eva are set against the older generation of dominating father figures, i.e., Pogner and Hans Sachs. In this configuration, the young generation is expected to win. Finally, however, it is Hans Sachs, a member of the older generation, whom the people (*Volk*) praise most. And he receives, in the end, the laurel from Eva's hands: "During the finale Eva takes the wreath from Walther's head and crowns Sachs with it."[31] Instead of the conventional shift of power from the old to the young generation, we have a reversal that contradicts both the generational and the aesthetic opposition while it confirms, in a surprising move, the social contrast. It is Hans Sachs, the representative of the *Bürger,* who stands out.

As it turns out, Hans Sachs is the pivotal figure in all three configurations. Most clearly, he mediates between the rigorous definition of *Meistersang* and Walther's practice of free expression. In Act I, he openly supports Walther's aspirations to join the school so that he can win the girl. In the third act, he helps Walther to define his own task in broader terms and encourages him to enter the competition on the terms of the *Meistersinger:*

> Then let the Master-rules now speed you,
> That they may truly guide and lead you,
> And help to keep untainted
> What spring and youth have planted
> Amidst youth's pleasure
> So the treasure
> Deep in the heart in secret laid,
> Through the power of song shall never fade![32]

Equally crucial is Sachs's intervention in the generation conflict. He encourages the connection between Walther and Eva, in spite of his friendship with Pogner, and thoroughly demolishes the aspirations of Beckmesser, who is socially much closer to him than Stolzing. He can do this because he withstands the temptation to enter the competition himself, although Eva suggests this in Act II, when she is threatened with marriage to Beckmesser.[33] Not only is Sachs the figure who helps to decide the outcome in the struggle between the opposing forces (he hinders Beckmesser and encourages Walther, he helps the young lovers against the older generation, and he is willing to favor the young nobleman over the *Bürger*), but he also connects the various levels on which these conflicts are situated. Although the conventional logic of the plot would give him only a supporting role, he is clearly the central figure; the various oppositions and tensions could not be resolved without him.

This role as the central mediator implies a number of significant shifts and ambiguities. As much as Hans Sachs presents himself and is viewed by the community as a firm, almost immovable agent, a closer look at his actions reveals that he accomplishes his role by not necessarily stating the entire truth to the person with whom he is dealing. Most obvious is his duplicity in his treatment of Beckmesser, when he offers him Walther's poem: he does this supposedly to help him; in reality, however, he knowingly destroys him, because he is certain that Beckmesser will fail in its performance. More benign is Sachs's interaction when he crushes Walther's attempt to elope with Eva. His support for the young nobleman depends on Walther's willingness to become a *Bürger* and citizen of Nuremberg, just as much as Sachs's encouragement of free poetry hinges on the acceptance of *Meistersang* rules. As a result, the resolution of the aesthetic, social, and generational conflicts is ultimately much more ambivalent than it seems. The consensus between Hans Sachs and the people (*Volk*) at the end of Act III, the praise of German art and its artists, affirms both the *Meistersinger* and Walther von Stolzing, the old as well as the new (which turns out to be a return to the truly old, i.e., the *Minnesang* of the 12th and 13th centuries).

9. The Festival Meadow in Act III, Bayreuth Festival, 1957. Stage design by Wieland Wagner. From Oswald Georg Bauer, *Richard Wagner* (New York, 1983), p. 176.

From the vantage point of liberal historiography, Wagner's vision of Nuremberg culture is confusing. It seems to point in the right direction, but there are also several elements which are not compatible with the liberal understanding of the 16th century. For instance, liberal historians like Gervinus perceive the rise of the free cities as a progressive development; yet it is a nobleman who wins the contest in *Die Meistersinger*. The strength of these towns came from their highly developed international trade, but there is no sign of commerce in Wagner's opera. However, a conservative observer would be equally confused. While the ending of the opera clearly affirms the *status quo,* and carefully integrates oppositional elements, the center of political power in the 16th century, the monarch, is clearly absent. A conservative praise of the arts would have to include the legitimate political authorities.

The aesthetic trajectory of the text is no less ambiguous than the social one. The confrontation between the rigid and narrow rules of the *Meistersinger* and the subjective inspiration of Walther encourages a solution which would affirm the emancipation from the rules as a legitimate breakthrough in the history of poetry and music, just as the breakdown of Gottsched's classicism was hailed by later critics as a positive and necessary evolution. The transition from craftsmanship to free expression, from artisan to genius, as it occurred in the theory of criticism during the 18th century, was understood as a logical development.

Yet Wagner, after celebrating Walther's victory in the third act, adds, through the voice of Hans Sachs, the praise of the *Meistersinger* and their legitimate rules. How do we explain these inconsistencies and contradictions? It has been suggested that the long gestation of the work, which lasted from 1845 to 1868, contributed to these tensions. Clearly, Wagner's outlook during the 1860s was different from the revolutionary radicalism of the 1840s. Still, some of the contradictions are already present in the 1845 draft, including the basic instance which combines an emphasis on political action (the new) with praise of Sachs (the old).

A comparison with Lortzing's opera might throw some light on these problems. Wagner's text is fairly similar to Reger's libretto. There is the competition for the prize, which is coupled with the competition for the hand of the rich goldsmith's daughter. Furthermore, there is the contest between two suitors: while one of them is familiar with the tradition but incapable of improvising, his victorious opponent wins the hand of the girl through his performative skills. The opposition between poetic rules and free expression also defines the aesthetic conflict in Reger's text. There is one significant difference, however, which has major consequences. The young man who competes for the hand of the daughter and the poetic prize is Hans Sachs himself—the young Hans Sachs who is in love with Kunigunde, his first wife-to-be. Wagner, on the other hand, portrays Hans Sachs the widower. Hence, the structure of Reger's plot is simpler. In his text, the aesthetic and the social/political conflict can be neatly resolved at the end since Hans Sachs represents aesthetic innovation. He defeats the patrician Eoban Hesse from Augsburg, thereby affirming the fame of his hometown and his own class (artisan) in the presence of the Emperor. Interestingly enough, class conflicts between the ruling elite and the craftsmen are explicitly foregrounded in Reger's libretto. Steffen, the father of the girl and mayor of Nuremberg, does not hesitate to ban Hans Sachs when the lovers resist to accept his decision to marry Kunigunde to Eoban hesse. Only the intervention of the Emperor is strong enough to change this decision. In Lortzing's opera, the monarch stands above class oppositions. His task is seen as that of a just mediator.

In Wagner's *Die Meistersinger,* this mediating role has been transferred, as we have seen, to Hans Sachs, while the monarch becomes absent. At the same time, Wagner transfers the task of the young Hans Sachs: that is to say, the task of challenging established and reified artistic practices, to the figure of Walther, who is both socially and aesthetically an outsider. The figure of Hans Sachs, on the other hand, who is now an older man and not the lover, is moved closer to the *Meistersinger* without, however, becoming a negative character. Unlike Lortzing's Hans Sachs, he is the insider from the very beginning. Neither his fame as an artist nor his social standing are ever in doubt. Hence, the victory of Hans Sachs at the end of the two operas has a different meaning. In Lortzing's case, it is entirely due to the intervention of Emperor Maximilian, who unmasks the false rival. Therefore, the *Schlußchor* celebrates the legitimate political power. In Wagner's opera, the lack of such a legitimate political power is the very theme of the final scene of Act III. Here, Hans Sachs invokes the potential decline of the German Empire because the prince is no longer one with the people.

> Take heed! Ill times now threaten all;
> And if we German folk should fall
> And foreigners should rule our land
> No king his folk would understand,
> And foreign rule and foreign ways
> Would darken all our German days . . .[34]

Of course, this warning refers both to the 16th century and the present. The place of the prince will be taken by art. In other words, the national myth of Nuremberg, as Wagner reformulated it after 1848, replaces the authority of the monarch with the authority of the artist. What is announced on the stage as a future event has actually already happened. Hans Sachs the artist has become the mediator and formal authority and is acknowledged as such by the people. This new task leads to a partial reversal of the liberal as well as the conservative interpretation of Hans Sachs. Wagner wants legitimacy for the aesthetic solution. Therefore, he underscores the popular element in Sachs, as it was defined by Gervinus; but his Sachs is less a transitional figure than a symbolic hero, a superior artist who

10. Design for the Nuremberg street in Act II. Used for the Bayreuth Festival of 1888, based on the sets of the Munich production (1868). From Oswald Georg Bauer, *Richard Wagner* (New York, 1983), p. 167.

is at the same time a popular leader. For this reason, Wagner also reinforces the conservative aspect, Sachs's proximity to *Meistersang*. Not only does Hans Sachs remind Walther that Meistersang is the legitimate basis for poetry, and that norms are indispensable for the practice of art, but even the *Meistersinger* themselves (in the person of Pogner, who kneels before Sachs) celebrate Hans Sachs as their leader. In this celebration, all divisions between the members of the community disappear; their feelings and hopes concentrate on the figure of the popular artist. This unity could not occur without the popular element in Hans Sachs. Again, he appears as the mediator between the *Zunft* and the people.

Obviously, the strong message of the final scene stresses the aesthetic and artistic sphere as the realm where social and political tensions can be resolved. Neither Gervinus nor Lortzing and Reger shared this view. For Gervinus, it was the transition from the aesthetic to the political sphere that defined the task of modern Germany. That is to say, politics has to replace art. In Lortzing's libretto, on the other hand, the legitimate power of the monarch gives art its proper place. In his final draft, Wagner was still rather close to Gervinus when Sachs advises the young artist to join Hutten's political struggle instead of competing for the prize. In the text of *Die Meistersinger* as it was worked out during the 1860s, however, the relationship between art and politics has been reversed. Now it is the artistic realm that subsumes the social and political. Yet we also have to keep in mind that the new configuration is predicated on the New Testament, specifically on the role of St. John the Baptist, whose patron's day is celebrated on the 24th of June. Hans Sachs, in the role of the Baptist, points to the Messiah. These unmistakably religious echoes clearly serve to legitimize the future in terms of the old and established. For this reason, Wagner's Nuremberg has to be more medieval than the historical Nuremberg of the 16th century, more inward-looking and more self-contained.

The stage functions as a contrast to social reality also on a different level: Wagner composed the opera at a time when the guilds of the craftsmen, which had been the backbone of the old free cities, were collapsing under the impact of the industrial revolution. As Timothy McFarland argues: "Out of the ashes of the social reality there was arising like a phoenix a potential cultural myth, of which Wagner's opera is the most complete expression."[35]

Wagner's Nuremberg is, to use Adorno's term again, a "Phantasmagorie," neither located in the present nor in the historical past. The historical core of the opera, which it was Adorno's aim to identify, is situated on a different level. It derives its meaning precisely from the confrontation between past and present, between medieval community and modern industrial society. Wagner's music quite consciously foregrounds this tension by using archaic forms as part of a modern composition. Yet this return to the old is, as Carl Dahlhaus has shown, just as modern as the entire opera. Dahlhaus speaks of a "geträumte Diatonik" and argues: "Nowhere, not even in *Parsifal*, is Wagner's music as artificial as when in *Die Meistersinger* it gives the appearance of simplicity."[36]

11. Design for the Festival Meadow (Act III, Scene 2), Court Opera, Vienna, 1875. This design was typical of the 19th-century perception of the Festival Meadow. From Oswald Georg Bauer, *Richard Wagner* (New York, 1983), p. 165.

This ambiguity invites interpretative appropriation. Clearly, Wagner himself could claim the role of the artist who creates the new aesthetic form, i.e., the *Musikdrama,* by reworking Goethe's and Schiller's drama theories. In fact, Wagner understood himself as the heir and *Überwinder* of Goethe. In its most radical formulation, in the essay "Kunst und Revolution" (1850), this claim moves towards a utopian reconciliation of art and life, a goal that resurfaces in Stolzing's prize song. In its later articulations, it postulates a new grounding of drama in *mythos.*

Later appropriations shifted the focus from a metaphysics of art towards a celebration of the German nation.[37] The fascist interpretation only radicalizes this tendency by underlining the *völkisch* character of Wagner's opera. In this reading, the community of Nuremberg prefigures the *Volksgemeinschaft* as much as Hans Sachs's invocation of German art anticipates the art of the Third Reich. Historically speaking, this claim is not legitimate. Wagner's vision of Nuremberg owes its force to a specific historical moment; that is, not simply to a nostalgic view of the Middle Ages, but to a highly modern transformation of the received source materials. Yet this historical separation leaves us with unanswered questions. Was Goebbels' praise of Wagner's *Die Meistersinger* nothing more than a misunderstanding and misuse of its terms?

Syberberg's controversial Hitler film might serve as an appropriate commentary,[38] since Syberberg, searching for a symbolic rather than a rational explication of German history, brings together the figures of Hitler and Wagner in such a way that their intrinsic connection becomes clear: Hitler rises from Wagner's grave. Their relationship is not understood as a question of influence or ideological similarity but seen as a rebirth of Wagner the artist in the person of Hitler — fascism as a reenactment of Wagner's operas. The reversal of the conventional point of view, i.e., the emphasis on Hitler's dependence on Wagner, foregrounds affinities which a strictly historical comparison will possibly miss. The Bayreuth productions of *Die Meistersinger* between 1933 and 1945 only accentuated the problematic and false moments of Wagner's myth. Through their closeness to the party rallies, these productions underscored the fateful appropriation of Wagner by the Third Reich. At the center of this claim, we find a radical extension of the aesthetic into the political realm. It is significant that Goebbels defined the identity of the new Germany in terms of its art. "All great art is rooted in the people. When it loses its connection with the people, the development of a bloodless artificial virtuosity is inevitable."[39] Yet this formulation, seemingly summarizing the message of *Die Meistersinger,* misses the core of Wagner's opera: i.e., the tension between the ideology of the medieval material and the modernity of the music; in other words, it fails to acknowledge Wagner's "Artistentum."

Notes

1 *Der Luftkrieg in Nürnberg: Quellen des Stadtarchivs zum 2. Januar 1945* (Nuremberg, 1985).
2 See Oswald Georg Bauer, "Die Meistersinger von Nürnberg," in *Richard Wagner* (Fribourg, 1982), 163–92; and Dietrich Mack, "Die Bayreuther Inszenierungen der *Meistersinger,*" in *Richard Wagner, Die Meistersinger von Nürnberg: Texte, Materialien, Kommentare,* ed. Attila Csampai and Dietmar Holland (Reinbek, 1981), 158–78. (Henceforth referred to as *Texte*).
3 See Richard Wagner, *Die Meistersinger von Nürnberg,* in *Texte,* 170–71.
4 Bauer, *Richard Wagner,* 175.
5 Mack, "Die Bayreuther Inszenierungen der *Meistersinger,*" in *Texte,* 169. (Unless otherwise indicated, all translations are mine.)
6 Bauer, *Richard Wagner,* 176.
7 Hans Mayer, "*Meistersinger* ohne 19. Jahrhundert," in his *Anmerkungen zu Richard Wagner* (Frankfurt, 1966), 76–90.
8 Marcel Reich-Ranicki, "Wieland Wagners Rechung ging nicht auf," in *Texte,* 188.
9 Theodor W. Adorno, "Wagners Aktualität," in *Texte,* 186–87.
10 See Peter Wapnewski, "Die Oper Richard Wagners als Dichtung," in his *Richard-Wagner-Handbuch* (Stuttgart, 1986), 320–32.
11 See Richard Wagner, *Dichtungen und Schriften,* ed. Dieter Borchmeyer (Frankfurt, 1983) 4:223–80; and Richard Wagner, "Eine Mitteilung an meine Freunde," (1851), in Richard Wagner, *Gesammelte Schriften,* ed. Julius Kapp (Leipzig, n.d.) 1:113–16.
12 See *Geschichte Nürnbergs in Bilddokumenten,* ed. Gerhard Pfeiffer (Munich, 1970).
13 "Brief eines jungen deutschen Malers in Rom an seinen Freund in Nürnberg," in Wilhelm Heinrich Wackenroder, *Sämtliche Schriften* (Reinbek, 1968), 71.
14 Georg Gottfried Gervinus, *Geschichte der Deutschen Dichtung* (Leipzig, 1871) 2:693.
15 Ibid., 694.
16 Ibid., 469.
17 Ibid., 472.

18 Albert Lortzing and Philipp Reger, *Hans Sachs* (Leipzig, n.d.) 206f.
19 See Richard Wagner, *Dichtungen und Schriften* 4:223–35.
20 See Gunter Reiß, "Schuhmacher und Poet dazu: Anmerkungen zur Kunst der Meister in Richard Wagners Meistersingerkomödie," in *Das Drama Richard Wagners als musikalisches Kunstwerk,* ed. Carl Dahlhaus (Regensburg, 1970), 277–302.
21 Richard Wagner, *The Mastersingers of Nuremberg,* ed. Nicholas John (London, 1983), 125.
22 Joseph Goebbels, "Richard Wagner und das Kunstempfinden unserer Zeit," in *Texte,* 196.
23 See Bauer, *Richard Wagner,* 171.
24 Ibid., 165; for Act II, see p. 167 (1888 Bayreuth production).
25 See Adorno, *Versuch über Wagner* (Berlin and Frankfurt, 1952).
26 See Horst Brunner, "Hans Sachs und Nürnbergs Meistersinger," in *Hans Sachs und die Meistersinger in ihrer Zeit* (Catalogue of the exhibition of the Germanisches Nationalmuseum, 1981).
27 Ibid., 161.
28 See Johann Christoph Wagenseil, *Von der Meister-Singer Hochseligen Kunst* (Altdorf, 1697).
29 Thomas Nipperdey, "Der Mythos im Zeitalter der Revolution," in *Wege des Mythos in der Moderne: Richard Wagner, Der Ring des Nibelungen* (Munich, 1987), 102.
30 Nipperdey, in *Wege des Mythos,* 104.
31 Richard Wagner, *The Mastersingers of Nuremberg,* 125.
32 Ibid., 103.
33 In a recent essay, Marc Weiner underscores the anti-Semitic aspect of Sachs's attitude towards Beckmesser; see his "Wagner's Nose and the Ideology of Perception," *Monatshefte* 81 (1989): 62–78.
34 Richard Wagner, *The Mastersingers of Nuremberg,* 125.
35 Timothy McFarland, "Wagner's Nuremberg," in *Die Meistersinger von Nürnberg* (London and New York, 1983), 33.
36 Carl Dahlhaus, *Richard Wagners Musikdramen* (Hildesheim, 1971), 77.
37 For the reception of *Die Meistersinger,* see Bauer, *Richard Wagner* 163–91; and Mack, *Der Bayreuther Inszenierungsstil 1876–1976* (Munich, 1976).
38 See Hans Rudolf Vaget, "Die Auferstehung Richard Wagners," in *Film und Literatur,* ed. Sigrid Bauschinger, Susan L. Cocalis, and Henry A. Lea (Berne/Munich, 1984), 124–55.
39 Joseph Goebbels, in *Texte,* 196.

Transgression and Affirmation: Gender Roles, Moral Codes, and Utopian Vision in Richard Wagner's Operas

Peter Morris-Keitel, Alexa Larson-Thorisch, and Audrius Dundzila*

I

"Our existing opera is a culinary opera. It was a means of pleasure long before it turned into merchandise."[1] Bertolt Brecht's remarks concerning opera, here in regard to his *Aufstieg und Fall der Stadt Mahagonny* (1929), seem to repeat the obvious: namely, that opera is as much an experience as a pleasure. As such, opera is a source of sensual gratification, which is not only a result of its form but also of its content. At the same time, Brecht maintained that the character of opera as merchandise prevented the formation of any critical stance with respect to its content. This situation may only be altered through the introduction of innovations at the base of which is the intention to provoke.

Similar suggestions for change, which led Brecht to his theory of epic theater, had been proposed earlier by Wagner. After all, Wagner, in his essays "Die Kunst und die Revolution" (1849) and "Das Kunstwerk der Zukunft" (1850), criticized the commercialized character of music and professed his devotion to an art for all people on a level bound to much higher communal ideals.[2] With such concepts of a "people's opera" (*Volksoper*), Wagner attacked the traditional aristocratic content of opera by emphasizing bourgeois notions of emancipation, not unlike similar attempts by Mozart and Beethoven.

In earlier centuries, the primary function of opera was the confirmation and affirmation of the supremacy of the court. The rise of the middle classes, however, changed this function considerably. Since the end of the 18th century, the purpose of opera has no longer been to glorify absolutism, but rather to serve as a means of bourgeois emancipation. In contrast to these ideological changes, the staging of operas in the 19th century was still largely dependent on the court. The emerging presence of a bourgeois mentality was tolerated by the aristocracy, especially in the second half of the 19th century, when the economic and social changes in Germany led to a convergence of the aristocracy and the upper middle classes.

The rise of the bourgeoisie also led to a change in and a polarization of gender roles. The striving of the preceding era for romantic and Young German ideals

---

* Parts I, II, and III of this chapter were written by Morris-Keitel, Larson-Thorisch, and Dundzila, respectively.

of emancipation were now replaced by a new ideological activism centered around and dominated by the masculine.[3] Art became an expression of self-assertion, and bourgeois artists conceived of themselves as geniuses; indeed, composers such as Franz Liszt referred to themselves as "Priests of Art."[4] Such models of masculinity dominated the art, the music, the philosophy, and the literature of the time. Prevalent were encounters with the heroic man, who embodied physical power, lust for hunting, readiness for battle, and a defiance of law and order. Within this context, a strong appeal to feelings of nationalism was made quite often, thereby presenting the great individual as the masculine role model.

This cult of the masculine inevitably led to new forms of repression regarding bourgeois women. If man, in general, constituted the outgoing, energetic, and active hunter, woman could only be understood as a naturally passive creature and, ultimately, as man's victim. Friedrich Nietzsche reduced such stereotypes even further in characterizing man by his wartime abilities and woman by her fertility:

> Everything about woman is a riddle, and everything about woman
> has one solution: it is called pregnancy. . . .
> Man should be trained for war and woman for the recreation of the warrior:
> all else is folly.[5]

Such a polarization imposed moral and sexual inhibitions on bourgeois women which functioned much more effectively than any external restraints. Nevertheless, these inhibitions must be viewed in light of the shaping of new values among the emerging middle classes invoking a redefinition of the female role. This led to the dogma of the "natural determination" of woman, whose niche was away from the active center of cultural development. In addition, the typification of male and female stereotypes had devastating effects on the morality of the bourgeoisie.

Their moral conduct, with its attempts, at least on the surface, at maintaining the guise of socially respectable behavior, soon led to prudery surrounding erotic questions. In the case of young men, there was greater denial of any time spent in brothels or with mistresses. Young women, on the other hand, were often left in a state of complete ignorance regarding erotic questions until their wedding day. Men were rarely able to marry before the age of 35 due to their careers. The marriages they then entered were seldom based on love, but rather on status and financial gain. This resulted in the complete economic, cultural, and sexual dependency of women.

In reaction to this oppression, middle-class "women's rights activists" soon demanded a reform of marriage and professional practices—without, however, setting any clear political goals. At first, they merely chose intellectual freedom over economic independence. Such attempts at emancipation were restricted to the liberating powers of the mind and increased access to education, which in turn were to secure women equal positions in society, as individuals. These intentions, however, did nothing to alter society's perception that women should remain the guardians of tradition and morality.

The obvious result of the rise of the bourgeoisie was the collapse of their traditional order of home and morality, which had long separated them from the aristocracy. The reason for this was the spread of capitalism: the middle class was convinced that by abandoning the existent order, optimal conditions could be established for a free market system.[6] Inevitably, this economic development also affected a breakdown and thus a change of the family structure. To what extent this had already occurred by the middle of the last century is illustrated by Wilhelm Heinrich Riehl's analysis of *Die Familie* (1855). In this context, Riehl's book needs to be understood as a conservative stance against the destructive powers of industry and capitalism, recommending a return to an idealized traditional family.

Wagner's operas reflect social reality by problematizing sexuality and morality. Very few married couples can be found in his works, and where they do exist, their situation is atypical. Elsa and Lohengrin separate already on their wedding night, Marke has been cheated on before he is married to Isolde, and Fricka and Wotan continuously argue about the state of their marriage. Only in the case of Stolzing and Eva does there seem to exist a possibility for a more positive future. Undoubtedly, Wagner's operas would not have had the resonance they still enjoy, if his reworking of medieval mythologies had not had some actual political, social, and erotic impetus, confirming and at the same time placing into question the moral roles of his time.

It is from this perspective that Wagner's use of medieval mythological sources and his goals must be understood. In the familiarity of the audience with this material, Wagner recognized a basis for reanalyzing history. In addition, these myths had been important in the search for a German national identity since the beginning of the 19th century, and Wagner wanted to contribute to this search. At the same time, however, he restricted his use of the medieval sources to the formative elements, which gave him room to establish a contemporary relevance. For the audience of the 19th century, Wagner's thematization of sexuality, which exposed the hypocrisy of bourgeois morality, was, without a doubt, shocking.

In order to portray this hypocrisy, Wagner used examples of various bourgeois stereotypes which contradicted the common conception the middle classes had of themselves and their moral and sexual behavior. If man was seen, in general, as active and unsurpassable in his striving for exemplary greatness, Wagner usually depicts him as a sinful seducer and patriarch. Woman becomes the goal of all male fantasies and is thereby, in contrast to reality, elevated onto a pedestal. This is achieved in most cases through subtly psychologizing well-known figures from German mythology. On the other hand, the result of this technique is a modernization which, in regard to gender roles, parallels those found in bourgeois realism.

Thus, Wagner's operas can be viewed in the same context as novels such as Flaubert's *Madame Bovary* (1857), Tolstoi's *Anna Karenina* (1873-76), and Fontane's *Effi Briest* (1895).

The absence of parents and families in Wagner's works implies, therefore, a criticism of the bourgeois conventions of marriage and love. Concepts for the improvement of this state of affairs are not, however, presented; on the contrary, at best, Wagner vaguely hints at such abstract ideas as humanity and true love. Consequently, the stereotypical roles of men and women still serve as figures of identification for the audience and cannot function as critical alternatives. Thus, Wagner is bound to this bourgeois-elitist audience, and his earlier plans for a grand opera for the people remain utopian.

To what extent gender roles were redefined by this approach, or remained untouched within the confines of bourgeois patriarchal thinking, is the central issue here. We begin by focusing on the role of men and their social responsibilities within a patriarchal society, and, in part two, by investigating the role of women in terms of three operas. Our position is a feminist one, in which it is argued that the survival of partriarchal order requires sexual subordination of women as well as their participation in their own oppression. If women try to leave the sphere of the loving wife and mother, thereby challenging male authority, severe punishment awaits them. Thus, within Wagner's operas, women seem to be condemned to the role of cultural remnants. This view is continued in part three, where we focus on the interplay between women and men, as well as between men and men, in *Tristan und Isolde* (1859). In this case, it will be shown that Wagner's portrayal of bourgeois sexuality and morality occasionally reaches beyond those stereotypes analyzed in the previous sections.

The major male roles in Wagner's operas for the most part follow a similar pattern with regard to manliness and action. Each seems to mirror bourgeois expectations either by succeeding in his goals and achieving greatness, or by failing and becoming even greater. Following this pattern, two stereotypical male roles can be differentiated. In the first category, the men – due to their social responsibilities and sense of social commitment – are able to overcome the traditional notions and demonstrate possibilities for a new era in gender relations. In the second, quantitatively greater category, such a redefinition proves not possible.

Exemplifying the latter situation are the Dutchman, Tannhäuser, and Tristan. These men are united not only through their own deaths and the deaths of their respective female counterparts, but also through their intentions towards love. Their escape into absolute love is destroyed by a conformist society and its principles of power and order.[7]

All three works are rooted in the romantic tradition. This can be seen most clearly in Tristan's mysticism of death and glorification of the night, which strongly reminds one of Novalis's *Hymnen an die Nacht* (1800). Wagner's reworking of the *Fliegender Holländer* (1843) significantly surpasses Heine's story of the Dutchman as the "incarnation of a damned person."[8] In Wagner, the motivation for the Dutchman's death wish lies in his despair of the state of humanity and his disgust with capitalist society. The lust motif in *Tannhäuser* (1845) is evidence of the influence of the *Junges Deutschland* and Heine and, moreover, reflects Wagner's anticapitalism, which was influenced by the theories of Proudhon and Feuerbach. The Dutchman, Tristan, and Tannhäuser fail because of their radicality in a patriarchal society that leaves no room for change.

Such a possibility for changes appears to exist for Lohengrin and Siegfried. At the beginning of the operas, both are committed to reforming society and accepting responsibility for it. This attitude is gradually reversed as they become increasingly entangled in the existing patriarchal power structures. Superficially, Lohengrin's marriage to Elsa fails because of a lack of understanding for one another and because of society's inability to accept their relationship. Lohengrin demands faithfulness and trust of Elsa in a society which claims to uphold these values, but which in reality has replaced them with a rationale of materialism. Wagner uses Lohengrin's retreat, already present in the medieval source, to make the audience aware of the sterility of their own society. Moreover, the reference to the Grail utopia in *Lohengrin* (1850) intimates that such values must be present in order to achieve a society which allows for humanism and an equal partnership between man and woman.

In contrast to this, there is Siegfried's physical power in *Der Ring des Nibelungen* (1849-76), which remains controversial to this day.[9] In Siegfried, the revolutionary and anarchist can be easily recognized. He is the personification of a free human being, free of fear, rules, and tradition, and is therefore capable of love. In short, he possesses the necessary qualities to change society. Thus, the battle with the dragon can be seen as Siegfried's introduction to his responsibilities; it also represents the beginning of his battle for power, which, in the end, will be his demise. Consequently, he heads straight into the trap that was laid for him, by offering his power to those against whom he should be fighting. In this way, Wagner demonstrates the susceptibility of idealists to fall prey to the hidden goals of those wishing to maintain the status quo. Such individuals are either absorbed into the realm of the powerful classes or destroyed.

A more positive development in gender relations can be found in *Rienzi* (1842), *Parsifal* (1882) and *Die Meistersinger von Nürnberg* (1868). The determining factor for Rienzi, Parsifal, and Hans Sachs is their idealistic espousal of their social responsibilities. At the same time, their actions are determined by asceticism, suppression of sexuality, and authoritarian attitudes, characteristics widespread among male bourgeois in 19th-century capitalist society.[10]

Their commitment to save the people or found a new state has various results. Rienzi fails because of the masses which have been incited against him, as well as because of his own search for power. Parsifal is the first figure who can distance himself from his own individual goals. His conduct towards the powers of the existing state proves successful, even if Wagner, by coupling Parsifal's actions with the myth of the Grail, presents this in terms of a vision. The obvious condemnation of the killing of animals in *Parsifal* shows the influence of evolutionary theories on Wagner, who argues in favor of a utopian society, determined by vegetarianism, animal rights, and moderation. It can be concluded that such a positively defined new order of society would inevitably effect gender relations as well.

The male role in Wagner's works that most closely mirrors reality is that of Hans Sachs in *Die Meistersinger von Nürnberg*. This work—free of medieval myth—is defined by practical politics, the goal of which is classless love. Even though Hans Sachs, in contrast to this poetic model, seems to appear here as "Plüsch-Sachs," as Hanns Eisler once derisively remarked,[11] the success of the practical politics is not solely made possible by his personal modesty and renunciation. The reason for success lies in the challenging of the rules and laws of the existing bourgeois society. The fulfillment of love between Stolzing and Eva plays a role here as well, and in the end helps to overcome bourgeois conventions. Through the cheerful ending, Wagner shows a new and different society and thereby demonstrates a human possibility which could minimize the social and economic inequality between man and woman.[12]

II

Opera's culturally laden messages, ritualized consumption, blatant conventions, and inevitable plots disquiet French philosopher and literary critic Catherine Clément. While she "loves" the magnificent female characters who dominate the opera stage, she is disturbed by the high price these women pay for their presence. According to Clément, opera consistently undoes its women:

> Women are [opera's] jewels. . . . No prima donna, no opera. But the role of jewel, a decorative object, is not the deciding role; and on the opera stage women perpetually sing their eternal undoing. . . . Look at these heroines. With their voices they flap their wings, their arms writhe, and then there they are, dead, on the ground.[13]

We may adapt Clément's observations regarding "jewels" to raise, with respect to Wagner's heroines, the following initial questions. Can we interpret these women as autonomous, self-creating beings? Can we embrace them as models, or should we hesitate, and consider Clément's perception of an operatic double message for at least a moment? Surely, the fact that all of Wagner's principal female characters but Eva, the "jewel" of a comedy, are dead by the end of the libretto means something. Do not the closed narratives within which Wagner's heroines struggle, captivate, frighten, and forewarn—narratives which, like history, would not exist without women—inform us that these beings are restricted by more than nature? Finally, does historian Gerda Lerner's identification of a fundamental tension "between women's centrality and active role in creating society and their marginality in the meaning-giving process of interpretation and explanation" elucidate Clément's ambivalent response to opera's traditions?[14]

In general, the creation of works of art is part of the "meaning-giving process" in which women have long had a marginal presence. Certainly, this is true of 19th-century opera. And yet, one can hardly imagine an operatic work whose plot is not centered on one or sometimes two female characters. By coupling Clément's study of how opera "defeats" women with Lerner's assessment of the reasons women have participated in their own subordination for centuries, it may be possible to develop a critical understanding of the women Wagner represents, an understanding which neither accepts them as universal proof of "how women are" nor tiresomely identifies them as victims, but which instead views them as cultural artifacts of a male-oriented system.

The survival of patriarchal order requires women's sexual subordination as well as their participation in their own oppression. According to Lerner, "force, economic dependency . . ., class privileges . . ., and the artificially created division of women" into respected and scorned groups are some of the means through which women's cooperation has been secured.[15] Works of art are another. Opera offers a particularly good example of art in the service of patriarchal ideology in that its heroines inevitably succumb to male authority.[16]

In the world of Wagnerian opera, women's submission takes four general forms: willing participation in the partriarchal order by a character who may or may not die (Eva, Sieglinde); a type of socially insignificant self-murder inspired by identification with a single male lover (Isolde, Elsa, Senta, Elizabeth); or both participation and death, in which case participation is secured through punishment, and death has a broader meaning than the romantic "Liebestod" (Kundry, Brunhilde). A final category moves the female to an abstract level, where a single male god rules over or replaces the multiple gods and goddesses of pre-Christian days (Venus, Ortrud, Erda, Fricka). Common to these libretti is a plot which ultimately affirms the continuation of male authority.

Once we recognize women's unfreedom as a precondition of patriarchal art, Clément's argument becomes a useful position from which to examine the affirmation of traditional gender roles inherent in Wagner's works. According to Clément, operatic heroines "end up punished — fallen, abandoned, or dead," either because in exercising their wills they "leave their familiar and ornamental function," that is, they challenge male authority; or because they fill supporting rather than "deciding" roles and are eventually expendable.[17] In the context of Wagnerian opera, the fates of three female characters, namely Brunhilde, Sieglinde, and Kundry, illustrate this thesis particularly well.

Let us begin with Brunhilde, the daughter Wotan loves almost as much as he loves himself, the daughter who desires no separate will ("What am I, if I am not your will?"), whose identity is so indistinguishable from his own that to confess his deepest fears to her is only to confess them to himself ("Myself I speak to, speaking to you").[18] Let us begin then with Brunhilde, her crime and her punishment.

Pledged to obey Wotan's command and about to claim Siegmund for Valhalla,

Brunhilde is engaged in a fairly routine mission, one she has diligently completed many times before. And yet, this time she falters. As she listens to Siegmund's refusal to abandon Sieglinde, Brunhilde experiences her first moment of psychological independence. When she then acts in the lovers' favor, she directly and openly defies the highest of male authorities. The consequences of her decision make it dramatically clear that the idea of self-governance Wotan carefully nurtured in his son Siegmund ("Boldly, I brought him up to flaunt the laws of the gods") are utterly unacceptable in a daughter's behavior.[19]

Dreading her father's wrath, and not strong enough to prevent Siegmund's death, Brunhilde flees. She seeks support from her sisters, but they are passive, obedient females who fear their father/master too much for a "linkage of sisterhood" to occur. Wotan finds her. His ego raging, his authority challenged, he declares himself Brunhilde's sole creator and proprietor; she has neither autonomy nor a mother ("my will alone woke you to life"). A ruler protecting his turf, a father asserting his supremacy, Wotan prepares to punish his daughter. He will punish her into mortality. He will punish her into sex. He will punish her into marriage. In short, he will pass her from his own authority to that of another man.[20]

As she fights for her integrity, Brunhilde knows her only hope lies in being discovered and taken by a hero, a man she can respect, a man she can love. A kiss on each eyelid, and this magnificent woman warrior is asleep, a dormant, passive, waiting female. A kiss on the lips, and she wakes. As a wife she is tame. She has been punished and now she cooperates. Once she served her father; now she serves her husband. And when Siegfried, a man, a hero, becomes restless with their narrow life and sets out in search of adventure, she accepts her inadequacy.

The wounding marks of Brunhilde's fall into womanhood are her jealousy and injured vanity. Finding herself replaced by another woman, she immediately becomes a murderous traitor and plots Siegfried's death with Hagen. However, as the family saga of *The Ring* finally draws to an end, she is reinstated, for she has one more task to perform. Accompanied by tongues of fire and a flood, Brunhilde restores order. She restores nature. She returns the ring. And because she was good, death reunites her with the authority figures in her life: her husband and her father.

As Brunhilde, representing "the eternal feminine," is engulfed by flames, her self-sacrifice is underscored by Sieglinde's melodic presence. Together, these half sisters share the feminine resolution of the cycle, enacting what Clément calls that "good old tradition that has woman neatening everything up at home."[21] Nor is this the first time they have collaborated. In the confrontation with Wotan, it is Brunhilde's courage and Sieglinde's tenacity which ensure the future. Although one would like to think they will change the course of history by interfering in the godhead's plan, it is difficult to believe Wotan was not anticipating the birth of yet another hero all along. If not, why did he separate and then reunite Siegmund and Sieglinde so strategically?

Sieglinde, the new hero's mother, is a model daughter and wife. For years, she has patiently awaited the man her father promised would come to claim Nothung, the sword which must be the central fixture of her home. Then one night he is there: Siegmund, her lost brother, Siegmund, her liberator, Siegmund, her heart's desire. The sword in his hand tells her to flee with him; nature tells her to love him. Then, after barely twenty-four hours of drama, passion, and bliss, Siegmund is dying and she is expecting a son. While her love for Siegmund is great, she is not allowed to die with him, for only Siegfried's birth can complete her supporting role. As she is delivered of her son, she expires.

Sieglinde is Wotan's good daughter. Metaphorically, her fate illustrates not only woman's vulnerability in male society but also the attitude that women who are "exchanged"[22] through violent rather than peaceful means should respond to their experience in terms of self-hatred rather than rebelliousness, anger, or suicidal despair. Sieglinde does not curse Hunding for abusing her; she curses herself for once obeying "a man she loved not at all." How can she forget that she was kidnapped and then raped into marriage? She does not curse the father who visited her on her wedding day, advising patience and endurance, and leaving behind a weapon intended for yet another man; she pours loathing upon herself. "Away! Away!" she tells Siegmund, "Flee the profaned one! Unholy . . . disgraced, dishonored. . . . Flee this body, let it alone!"[23] While titillating his audience by romanticizing adultery and incest, Wagner does not miss the opportunity to enforce the notion that sexually abused women have only themselves to blame. How easy to obscure Wotan's part in Sieglinde's misery!

As unsatisfying as it is to find heroines like Brunhilde and Sieglinde forever caught in supporting roles, Wagner's oeuvre does contain a worse alternative for women: in the opera he called his "Weltabschiedswerk," his swansong, salvation hinges not on keeping women in their place, or some sort of final redemption brought on by female self-sacrifice, but instead on overcoming woman altogether. Let us look, then, at *Parsifal,* Wagner's "final reckoning."

Gone is the young man's critique of the destructive effects of 19th-century capitalism. Gone is the usual Wagnerian reverence for private, heterosexual love, as well as the much broader conception of love which informs *The Ring.* Edward Downes, for example, holds that Alberich renounces "not only romantic love but [also] love of one's fellow man, and love as a symbol of all beneficent creative activity," to gain the Rheingold. In the "conflict between love and the lust for power" which takes place in *The Ring,* human rights are abused and disregarded.[24]

In *Parsifal,* Wagner withdraws such broadly defined love from at least half of humanity and replaces the richness of *The Ring* with hollow religious asceticism: the lust for gold, a lust to which both men and women fall prey, is replaced by man's lust for woman's sinful flesh; and if one work views the renunciation of love as the beginning of evil human activity, the other views the renunciation of woman as the source of a new and beneficent social order.

While it is hardly surprising that Otto Weininger and others of his misogynist ilk hail Kundry as 'the most profound conception of woman in all literature,"[25] it is disturbing that contemporary scholarship is little inclined to acknowledge the work's relentless gender system. In discussing Kundry, Michael von Soden, for example, offers only obscurities, calling her "Wagner's most multifaceted stage figure," a "seemingly schizophrenic woman, who, now lust, now humility, wanders through the world for centuries."[26] He prefers philosophical reflection on the briefest of lines—"time changes here to space"—to the direct admission that Kundry's tormented presence is more animal than human.

Listen to Kundry: she groans, she moans, she shrieks, she screams. She speaks hardly a sentence that is complete. Then she coos, disarms, seduces. She begs for sex and curses the man who rejects her. Finally, she looses her voice altogether, to become that most desirable of things, a silent, humble, hard-working female. Early in scene three, she utters one word: "to serve . . . to serve" (*dienen . . . dienen*). And until her life expires she will speak no more.[27]

Look at Kundry: a disheveled, unkempt hag whose eyes roll, burn, go blank. Her body tense, she crouches close to the ground, tosses her wild dark hair, and clenches her fists. She sleeps outside, under thorny bushes. Transformed, she is devilishly beautiful, transparently clothed, surrounded by gentle flowers. Finally, she is plain, neat, penitent; a servant with long, soft hair and eyes that beg for death.

Of course, Kundry is not a real woman but a compilation of male fears and desires, an oxymoronic fantasy figure made to satisfy and appall the male gaze. Like Brunhilde, she is punished for transgressing against male authority. Though her sin would seem minor (she once saw Christ "—and—laughed"), her punishment is so severe that she must be tremendously evil. Perhaps we are to associate her with Lilith, Adam's sexually independent first wife, whom celibate monks feared and who was said to laugh "every time a pious Christian had a wet dream."[28] We are certainly meant to associate her with the medieval Christian notion of witchcraft, for one of the names her "master" Klingsor heaps upon her is "Herodias," a synonym for Hecate, Queen of Witches.[29] Unlike Senta, Elizabeth, Brunhilde, and Sieglinde, Kundry is not allowed a final redemptive role. On the contrary, she must thrice be redeemed by male figures. Only a man, a physical complete male virgin, can free her from Klingsor's curse. Only a man can effect her entrance into the fold, baptizing her in the name of Christ, and thus granting her tormented being the peace of death. Only Christ, uninfluenced by a female saint, awaits her in heaven.

How different from the resolution of *Tannhäuser,* the opera in which Wagner first represented the "antagonism between sensuality and asceticism," and in which women play significant roles![30] Elizabeth, the chaste lover who will die upon his breast, prays for the soul of Tannhäuser, a man so sinful the Pope himself has refused him absolution. She prays to Maria, whom people in the Middle Ages persisted in viewing "as their defender" while they saw God "as their persecutor."[31] The journey from *Tannhäuser* to *Parsifal* can be seen as a journey from the Hebrew to the Christian Scriptures. The god who once was wrathful, but who would listen to a female mediator, has been replaced by his gentle son who reigns alone. On earth, it is now only celibate men, the elite members of a spiritual brotherhood, who perform good works. Woman, if she is humble enough, may be forgiven her sins, but however devoutly she may wish to participate in the existing social order, she can be no more than a servant to man. And since she has no place at all in the projected social order, a silent death will be her fate.

Susan McClary's introduction to Clément's study suggests two crucial reasons for applying a feminist reading to opera. Firstly, opera is not merely a phenomenon of the past; today, at the end of the 20th century, canonic operas exert "extraordinary," even archetypal, "prestige and influence" on Western culture. Secondly,

> opera was one of the principal media through which the nineteenth-century bourgeoisie developed and disseminated its new moral codes, values, and normative behaviour. . . .[32]

Consequently, opera is an important "source of information" for scholars interested in tracking the evolution of "European middle-class constructions of gender."[33]

III

The first part of this study considered the kinds of roles typically played by men in Wagner's operas, while the second part interpreted Wagner's patriarchal iconography of women from a feminist perspective. As we have seen, most of the men and women in Wagner's operas reflect ideological positions typical of the bourgeois capitalistic society of his time. In the case of the male characters, however, there is an attempt at reforming the socioeconomic patterns by means of utopian thought, which results in the breakdown of class barriers. Wagner's affirmation of traditional gender roles, on the other hand, perpetuates male authority, which women may challenge, but are never allowed to overcome. In this final section, we shall further expand the analysis of gender roles by examining both the reduction of woman to an object of exchange, and male homoeroticism in *Tristan und Isolde* (1859).

Invoking 19th-century middle-class gender stereotypes and male fantasies about women and at the same time eliciting the complexity of his medieval source,[34] Wagner subtly portrays Isolde as both a seductress seeking the ruin of men and as a commodity guaranteeing the stability of male society. As the feminist anthropologist Gayle Rubin has noted, patriarchal society is based on the ritual exchange of women by men as gift objects in order to establish kinship ties.[35] Wagner relegates Isolde to the status of an exchange object, describing her as a "Schatz," a "schmucke Irin," or, in other words, mere "Zins," to be paid to King Marke in a marriage that will establish permanent kinship and political ties.[36] One woman pays the price of uniting two kingdoms in order to maintain the supreme world order of men. Patriarchal rule, be it feudal, capitalist, or socialist, "civilizes" the world at the expense of women (and sometimes, at least in Wagner's case, at the expense also of Jews).

Wagner tendentiously meddles with medieval myth: by having Isolde provide the fateful love potion, he blithely ignores Tristan's amorous predisposition toward her. Wagner also makes Isolde responsible for Tristan's death and death wish by having her suggest *Liebestod* while ignoring Tristan's rapturous desire for death in his lover's arms. Isolde heals Tristan because, as she says in her own words: "Seines Elends jammerte mich."[37] But Wagner perverts her gift of compassionate healing by depicting the strong, powerful healer as a weak, frail woman. Moreover, he depicts Isolde as an unstable character. Love makes Isolde take leave of her senses, as her closest companion, Brangäne, cautions: "der Minne tückischer Trank [wird] des Sinnes Licht dir verlöschen."[38] Wagner even has Isolde blame a woman (albeit a goddess) for her infatuation with Tristan: "Frau Minne hat meiner Macht es entwandt."[39] A sailor apostrophizes Isolde as "mein Kind! Irische Maid, du wilde, minnige Maid,"[40] and Clément emphasizes that "Isolde's wildness" becomes the source of all misfortune for Tristan.[41] By her very presence, Isolde intervenes in the male transaction that has made her into a mere object, thus disrupting the patriarchal order. Wagner does not blame Isolde for her deeds and potions alone: he blames her for her existence.

Finally, Wagner damns Isolde for being a woman, and destroys her to reproach all women and to vanquish all men. Nevertheless, the men continue to circle around Isolde even after her obscure disappearance halfway through the opera. The feminist theorist Luce Irigaray has noted that "the circulation of women among men is what establishes the operations of society, at least of patriarchal society."[42] In other words, Isolde's presence binds the men together for the duration of the opera, and, consequentially, her meaningless death reveals the destructiveness of male desires and male lust. A woman cannot exist without a male counterpart—owner, protector, husband, or father—even though she serves as an important strategic object in patriarchal society.

The love affair and death wish of Tristan and Isolde transgress patriarchal norms. The mythologist Joseph Campbell points out that by falling in personal love (*amor*) and in rapturous love (*eros*), Tristan and Isolde reject the compassionate love (*agape*) of the patriarchal marriage system, which requires neither the consent nor the love of the contracted parties.[43] Tristan and Isolde seek that which patriarchy prohibits. Violating the cultural taboo of forbidden love can lead only to death, which Isolde suggests and Tristan welcomes. In fact, Isolde describes her love with an echo of love and death: "Leben und Tod . . . Lust und Leid."[44] The Marxist Freudian Herbert Marcuse interprets eros and the death instinct as representations of a single drive since both "strive for a gratification which culture cannot grant."[45] Tristan and Isolde choose death because they cannot satisfy their amorous desires.

Actually, it is Tristan, and not Isolde, who violates the patriarchal norms of culture, though Wagner conveniently ignores this. Whereas Isolde remains in the stereotypical female realm, Tristan crosses defined gender (not sexual) boundaries. Rubin untangles sex from gender: nature determines biological sex, termed male or female, whereas patriarchy arbitrarily defines the gender roles of man or woman.[46] By accepting Tristan's sword and by killing him with it, Isolde would have the opportunity to cross gender boundaries, but she rejects this. Instead, she intends to offer Tristan a chalice of poison. The feminist historian Riane Eisler defines the sword as a historically and culturally male symbol and the chalice as the female one.[47] By shunning the stereotypical male sword in favor of the stereotypical female chalice, Isolde remains consistent with the gender role patriarchy has assigned her.

Tristan differs. Initially, he embodies his gender perfectly by fighting and defeating Morold. Tristan's flesh wound and damaged sword, besides indicating a personal loss for him, eventually symbolize his transformation. Through the wound, Tristan initially submits to Isolde's healing power, i.e., the wound makes Tristan surrender to a woman. Although Isolde cures his wound, love prevents its complete healing, and her love potion reopens the wound. Tristan, by drinking from Isolde's chalice, not only accepts the device of his wounding, but also receives communion with the opposite gender, thus migrating across established gender boundaries. Furthermore, the wounded Tristan emotionally expresses passionate love, which contradicts the male suppression of emotion and denial of love (other than lust). He eventually dies from the selfsame wound that symbolizes his femininity.

The sword also indicates Tristan's gender, and the chip on Tristan's sword parallels his wound. Initially, after his battle with Morold, Tristan's public symbol of male power—irreparably damaged—symbolically questions Tristan's manhood. Later, when Isolde wants to kill Tristan, he patronizes her by offering her his own sword, thus relinquishing his symbol of power. He repeats the same relinquishment when Melot challenges him. In fact, the sequence of events in Melot's challenge perfectly repeats the sequence in Isolde's challenge. By paralleling Tristan's initial struggle with Isolde, this duel stresses Tristan's passion for Melot. Enthralled by his friend and comrade Melot, Tristan resigns his sword to him, making himself vulnerable. Tristan actually fosters his gender transmutation during the encounter with Melot when he deliberately falls on Melot's sword, but lands on his old wound, again emphasizing his new gender role. From the patriarchal perspective of Wagner's time, Tristan loses his manly virtue by abandoning his sword and by refusing to defend himself.

Besides Tristan's illegitimate affair with Isolde and his transgression of gender, Tristan engages in homoerotic friendships with both Melot and Marke. Tristan's illegitimate affair with Isolde legitimizes and displaces the violated sexual norms of these enigmatic relationships. Wagner exposes the public, superficial nature of heterosexual relationships in order to redeem the vulnerable, confused, androgynous men who engage in veiled, sincere homoerotic friendships. In a double entendre which merges the Greek *homo* ("same") with the French *homme* ("male"), Irigaray calls the combined homosocial and homosexual interaction between men "hom(m)o-sexual," which "is played out through the bodies of women."[48] The same-sexed interaction among men expedites the manipulation of Isolde.

Wagner's characters with homosexual leanings appeared at a time of intense repression of homosexuality in Germany.[49] At best, Tristan, Melot, and Marke illustrate a pre-homosexual or a homoerotic sensibility, even though the patriarchy, which Tristan, Melot, and Marke do indeed epitomize, creates a new category of social, economic, and political exclusion with the term "homosexual." According to the cultural philosopher and historian Michel Foucault, the term incorporates all "peripheral sexualities" and "perversions," which includes all unlabeled categories of sexual expression.[50] As such, the term does not apply to Tristan, Melot, and Marke. Furthermore, the cultural critic Eve Kosofsky Sedgewick demonstrates that the binary operation of the artificial terminological pair "homo/heterosexual" perfectly parallels the patriarchally defined gender roles of "woman/man."[51] In other words, patriarchy denigrates the "homosexual" much in the same way it denigrates woman. Again, the term does not apply to Tristan, Melot, and Marke. Calling Wagner's characters homosexual or homoerotic poses an irresolute problem, because the term does not describe them appropriately, and an adequate term does not exist.

Brangäne reveals the first homoerotic index between Tristan and Melot when she notes that Melot had stolen secret passionate glances "mit böslicher List, lauerndem Blick" at Tristan.[52] Isolde only confirms Brangäne's suspicions: "Muß mein Trauter mich meiden, dann weilt er bei Melot allein."[53] Tristan's time with either Isolde or Melot infers a parallel relationship between Tristan and either Isolde or Melot. Finally, Melot's death reaffirms Melot's and Tristan's clandestine relationship when Melot dies with Tristan's name on his lips: "Weh' mir! Tristan!"[54]

Melot challenges Tristan because Tristan's love for Isolde threatens his friendship with Tristan. He acts jealously, indicating the unusual nature of his relationship to Tristan, when he interprets Tristan's tie to Isolde as a rival relationship. Melot's patriarchal dualism surmises that Tristan can engage in only one romantic pursuit: either with Isolde or with Melot.

The second, even more foreboding, aspect of the homoerotic entanglement pertains to Tristan and Marke. When Marke discovers Tristan and Isolde in each other's arms, he chastises Tristan alone. As Robert Gutman explains, Marke's tirade "is directed to Tristan alone, his references to the lady being, in fact, rather gallant."[55] Wagner's prose drafts confirm a friendship between Marke and Tristan that goes beyond emotional male-bonding.[56]

Tristan angers Marke, in addition to Melot. Instead of challenging him, Marke censures Tristan out of jealousy, ignoring the fact that Tristan seriously abrogated the medieval code of honor. Marke blames the man, the friend, the comrade-in-arms of disloyalty, and not his bride-to-be of premarital infidelity. Tristan's love for Isolde undermines Marke: Tristan loves Isolde, whereas Marke only intends to love her for the sake of spectacle.

Tristan's love for Isolde exposes the insecurity of the men at Marke's court. Tristan personally threatens both Melot and Marke on an emotional level. Melot assumes that Tristan has abandoned him, while Marke feels Tristan has betrayed him. The misogynistic explanation that Isolde's love potion made Tristan do what he did eventually corrects the strained situation, erasing Tristan's emotional impropriety. Subsequently, Marke forgives Tristan, thus reestablishing patriarchal order and culture. Tristan's *Liebestod,* in spite of the pardon, underscores the invalidity of the patriarchal mechanization that publicly restores honor and condemns Isolde.

Ultimately, woman serves male society by disguising authentic homoerotic relationships in Wagner's *Tristan und Isolde,* although she also disturbs society. Patriarchy has no defense against woman's meddling except through her death, which easily reestablishes order. Wagner documents the Marcusian interpretation of the Freudian dictum that society imposes two acts of repression concurrently: it represses the individuals in order to make them acceptable elements of society, and it represses social structure in order to maintain its own definition of social acceptability.[57]

In conclusion, most of the men and women in Wagner's operas reflect the bourgeois capitalistic society of the time. However, at least for the males, there is an attempt at restructuring socioeconomic patterns by means of utopian thought and a breaking down of class barriers. The affirmation of traditional gender roles ensures the preservation of male authority. Women may challenge this authority, but they are not allowed to overcome it. Furthermore, women are used and manipulated in order to mask male transgressions of gender roles and moral codes through veiled homoerotic relationships.

Notes

1 Bertolt Brecht, *Schriften zum Theater* (Frankfurt, 1957), 16.
2 Cf. Jost Hermand, "Avantgarde, Moderne, Postmoderne: Die Musik, die (fast) niemand hören will," in *Kunst und Politik der Avantgarde,* ed. syndicat anonym (Frankfurt, 1989), 13–30. For Wagner's relationship to socialism, cf. Frank Trommler, *Sozialistische Literatur in Deutschland* (Stuttgart, 1976), 136ff.

3 Cf. Richard Hamann and Jost Hermand, *Gründerzeit* (Munich, 1971), 88ff.
4 Eva Rieger, "Feministische Ansätze in der Musikwissenschaft," in *Feminismus: Inspektion der Herrenkultur,* ed. Luise F. Pusch (Frankfurt, 1983), 109.
5 Friedrich Nietzsche, *Also sprach Zarathustra,* ed. Giorgio Colli and Mazzino Montinari (Munich, 1988), 84f.
6 Cf. Eckart Pankoke, *Soziale Bewegung—Soziale Frage—Soziale Politik* (Stuttgart, 1970), 13.
7 Cf. Jochanaan Christoph Trilse, "Antikapitalismus bei Heinrich Heine und bei Richard Wagner: Über Säkular-Gleiches und Säkular-Verschiedenes," in *Heinrich Heine und das neunzehnte Jahrhundert: Signaturen,* ed. Rolf Hosfeld (Berlin, 1986), 170.
8 Hans Mayer, *Richard Wagner* (Hamburg, 1959), 24.
9 Cf. Peter Morris-Keitel, "Siegfried as Idol? The Role of the Hero in Recent West German Adaptations of the *Nibelungenlied,*" in *"Was sider da geschah": American-German Studies on the Nibelungenlied,* ed. Ulrich Müller and Werner Wunderlich (Göppingen, 1991).
10 Wilfried Gottschalch, *Vatermutterkind* (Berlin, 1979), 85.
11 Hanns Eisler, *Gesammelte Werke.* Musik und Politik: Schriften 1948-1962, ed. Stephanie Eisler and Manfred Grabs, series 3, vol. 2 (Leipzig, 1982), 239.
12 Cf. Trilse.
13 Catherine Clément, *Opera, or the Undoing of Women,* trans. Susan McClary (Minneapolis, 1988), 5.
14 Gerda Lerner, *The Creation of Patriarchy* (Oxford, 1986), 5.
15 Ibid., 9.
16 See Clément.
17 Ibid., 7.
18 Richard Wagner, *The Ring of the Nibelung,* trans. Stewart Robb (New York, 1960), 107.
19 Ibid., 111.
20 Ibid., 142.
21 Clément, 162-69.
22 See Gayle Rubin, "The Traffic of Women: Notes on the 'Political Economy' of Sex," in *Toward an Anthropology of Women,* ed. Rayna R. Reiter (New York, 1975), 157-210.
23 Wagner, *Ring,* 116.
24 Ibid., xii-xiv.
25 Otto Weininger, *Sex and Character* (New York, 1975), vii.
26 Richard Wagner, *Parsifal,* ed. Michael von Soden (Frankfurt, 1983), 9, 21.
27 Except for the reference to childbirth, Kundry's submission recalls I Timothy 2, 8-15: "I desire . . . that women should adorn themselves modestly and sensibly in seemly apparel . . . by good deeds, as befits women who profess religion. Let a woman learn in silence with all submissiveness. I permit no woman to teach or to have authority over men; she is to keep silent. For Adam was formed first, then Eve; and Adam was not deceived, but the woman was deceived and became a transgressor. Yet woman will be saved through bearing children if she continues in faith and love and holiness, with modesty."
28 Barbara G. Walker, *The Woman's Encyclopedia of Myths and Secrets* (New York, 1983), 542.
29 Ibid., 399.
30 Wagner, *Parsifal,* 9.
31 Walker, 604.
32 Clément, xviii.
33 Ibid., xi.
34 For an appraisal of the relationship between the medieval *Tristan und Isolde* and Wagner's version, see Dagmar Ingenshay-Goch, *Richard Wagners neu erfundener Mythos: Zur Rezeption und Reproduktion des germanischen Mythos in seinen Operntexten* (Bonn, 1982); and Arthur Groos, "Appropriation in Wagner's *Tristan* Libretto," in *Reading Opera,* ed. Arthur Groos and Roger Parker (Princeton, 1988), 12-33. Groos successfully demonstrates that Wagner used Gottfried von Straßburg's unfinished poem as an inspirational source, and that he did not feel obligated to maintain the integrity of the original plot. Nevertheless, the famous plot of the original myth echoes in the minds of Wagner's audiences, creating a secondary text that contrasts and critiques Wagner's libretto.
35 Rubin, 173.

36 Richard Wagner, *Tristan und Isolde,* ed. Nicholas John (London/New York, 1981), 52–53.
37 Ibid., 52.
38 Ibid., 66.
39 Ibid.
40 Ibid., 47.
41 Clément, 34.
42 Luce Irigaray, *This Sex Which is Not One,* trans. Catherine Porter (Ithaca, 1985), 184.
43 Joseph Campbell, *The Power of Myth,* ed. Bill Moyers (New York, 1988), 189.
44 Wagner, *Tristan und Isolde,* 66.
45 Herbert Marcuse, *Eros and Civilization: A Philosophical Inquiry into Freud* (Boston, 1955), 11. See also Roland Barthes, *A Lover's Discourse: Fragments,* trans. Richard Howard (New York, 1978), 218. Barthes discusses the unity of love and death in *Liebestod* at great length, cleverly noting that suicide for lovers is but a trifle. Such a suicide does, however, provide an escape from an otherwise impossible situation.
46 Rubin, 178.
47 Riane Eisler, *The Chalice and the Blade: Our History, Our Future* (San Francisco, 1987), xviii.
48 Irigaray, 172.
49 For an analysis chronicling the first stages of a public homosexual sensibility, see James D. Steakley, *The Homosexual Emancipation Movement in Germany* (New York, 1975), 1–19. Manfred Herzer, *Bibliographie zur Homosexualität: Verzeichnis des deutschsprachigen, nichtbelletristischen Schrifttums zur weiblichen und männlichen Homosexualität aus den Jahren 1466 bis 1975 in chronologischer Reihenfolge* (Berlin, 1982) provides an exhaustive list of publications that broach the subject of homosexuality.
50 Michel Foucault, *The History of Sexuality: An Introduction,* vol. 1, trans. Robert Hurley (New York, 1980), 42–43.
51 Eve Kosofsky Sedgwick, *Epistemology of the Closet* (Berkeley, 1990), 8–9.
52 Wagner, *Tristan und Isolde,* 64–65.
53 Ibid., 65.
54 Ibid., 90.
55 Robert W. Gutman, *Richard Wagner: The Man, His Mind, and His Music* (New York, 1968), 251. Gutman diverges from established Wagnerian analysis in that he critically investigates the locus of homosexuality in Wagner's texts, and not in his life alone. Hanns Fuchs, *Richard Wagner und die Homosexualität: Unter besonderer Berücksichtigung der sexuellen Anomalien seiner Gestalten* (Berlin, 1903) furthered the biographical approach to homosexuality in Wagner with his exhaustive catalogue of Wagner's homosexual acquaintances and friends. However, Wagner's characters suspected of homosexuality came under public moral scrutiny, as in Oskar Panizza, "Bayreuth und die Homosexualität," *Die Gesellschaft* 11.1 (1885): 88–92.
56 Ibid., 250.
57 Marcuse, 20, 55–77.

Wagner and the Vocal Iconography of Race and Nation

MARC A. WEINER

> No break anywhere, no coloratura,
> And not a trace of melody![1]

Beckmesser's condemnation of Walther von Stolzing's new music is set to a pliant vocal line that lies predominantly above the staff and that, characteristically, rises through florid melismas to a high G-flat (see illus. 1). Beckmesser's music thus demonstrates the very kind of vocal production the influential critic so misses in the aesthetically different song of the future. It is no coincidence that Wagner's musical material here associates elevated pitch with a figure universally recognized as a caricature of a Jew, because for Wagner the physiological makeup of the human voice revealed national and racial identity, and a high voice was a foreign, a non-German instrument.

Kein Ab-satz   wo, kein Co - lo-ra-tur, von Me-lo - dei auchnichtei-ne   Spur!

1. Beckmesser's high-pitched rejection of Walther von Stolzing's music. From *The Mastersingers of Nuremberg: An Opera in Three Acts.* Complete vocal score in a facilitated arrangement by Karl Klindworth. English translation by Frederick Jameson (New York, 1932), p. 157.

This notion did not first appear in *Die Meistersinger von Nürnberg;* it had already emerged on numerous occasions throughout Wagner's expository and dramatic production from his initial essays of 1840 on the Parisian culture industry to his more celebrated tracts of 1849–51 concerning aesthetic reform and the need for the transformation and purification of German society; and it would reappear in his analysis of the legitimate theater, penned in the early 1870s following the formation of the *Reich.* [2] The notion of the voice as an acoustical icon of race and nation also decidedly influenced the composition of the vocal music with which Wagner would come to be most closely identified: that of the *Ring, Tristan und Isolde, Die Meistersinger,* and *Parsifal.* Regardless of the extent to which Wagner's understanding of the voice reflects an iconography of the body that was widespread in European culture of the mid-19th century, it has been virtually ignored by his modern critics, who thus disregard the central role such corporal images play in Wagner's conception of a new art and of the new society in which he hoped his music of the future would sound.[3] Though much scholarship to this day disavows the connections between Wagner's anti-Semitic tracts, his aesthetic theory, his dramatic texts, and his music, an examination of the motif of the voice as icon highlights the uniformity of the ideological forces that informed Wagner's theoretical and dramatic works.

Wagner's search for his own voice began in Paris in the employment of a wealthy German Jew and music publisher, Moritz Adolf Schlesinger, and from this experience emerged his never-ending association of Jews with the nascent culture industry and, perhaps, his characterization of Jews as vocally different.[4] Moritz Schlesinger was the son of Adolf Martin (actually Abraham Moses) Schlesinger, whose Berlin publishing house ranked as one of the most important of its kind in Prussia.[5] Moritz Adolf enjoyed a similar success in Paris, Europe's operatic center, where he specialized in publications of the very composers Wagner despised: by his retirement in 1846, Schlesinger had produced more than fifty piano-vocal and two dozen full orchestral scores to such works as Meyerbeer's *Robert le diable* and *Les Huguenots,* twelve operas of Halévy, among them *La juive,* and operas by Adam and Donizetti. He also published complete editions of Beethoven's piano works, string trios, quartets and quintets, and early works of Mendelssohn and Berlioz, including the first edition of *Huit scènes de Faust* and the full score of *Symphonie fantastique.*[6]

In his vindictive autobiography, Wagner characterized Schlesinger as a "monstrous acquaintance" who exploited the young composer's destitution and forced him to accomplish tasks he detested, such as providing the publisher with operatic piano-vocal scores, arrangements for trumpet, guitar, and string quartet, potpourris, and even a pedagogical manual for the *cornet à pistons.*[7] Wagner doubtless envied Schlesinger's position in Parisian society, secured in part through the prestigious journal *Gazette musicale de Paris,* which Schlesinger had founded in 1834, and which had merged, in the following year, with the successful *Revue musicale de Paris.*[8] The new journal subsidized a series of concerts especially for Schlesinger's favorite composers, many of them Jews, and provided him with a printed forum for their works.[9] Both the concerts and the journal were vehicles Wagner was never able to exploit successfully for the furthering of his own fame as a composer, despite his repeated attempts to that end. The performance of his *Columbus* overture in the series "bored everybody," and the publication of his setting of "Deux grenadiers" in the *Gazette musicale* only brought him a debt of fifty francs, payable to Schlesinger, and failed to attract the attention of the influential singers Wagner had longed for.[10]

Wagner's career as a critic and feuilletonist was furthered when Schlesinger commissioned from him an article on German music for the *Gazette musicale,* which first appeared in two installments, on 12 and 26 July 1840, as "De la musique allemande" ("On German Music") and was later republished in Germany under the title "Über deutsches Musikwesen."[11] As late as 1871, Wagner deemed the essay important enough to include it in volume I of his *Gesammelte Schriften und Dichtungen,* while he omitted there most of the reviews and essays he had written in Paris for the German press: for August Lewald's *Europa: Chronik der gebildeten Welt* in Stuttgart, Schumann's *Neue Zeitschrift für Musik* in Leipzig, and for Theodor Winkler's *Dresdner Abendzeitung*. Thus, "On German Music" must have represented even to the older Wagner a valid expression of fundamental constants in his thinking. When Schlesinger commissioned "De la musique allemande," Wagner found a vehicle for theoretically justifying his never-ending resentment of the institutional forces governing the arts in the modern world, forces he associated explicitly with the Jews, as he made clear ten years later in his anti-Semitic diatribe "Judaism in Music" ("Das Judentum in der Musik").[12]

Though Wagner's essay contains many complimentary remarks on the French appreciation of German music and on his recognition that the political centralization of France contributes to the strength of French cultural life, and though it closes with the hope that the Germans and French will work together to enhance their differing approaches to art for the betterment of both nations, such passages were most likely intended to forestall consternation over the text's pervasive Francophobic sentiment.[13] "On German Music" unfolds within the very tension between dependence, envy, and resentment that Wagner experienced in his work for Schlesinger, and opens with the concern that German art is all too easily overpowered by foreign influence:

> [One] can say that the French, through their proven willing acknowledgement of foreign productions, have distinguished themselves more than the Germans, who succumb faster and with less opposition to every foreign influence than is good for the preservation of a certain independence. The difference is this: — the German, who does not possess the ability to initiate a fashion, adopts it without hesitation if it comes from abroad; in this weakness he forgets himself, and blindly sacrifices his own judgment to the foreign impression. (7:84 / 5:152)

The struggle for power that Wagner discerns within the cultural life of Europe sets up an unequal exchange between diverse national forces. The despairing martial imagery of overrun borders and impending subordination underscores the plight of the German artist, for it is he who must strive to preserve the integrity of the besieged homeland. This cognitive model of culture as a vehicle for national attack and defense will infuse Wagner's writings to the end of his life, and is as readily apparent in the anti-Semitic "Know Thyself" ("Erkenne dich selbst") of 1881 as it is in the xenophobic tract here.

To counter this threat, Wagner develops a compensatory argument that robs the competing culture of its validity, though the assessment of foreign culture as superficial, mercantile, and as lacking in populist support further accentuates the peril facing Germany. Each national identity is coupled with its representative culture:

> The Italian is a singer, the Frenchman is a virtuoso, the German a — musician. The German has a right to be called exclusively "Musician," for of him one may say that

he loves Music for its own sake—not as a means of charming, of winning money and respect. . . . The German is capable of writing music merely for himself and his friend, completely oblivious as to whether it will ever be executed and presented to a public. . . . Go some winter night and listen to them in their cozy little room: a father and his three sons sit there at a round table; two play the violin, a third the viola, the father the cello; what you can hear being performed in the deepest and most heartfelt manner [*so tief und innig*] is a string quartet which that little man composed who is beating time. . . . [The] quartet that he composed is artistic, beautiful, and deeply felt [*kunstvoll, schön und tiefgefühlt*]. (7:85–86 / 5:153–54)

A number of consistent oppositions emerge here that provide the basis for the development of Wagner's argument.[14] The specific nature of the foreign danger is underscored in polarizations which stress the difference between Latinate and German culture: the virtuoso versus the artisan, the implied aristocratic society versus the explicit Biedermeier setting, the public audience versus the private domestic sphere, and, above all, the superficial *Ausland* opposed to the image of Germany's cultural essence as deep—*tief, innig,* and *tiefgefühlt.* It is no coincidence that Wagner's Hans Sachs will later extol his *liebes Nürnberg* as lying *in Deutschlands Mitten,* nor that the Rhinemaidens will lament at the conclusion to *The Rhinegold:* "Trusted and true / is only in the depths: / false and cowardly / is what rejoices above!"[15]

Wagner's image of the human voice, introduced in this essay, must be understood within these ideologically significant oppositions. For Wagner, the voice is both a physiological reality reflecting racial difference and the metaphorical representation of national identity. The notion of deep as better, as more natural, communal, familial, and untouched by the alienation of an inferior and different "higher" modern civilization, reemerges in his description of the physiological basis of art south of Germany, specifically of Italian vocal music.[16] Culture as metaphor has for Wagner a realistic, literal component based on the physical properties of those who create, experience, and share it:

Both nature and the makeup of his homeland set strict boundaries for the German artist. Nature denies him the light and supple development of a head organ, of song [*die leichte und weiche Bildung eines Hauptorganes, des Gesanges*] which we find in the lucky Italian throats—the political makeup prevents him from [attaining] higher publicity. The opera-composer is forced to learn an advantageous singing technique from the Italians, to seek however foreign stages for his works, because he can find none in Germany on which to present himself to a nation. (7:87–88 / 5:155)

The Italian is a singer and the Frenchman is a virtuoso, but only the German, it seems, with his communal life based on a domestic harmony reflected in the physical makeup of his deep vocal registers, is a genuine musician. Ensconced in the center of Europe, he must acquire the superficial eccentricities of foreign culture in order to succeed in the "higher public arena" located in the outer geographic extremities surrounding Germany. High voices are Mediterranean, cultivated, hypercivilized, foreign, and far removed from the lower reaches of the German masses, comprised apparently of bass-baritones, who live in the lower center of the European map.

Such physiological metaphors of culture underscore the urgency behind the perception of a purportedly genuine threat to the German nation. To the fantasy of cultural despair that views modern civilization as corrosive and antithetical to a legitimate art and to its reception, the arenas of economic and political power in which inauthentic "high" art is disseminated are remarkably similar. While the Frenchman is a virtuoso and the Italian a singer, the commodification of inferior art in France, England, and Italy makes all three countries essentially similar, related, and fundamentally different from Germany as well. Wagner's ironic description of the Italian tenor Giovanni Rubini, for whom Bellini and Donizetti wrote many operatic roles and who enjoyed great success in both Paris and London, makes it clear that the virtuoso is equally at home in the culture industry of all three countries, but not in Wagner's homeland.[17] Morally, these nations resemble one another and are different from Germany. The pious religiosity so apparent in the German's attitude to his national art is missing in the sensual, titillating frivolity of Italian and French music and in its reception in the cultural centers of England and France. For this reason, in describing the musical life of Paris, Wagner stresses the notion that the English and the French have mistresses there, who are often found among the artists and dancers of the Opera, while the Germans do not.[18] They are morally upstanding, chaste, and baritonal.

Therefore, Wagner suggests, when the German musician elevates his voice, he degenerates morally. He loses his sincerity when he adopts the immoral Italian virtuosity so applauded in Paris, because he has neither the requisite vocal cords nor the vocal technique to effect the pyrotechnics of foreign musical sensuality:

> [The German musician] is pure and innocent, but, for that very reason, noble and sublime. — But set these glorious musicians before a large audience, in a sprawling salon — and they will no longer be the same people. . . . Now they will fearfully attempt to perform for you glittering passages as well; the same voices which sang the lovely German *Lied* so touchingly, will quickly study Italian coloratura. But they cannot succeed with these passages and coloratura. . . . These bunglers are the truest artists . . . [and were] ashamed of their own true nature. (7:87 / 5:154–55)

Beckmesser can sing such passages, and even prefers them, but the genuine German *Musiker* cannot and does not. Culture, then, is understood as related to the physiological characteristics of a people, and, as such, it is the hallmark of the nation. It is as indelibly inscribed upon the national character as is the physiognomy of the national appearance. Wagner implies that you can no more change your innate cultural identity than you can transform your face or the material of your voice, and, for him, the attempt to do so brings with it a loss of traditional values associated with a physiologically circumscribed and defined people.[19]

Wagner's remarks concerning the tessitura of vocal music as a criterion of national identity are consistent with his many pronouncements concerning vocal production per se. For Wagner, sounds reflect national essence, and therefore the tessitura of speech, like that of song, also provides a sign of national identity. This is true both of the sounds of everyday conversation and of declamation heard in the theater. In his essay "Actors and Singers" ("Über Schauspieler und Sänger"), written in 1872, one year after he had republished "On German Music," Wagner argues that the higher culture of French theater that has been adopted by the German stage, and that is so antithetical to the German spirit, is based on the different physiology of the French vocal chords. The Frenchman on the street speaks in a theatrical, false manner emblematic of his national-cultural essence and inimical to the linguistically and vocally different German:

> [This is how] the Frenchman speaks and behaves. . . . But to the German any pathos which somehow comes close to this French [behavior] is completely unnatural; if he feels it is necessary to employ it, he must attempt to imitate it through the ridiculous disguising of his voice and an elevation of all his usual speaking habits [*durch lächerliche Verstellung seiner Stimme und Heraufschraubung seiner Sprachgewohnheiten*] (5:178–79 / 9:206)

This metaphorical image of foreign culture as higher is meant literally when it is applied to the vocal apparatus producing speech, for these sounds are metabolically *wesensfremd* to the German. Wagner goes on here to decry the fact that foreign declamatory art has influenced even Germany's greatest poets: "Yes, even if one has our best poet read his verses to us, he immediately stumbles into the falsetto of his vocal instrument [*verfällt er in ein Falsett seines Sprachorganes*] and uses all those pompous and foolish distortions . . ." (5:179 / 9:207). If you try to sing like an Italian or to speak like a Frenchman, you will lose your identity, sound like a sex-starved eunuch (reminiscent of the castrati so central to the development of foreign opera, and anticipating the foreign nature of Wagner's malevolent Klingsor), and make a fool of yourself. Higher speech, then, is unnatural both to the German voice and to the German *Volksgeist* reflected in the voice of the people and in its art.

Yet the social implications of pitch in Wagner's reflections on speech and music in the modern world are not solely related to the nationally identifiable, to the French, the English, and the Italians. This criterion of inclusion in and exclusion from the German *Volk* plays a prominent role not only in the xenophobic tracts, but in the anti-Semitic writings as well, especially in "Judaism in Music" of 1850, in which Wagner discusses the Jews' purported lack of national identity. Wagner claims that the German's antipathy to the Jew is attributable to the foreigner's different speech patterns which reflect the absence of national-folkish roots:

> It is of central importance . . . to consider the impression that the Jew makes on us through his language. . . . The Jew always speaks the language of the nation as

a foreigner. . . . To our ear the hissing, shrill, buzzing and gurgling sound of the Jewish manner of speech appears quite foreign and unpleasant. (3:84–85 / JM:12–13)[20]

As is well known, language for Wagner is the singular product of a unified people, as he here states: "A language . . . is not the work of individuals, but rather of a historical community: only he who has unconsciously grown up in this community also takes part in its creations" (3:84 / JM:13).[21] This explicitly anti-Semitic idea had already appeared more covertly in "The Art-Work of the Future" ("Das Kunstwerk der Zukunft") of 1849, in which the Jew-as-intellectual is divorced from those that bond together through language: "Not you intellectuals . . . are inventive, but the Folk; because need drives it to invention. . . . It was not you who invented language, but the Folk" (1:80 / 6:20). Beckmesser is intelligent, but he has less affinity with his borrowed mother tongue than does the *Volk* that surrounds him in the penultimate scene of *Die Meistersinger*. With language a communal construct available only to those from whose bond and common need it arises, it will, for Wagner, always be imperfectly accommodated by those who are foreign and, for him, physiologically different. This notion provides an important link between Wagner's anti-Semitic writings and his reflections on the social implications of art. Just as the Jew's speech is perceived as shrill, and therefore higher than the German's, so, too, is his singing, which is also based on his purportedly natural difference, as a passage from "Judaism in Music" explicitly states: "[The] peculiarities of this Jewish way of speaking and singing, in all its most shocking abnormality, is to be explained solely on physiological grounds . . . [*ist rein physiologisch zu erklären*]" (3:89 / JM: 17–18).

It was Wagner's argument that the Jews, through their prominence in banking institutions and the growing publishing industry, were non-Germans who exerted an unprecedented influence on the musical institutions of Europe. In his essay "Parisian Fatalities for the German" ("Pariser Fatalitäten für Deutsche"), written not for a French, but for a German readership under the pseudonym V. Freudenfeuer, Wagner directed anti-Semitic remarks at Meyerbeer and, implicitly, at Schlesinger as well, who had attained wealth and success in Paris and who influenced the makeup and reception of music in the international culture scene:

[If the German musician] attains to higher levels of achievement, for instance if he becomes a composer who sets precedents [*gesetzgebender Komponist*] at the Grand Opéra, like Meyerbeer, he will have achieved this only as a banker, for a banker can do everything in Paris, even compose operas and have them produced. . . .

Yet the *German bankers,* of whom there are a good many here, no longer count as Germans; they are above all nationality, and therefore above all national prejudices; they belong to the Universe and the Paris stock exchange. . . . In the eyes of the French, Rothschild is more a universal Jew than a German. (8:102–3 / 5:62)

As wealthy Jews influential in the music world, Meyerbeer and Schlesinger lose for Wagner their national identity and implicitly endanger German art through their commodification of culture in the modern world. In "Judaism in Music," Wagner states emphatically that the Jews' financial control of cultural institutions had come to corrupt the public taste, and hence the public reception of music.[22]

> That the impossibility further to create natural, necessary and true beauty without completely changing the basis of the level to which the development of art has now advanced has brought the public taste in art under the mercantile fingers of the Jews, for that we have now to examine the causes. . . . (3:81–82 / JM:10)

Thus, it is only consistent that for Wagner the virtuosic music performed in the cultural institutions of France, Italy, and England—all controlled, according to him, by Jews—had come to resemble the vocal production of the Jews itself, which he radically separates from music of the German *Volk:*

> [The] melismas and rhythms of synagogue chant captivate the musical imagination of the Jew in the same way that the instinctive perception of the melodies and rhythms of our folk song and folk dance [captivate] the actual creative power of the creators of our art song and instrumental music. (3:91 / JM:20)

Jewish singing, with its melismas and extended pitch, recalls the coloratura of Italy and France. Though musicologists distinguish between the melisma ("an expressive vocal passage sung to one syllable") and coloratura ("a rapid passage, run, trill, or similar virtuoso-like material, particularly in vocal melodies of 18th- and 19th-century operatic arias"), these kinds of vocal writing had a similar, at times even identical, ideological significance for Wagner.[23] No wonder Beckmesser's criticism of Walther and his own nocturnal serenade in Act II of *Die Meistersinger* are based on a preference for florid, melismatic, high-pitched singing which shows little feeling for the German language (illus. 2). Beckmesser sings the "melismas . . . of synagogue chant" and accompanies himself with coloratura "ornamentation formulas of 16th-century keyboard and lute music."[24] And it is precisely this high-pitched singing that incites the riot at the conclusion of the act, because, in Wagner's world, the healthy German *Volk* must react violently to the vocal production of those who are racially foreign: "Who's howling there? Who cries so loud? / So late at night, is that allowed? . . . / That donkey's bray would wake the dead!"[25] Wagner's audience got the message: when the music drama was first performed in Berlin and Vienna, the Jewish communities of both cities protested, because they understood Beckmesser's serenade to be a parody of Jewish chant.[26] Did they also recognize the notary's high and florid singing to be Wagner's ridicule of Jewish influence in the international institutions of culture?

Wagner's alternative to the high voices based and foreign cultural production favored by the Jews is also on the interrelation of race and vocal pitch. The authentic reception of German music excludes precisely those elements Wagner despised in the Judaized music world, as he implies in "On German Music":

> We . . . may rightfully assume that Music in Germany branches out to the lowest and most inconspicuous social strata, yes, perhaps has its roots here. . . . Among

2. A passage from Beckmesser's elevated and melismatic serenade in *Die Meistersinger*, Act II. From *The Mastersingers of Nuremberg: An Opera in Three Acts*, p. 302.

these simple, unadorned souls, where the goal is not to entertain a large, *mixed* audience, art divests itself of every coquettish outward trapping. . . ." (7:89 / 5:157; my emphasis)

While the virtuoso performs before a heterogeneous (*gemischtes*) audience in the "Ausland," German art explicitly requires a uniform reception which does not transpire before a mixed and public crowd, but within the national family of like-minded, musical, and similar individuals. This is the very idea Wagner later emphasizes in "Know Thyself" when he argues that Germany must breed from herself if she is to stave off the threat of Jewish influence.[27] I have argued elsewhere that Wagner views incest positively in part because the family provides for him a model of racial and national purity; if the unpolluted Teutonic family is a metaphor for Germany, breeding within domestic boundaries preserves the national essence from the filth of foreign invasion.[28] The homogeneity of the authentic aesthetic experience thus mirrors the preferred image of the German nation. Mixed means more, and more means different, and different means dangerous and higher. Better to have an inbred national family of musicians than to have the high melismas of a slimy Beckmesser win the German maiden.

Wagner's alternative to contemptible cultural practices not only unfolds before a different kind of audience, but also encompasses a different kind of aesthetic material. The German, non-Jewish work will be available to all members of a uniform community because its aesthetic makeup will be suited to the community's Germanic physiology. This idea is discernible in Wagner's description from 1840 of a Protestant congregation participating in its musicial traditions. The Lutheran congregation is able to participate, because its non-virtuosic music is written for the voices of the common people who constitute the legitimate *deutsches Musikwesen*. Everyone can sing the Lutheran chorale. The vox populi thus emerges in the deeper vocal lines of the German liturgy available to all members of the nation:

> The glory of German vocal music blossomed in the Church; the Opera was left to to the Italians. Even Catholic church-music is not at home in Germany, but instead exclusively Protestant church music. . . . In the older Protestant churches . . . in place of fancy trappings, the simple Chorale sufficed, sung by the whole congregation and accompanied on the organ. . . . The Passion-music [of Bach] is based on the Savior's sufferings as told by the Evangelists; the text is set to music, word by word; but between the divisions of the tale, verses from the Church's hymns, appropriate to the special subject, are woven in, and at the most important passages even the Chorale itself, which truly was sung by the whole assembled congregation. Thus the performance of such Passion-music became a great, religious, solemn occasion in which artists and congregation participated equally. . . . . Thus Church-music had the needs of the folk to thank for both its origin and its highest flowering. (7:92–94 / 5:161–63)

In order to appreciate the bond here between communal music, language, speech, and race, we have only to recall that for Wagner the people create language out of "need." All forms of vocal expression emerge from a common source and

First Act.

First scene.

The stage represents an oblique view of the church of St. Katharine; the last few rows of seats of the nave, which is on the left stretching towards the back, are visible: in front is the open space of the choir which is later shut off from the nave by a black curtain.

In the last row of seats Eva and Magdalena sit; Walther von Stolzing stands at some distance at the side leaning against a column with his eyes fixed on Eva, who frequently turns round towards him with mute gestures.

3. The Pseudo-Lutheran Chorale in *Die Meistersinger*, Act I. From *The Mastersingers of Nuremberg*, pp. 14–15.

wil - lig dei - ne Tau - fe nahm,
by thy hand bap-tised to be,

wil - lig dei - ne Tau - fe nahm,
by thy hand bap - tised to be,

wil - lig dei - ne Tau - fe nahm,
by thy hand bap - tised to be,

wil - lig dei - ne Tau - fe nahm,
by thy hand bap - tised to be, (Eva's Blick und Gebärde sucht zu
(Eva by look & gestures attempts to
Belebend.

dim.

P.

weih - te sich dem Op - fer -
chose the Cross for man's re -

weih - te sich dem Op - fer -
chose the Cross for man's re -

weih - te sich dem Op - fer -
chose the Cross for man's re -

antworten; doch beschämt schlägt sie das Auge wie- weih - te sich dem Op - fer -
der nieder.)
answer him, but casts her eyes down again ashamed.) *chose the Cross for man's re -*
nachlassend

più p pp p cresc.

provide authentic vehicles for the confirmation of racial and national identity.[29] This idea informs Wagner's portrayal of the *Wälsungenpaar,* his allegory of the German *Volk,* who out of "need" merge to create the racially pure being, Siegfried. It is listening to Siegmund's voice which causes Sieglinde to recognize herself when she gazes upon her physiologically so similar twin brother: "But you came / and all was clear: / for I knew you were mine / when I beheld you. / What I hid in my heart, / all I am, / bright as the day, / all was revealed; / the sound of this truth / rang in my ear, / when in winter's frosty desert / my eyes first beheld my friend. . . . / Be still! Again / that voice is sounding, / the voice that I heard / once as a child— / But no! I know when I heard it: / when through the woods I called, / and echo called in reply."[30] To "know thyself" is to recognize oneself in the physiological similarity of one's compatriots, in their voices and in the voice of the nation's art fashioned through common need. The confirmation of the homogeneity of the nation typified for Wagner both the role of art in ancient Greece, as described in *Opera and Drama* of 1851, and of the artwork of the future as well, and it is suggested in this passage on the congregation's participation in German art.[31] No wonder *Die Meistersinger,* the work most concerned with preserving the homogeneity of Germany, opens with a pseudo-Lutheran chorale (illus. 3).

Yet the communal chorale is a remnant of a moment in Germany's folkish past; it no longer corresponds to the needs of the present, and thus is not the modern vehicle for the reestablishment of a cultural and national unity threatened by foreign countries and by the racially foreign living within 19th-century Germany; if it were, this wouldn't be Wagner. "On German Music" also locates such folkish commonality in another, different, and yet specifically German art that also requires the communal efforts of like-minded, musically-inclined members of the nation, and that is found throughout the provincial makeup of Wagner's contemporary Germany: in German orchestral music, especially that of Beethoven. Wagner explicitly equates the turn to instrumental music, above all Beethoven's, with a national message: a rejection of foreign voices and of a foreign vocal technique suited to the expectations of the international music scene:

> [The] lack of beautiful vocal training directs the German to instrumental music
> . . ., where the artist [is] free of every foreign and confining influence. . . . To realise
> the masterpieces of this genre of art there is no need for precious foreign singers.
> . . . And is it possible, with the most lavish additions of all the other arts, to erect
> a more sumptuous and sublime building than a simple orchestra is capable of
> constructing in the performance of one of Beethoven's symphonies? Most surely not!
> (7:90–91 / 5:158–59)

Beethoven's instrumental music provides for modern Germany the same communal aesthetic experience once integral to the reception of art in ancient Greece and to the pious *Volk* participating in the liturgical singing of the Bach Passions because, one assumes, Germans are innately musical and naturally bond together as a community when they experience the collective performance of an authentically and quintessentially German work of art. Beethoven's symphonies provide a model of hope for modern Germany and for its future.

Therefore, it is not surprising that Beethoven is the German artist par excellence in Wagner's short story "A Pilgrimage to Beethoven" ("Eine Pilgerfahrt zu Beethoven"), published shortly after "De la musique allemande" under the title "Une visite à Beethoven: épisode de la vie d'un musicien allemand" in four issues of the *Gazette musicale* in November and December of 1840.[32] Indeed, the short story may be read as a fictional representation of concepts expressed more explicitly in the earlier essay. Though the theme of vocal pitch as an icon of racial and national identity is less overt in the "Pilgrimage," it can be discerned there as well within a context of competing national characteristics, and the short story, too, is redolent with Francophobic and anti-Semitic sentiment, though Wagner strove to mask them more than he did in his expository writing.

When Wagner's protagonist "R.," who describes himself as "a simple German soul" (7:33–34 / 5:100), meets a group of Bohemian musicians at the outset of his pilgrimage to Vienna, they perform together a septet by Beethoven with the naive spontaneity unique to the German character and antithetical to the superficiality of the international institutions of culture. When they make music, they recall the small domestic ensemble idealized in "On German Music": "O what delight! Here on a Bohemian country road, under an open sky, Beethoven's Septuor played by dance-musicians with a purity, a precision, such depth of feeling seldom found among the most masterful virtuosi!" (7:25 / 5:90).

Immediately following this performance, the nemesis of the story, the villainous Englishman who threatens R.'s pilgrimage at every step of his journey, makes his first appearance and offers the musicians "a gold coin," which they refuse. The opposition of superior German musicality and the corrupt mercantilism of the modern, non-German music aficionado is blatantly manifest, and will be present with every reappearance of the Englishman throughout the tale. Wagner associates the Englishman with the Jews, the Italians, and the French. Like the internationally foreign and well-to-do Jews, he is wealthy and is himself a composer; at the end of the story, he's off to pay his respects to Italy for the same shallow reason he has visited Beethoven—"I wish to know Mr. Rossini, as he is a very famous composer" (7:45 / 5:112)—an example of musical taste that also links him to the Parisians, characterized elsewhere in the story as culture vultures. R., on the other hand, represents the German antithesis to England, Italy, France, and international wealth; he turns "to the north, uplifted in heart and ennobled" as the "Pilgrimage" closes. For the purposes of his cultural criticism, Wagner could of course have made the foreign nemesis a Frenchman, but he chose to make him English and to associate him with Italy because he was writing for a French audience, who could not know that the three countries were ideologically indistinguishable in Wagner's cosmology.

For Wagner, the central theme of German musicality threatened by the alienating forces of modern, foreign civilization is played out in Vienna, the goal of R.'s pilgrimage, and it is there that Wagner presents two antithetical images of the human voice, one virtuosic and French, and one part of a community, and hence *urdeutsch*. In order to underscore the besieged and tenuous position of authentic German art and artistic feeling in 19th-century Europe, Wagner portrays Vienna as both German and non-German, as both sharing, through its language, a tie with Germany's cultural traditions and as revealing, through the superficiality of its Parisian-like culture industry, a dystopic vision of a future possible for Germany as well.

Wagner's Beethoven—"a poor German musician" (7:23 / 5:88)—describes the reception of his works in Vienna in terms recalling "On German Music." "'I do believe . . . that my compositions speak more directly to Northern Germany. The Viennese annoy me often; daily they hear too much bad stuff ever to be disposed to approach in earnest something that is serious'" (7:40 / 5:106). This assessment is initially shared by R., who speaks of the "somewhat shallow sensuousness of the Viennese" (7:35 / 5:102), but at one point, not coincidentally during a performance of *Fidelio,* the narrator describes the Austrians explicitly as German: "Wilhelmine Schröder . . . [has] the high distinction of having revealed Beethoven's work to the German public; for truly I saw on that evening even the superficial Viennese seized by the most powerful enthusiasm" (7:36 / 5:102). There is hope for the Viennese after all! They are at least capable of the kind of reception commensurate with German art, and might be saved from the influence of foreign culture if they only attended more often to the genius in their midst. But their taste has come to resemble perilously that of the Parisians. Galops and potpourris, says Beethoven, the very music Wagner wrote for Schlesinger, are popular in the Austrian capital (7:44 / 5:111), and in lamenting the trials of an opera composer writing for a Viennese audience with Parisian expectations, Beethoven makes the connection between the two cities explicit: " 'He who has to stitch all kinds of pretty things for ladies with passable voices to get *bravi* and applause should become a Parisian lady's-tailor, but not a dramatic composer' " (7:41 / 5:107). The notion of the virtuosic voice as an instrument suited to the disjointed and heterogeneous Grand Opera is a notion associated with the French culture industry and, by extension, with its Jewish bankers and publishers. The nefarious influence of such forces pervades not only German-speaking Austria, but (Northern) Germany as well, R.'s homeland and the site where his pilgrimage originates. That the Franco-Jewish commodification of culture has emerged even there is made manifest in R.'s dealings with his German publisher, which recall in vivid detail Wagner's frustrated relationships with Schlesinger:

> A few pianoforte-sonatas, which I had composed following the master's model, I carried
> to the publisher; in a word or two the man made clear to me that I was a fool with
> my sonatas. He gave me the advice, however, that if I wanted some day to earn a

thaler or two with my compositions, I should begin by establishing for myself a little reputation through galops and potpourris. . . . To my misfortune, however, I was not even paid for these earliest sacrifices of my innocence, for my publisher explained that I first must earn myself a little name. I shuddered again and fell into despair. That despair, however, brought forth some capital galops. I actually received money for them. . . . (7:23 / 5:88–89)

The pilgrimage thus constitutes a search for redemption (that Wagnerian *idée fixe*) for German music from a mercantile approach to art such as this, associated with higher, and thus superficial, culture. After meeting Beethoven, R. will never again succumb to the demands of those who exploit culture as a commodity. This evocation of Schlesinger is more than a coincidence, because Wagner conceived "A Pilgrimage to Beethoven" as a surreptitious attack specifically on Jewish influence in the modern music world, typified for him by his Jewish employer.

While Schlesinger is discernible behind the characterization of R.'s publisher, it was primarily through the Englishman that Wagner ridiculed the entrepreneurial Jew. The Englishman is none other than Moritz Schlesinger himself, who had journeyed to Vienna in 1819 on behalf of his father's publishing house in order to secure from the composer the rights to Beethoven's opera 108-112, 132, and 135. After successfully completing his mission, Schlesinger moved to Paris and there published simultaneous first editions of Beethoven's piano sonatas opera 110 and 111 in 1822-1823, followed in 1827 by the string quartets opera 130, 132, 133, and 135.[33] Thus, in the very period in which Wagner's narrative is set (the early months of 1824, during which Beethoven's Ninth Symphony was completed, but not yet performed), the Jewish entrepreneur was involved in the very activities it denounces.[34]

How could the owner of the *Gazette musicale* have so missed the criticism directed at his person, his adopted country, and his race? The answer may lie in the fact that Schlesinger undoubtedly associated Wagner's narrative with another, far more flattering fictional depiction of his journey to Beethoven which he had published in his journal six years earlier and which he himself very likely commissioned. The first two issues of his *Gazette musicale* in 1834 had contained a short story by Jules Janin, entitled "Le diner de Beethoven: Conte fantastique," which transpires in 1819 and depicts the visit to Beethoven of a Frenchman who alone, unlike the insensitive Germans, appreciates the musician's genius.[35] Janin's work was obviously a veiled homage to Schlesinger, which the publisher was not averse to distributing in his newly-founded journal. Wagner either became acquainted with the piece through Janin himself, whom he mentioned twice in print during his stay in Paris, and who, as a colleague of Berlioz and an influential critic with the *Journal des Débats,* was a well-known figure in the Parisian music world, or Schlesinger may have directed his attention to it, implying or stating outright that the text had proven successful with his French readership and could provide a model for Wagner, a young and, at that time, still inexperienced writer of fiction.[36]

Wagner intentionally preserved numerous superficial motivic similarities to Janin's text in order to appeal to his publisher and to his French audience, while fashioning a story which clandestinely ridiculed Janin's Francophilic and implicitly pro-Jewish sentiment. Wagner's text, like Janin's, glorifies a visit to Beethoven, but it covertly associates its biographical model, the Jew Schlesinger, with an understanding of art that Wagner despised. Structurally, his most fundamental departure from his model was his bifurcation of Janin's narrating Frenchman into two figures, the Englishman and R., which enabled him to fashion a plot similar to that of the 1834 text while shifting its ideological affiliations.

Janin never identifies the profession of his narrator, but his Beethoven remarks that he is a Frenchman, while Wagner introduces R. at the outset as an aspiring musician, that most German of callings. Janin's narrator claims that Beethoven is the *only* true German musician ("le pauvre malheureux Beethoven est encore le seul musicien de l'Allemagne . . .," 10), but such a statement would be unthinkable in the universe of Wagner's story, in which the musical genius is best understood in his fatherland because of the common, shared, and innate musicality of all Germans. Such implications are antithetical to "Le diner de Beethoven: Conte fantastique," at the conclusion of which the narrator exclaims that Beethoven's isolation and neglect make the Frenchman ashamed for Germany and for Europe ("honteux pour l'Allemagne et pour l'Europe de la misère et de l'abandon où je le voyais," 11). Janin implies that only the Frenchman (like Schlesinger?) is capable of appreciating Beethoven's genius, as well as, paradoxically, the English, who have sent the composer a piano as a gift. Equally un-Wagnerian is Janin's description of Beethoven's performance on this untuned instrument as the "plus abominable charivari qu'on put entendre" (10). Wagner's Beethoven would never make such a fool of himself; indeed, the most unmusical figure in the "Pilgrimage" is the Englishman, Wagner's surrogate representative of the Judaized culture of France. With Schlesinger's visit to the real Beethoven as a backdrop to the story, the Englishman recalls the publisher racing towards Vienna in a coach with little on his mind but money and prestige, while R. traverses the entire route by foot with the purest of intentions. Wagner thus polarizes Beethoven and the commercialization of art in France, but Schlesinger's journey and Janin's fictional depiction of it had merged the two, and Wagner's only recourse was to invent an artistic allegory which would remove the blemish visited upon the figure he wished to preserve as truly accessible only to the Germans.

And it is only to a German, to R., and not to the Englishman (or Schlesinger), that Wagner's Beethoven reveals the secret of his new aesthetic of the human voice. Beethoven's remarks provide a counter to the Parisian commodification of the virtuosic vocal instrument, and thus the polarization of two kinds of voice in the story accompanies the bifurcation of Janin's narrating Frenchman into the two figures of the Englishman and R.:

> "Why should not vocal music, as much as instrumental music, form a grand and serious genre, and its execution meet with as much respect from the thoughtless race of singers

as, say, is demanded from an orchestra for a symphony? The human voice . . . is a far more beautiful and nobler organ of tone [*Ton-Organ*] than any instrument in the orchestra. . . . [The] very character that naturally distinguishes the human voice from the character of the instruments would have to be given special prominence, and that would lead to the most varied combinations. . . . May these two elements be brought together, may they be united!" (7:41–42 / 5:108–9)

If one considers Wagner's writings both immediately prior to his short story and those from the postrevolutionary period, the new vocal production described here by Beethoven comes to imply a vehicle for the emancipation of German music from foreign nations and from the Jews. For this reason, Beethoven tells only R. of the Ninth Symphony, the first example of the new German vocal writing which will provide the aesthetic and ideological model for the artwork of the future:

"You soon will become acquainted with a new composition of mine, which will remind you of what I have just discussed. It is a symphony with choruses. . . ."

To this day I can scarcely grasp my happiness at thus being helped by Beethoven himself to a full understanding of his titanic Last Symphony, which then at most was finished, but known as yet to no man. (7:42–43 / 5:109)

Beethoven's vision of a new kind of artwork of the future is intended for a different Germany, for an aesthetic that seeks to unite the voice and the orchestra and to treat them as equal partners is based on the notion that these are elements whose unity reflects the unification of the community. While the hierarchical proclivities of the foreign Grand Opera privilege the voice, which it views as a virtuosic instrument, Beethoven sees such an "organ of sound" as but one component in a group of elements and refuses to characterize it as instrumental. The foreign Opera reflects the disjointed makeup of a heterogeneous society comprised of Frenchmen, Jews, and others, while Beethoven's vision is intended for an homogenous German audience alone. Because of its nationalist undertones, the Ninth Symphony must remain a secret to be kept from the Jew-as-Englishman in the short story, though it will later emerge as the cornerstone of Wagnerian aesthetics.

These early theoretical and fictionalized discussions of a national and racist agenda of German music in general, and of vocal music in particular, do more than illuminate the ideological implications of Wagner's understanding of art in the early 1840s, for they bear direct comparison with the vocal music he composed after he had turned his back on Schlesinger and on the kind of singing associated for Wagner with the Jew. "On German Music," "A Pilgrimage to Beethoven," and the postrevolutionary essays shed light on the ideological underpinnings of Wagner's conception of a new kind of singer, the *Heldentenor,* whose new and different sound was the aesthetic product of a xenophobic and anti-Semitic iconography of the human voice.

The music Wagner composed for the heroic tenor following the publication of his "Artwork of the Future" and "Judaism in Music" constituted a rejection of the sounds associated with Schlesinger and the Parisian culture industry. The vocal demands of the *Heldentenor* roles in the *Ring, Tristan,* and *Parsifal* required a kind of singer with a vocal apparatus ill-suited to much of the Italian and French operatic repertoire of the mid-19th century. While the high, lyric Italianate tenor had to be able to sing an extended tessitura and to execute ringing high Cs, the *Heldentenor* required a powerful low C, an octave below middle C and two octaves below the Italian's celebrated high note (illus. 4). His imagined sound was new, darker, and deeper, and was associated for Wagner with a purer, more natural Germany unpolluted by the high culture of foreign nations and foreign races.

The *Heldentenor* often begins his career as a baritone, and the timbre of his mature singing reflects its deeper beginnings. The Danish singer Lauritz Melchior, for example, generally considered the greatest interpreter of Wagnerian heroic tenor parts in the 20th century, sang fifteen bass-baritone and baritone roles before making the transition to the higher vocal category.[37] The kind of singing for which he later became famous was always associated with an unusually dark and heavy sound. Melchior's biographer Shirlee Emmons describes the Wagnerian tenor thus:

> The *Heldentenor Fach* demands a tenor voice of large size, exceptional stamina, and more strength in the lower register than other tenors can summon. This voice often evolves, with maturity, from a high baritone voice. Indeed, it could be characterized as a tenor/baritone. Wagner wrote his tenor roles almost exclusively for this voice. . . . [Melchior's] conviction that a *Heldentenor* could never be found among lighter-voiced lyric tenors, who lack lower register strength, . . . became well-known. . . . One of Melchior's last accompanists, Leonard Eisner, recalls that "Melchior believed it was almost mandatory for a real *Heldentenor* to have been a baritone first. He considered it a logical sequence."[38]

The *Heldentenor* is only seldom called upon to sing above a high A, a note that Siegmund (the first heroic-tenor role Wagner composed after publishing "Judaism in Music") sings only *once* in the course of *Die Walküre* and that the young Siegfried and Parsifal, too, must never exceed, but a note that Beckmesser the baritone sings for four bars in Act III of *Die Meistersinger.*[39] Wagner's Jewish notary, like most of his pseudo-Semitic figures, likes to sing high, but his Germanic heroes generally do not. (The juxtaposition of Mime's higher tessitura and Siegfried's lower music in Act II, sc. 3 of *Siegfried* is a case in point.)[40] Interpreters of Siegmund often complain that the role requires power in the lower portion of the voice, where it is vocally damaging for a lyric and/or spinto tenor to sing consistently with great force, and some singers do not warm up extensively before going on stage because the singing voice normally rises in the course of a performance.[41] When *Die Walküre* was recorded under George Solti in the 1960s, the role was first offered not to a *Heldentenor,* but to a baritone, who declined, before the management engaged a tenor with a powerful middle and

4. Siegmund's baritonial tessitura in *Die Walküre,* Act I. From *Die Walküre.* Complete vocal score in a facilitated arrangement by Karl Klindworth. English translation by Frederick Jameson (New York, n.d.), p. 42.

lower register and who himself, like Melchior, had begun his career as a baritone.[42]

Certainly Wagner was aware of the unusual demands he was making in inventing a new kind of vocal category for the operatic stage, but that is precisely the point; the new work, the artwork of the future intended for a different world and for a different audience, rejects the voices associated with those portions of the heterogeneous world Wagner so detested. The low, dark sounds of the writing for the *Heldentenor* express a national and racial identity which defines itself through its rejection of a higher, different kind of writing associated for Wagner with Italy, France, England, and with the international Jews. With his early expository and narrative texts in mind, the very sound of his mature vocal music emerges as the sign of an ideology firmly established in the early 1840s and later manifested in a vocal writing based on a phonics of hatred.

Yet it would be foolish to suggest that Wagner's remarks concerning the human voice constitute a strict program, for, at most, they serve to illuminate repetitive tendencies and implications within his dramas, rather than to reveal a consistent equation of pitch and race. Wagner's conception of the human voice undoubtedly influenced his musical portrayals, but it did not provide a blueprint for composition. If it had, that is, if Wagner had been consistent, all his heroes would have been *bassi profondi* and his figures evincing purportedly Semitic features (Alberich, Hagen, Beckmesser, and Klingsor, as well as Mime) would have been cast as high lyric tenors.[43] Conversely, in the most explicitly anti-Semitic work for the stage, *Die Meistersinger von Nürnberg,* Wagner would not have written such an unusually high tenor part for his young poet Walther von Stolzing, a role that Melchior and numerous other Wagnerian tenors never sang on stage, if he had been consistently guided by the notion of a high voice as non-Germanic.[44] Clearly, the demands of operatic traditions—as seen, for example, in the works of Mozart, Beethoven, and Weber—associating villains with bass-baritones exerted another, vocally different, influence on Wagner's compositional strategies. But Wagner's caricatures of Jews do sing a music that sounds different in part because much of it lies at the top of their vocal register, regardless of whether the register in question is that of a bass, a baritone, or a tenor.

This leads to a final point which I have not pursued here, but which bears mentioning: Wagner's implicit feminization of the Jew. When Wagner writes about and portrays Jews, he usually means male figures who pose a sexual threat. Could the high voice, from Wagner's perspective, have been a slanderous counter to such a danger, a characterization of the Jew as effeminate? This might explain why most of his heroic women are called upon to sing well above high A, while his *Heldentenöre* are not. The conflation of the Jew and the feminine may have been widespread in German culture of the mid-19th century; it is explicit in Nietzsche's work of the early 1870s and, of course, became pervasive in Austrian culture by the end of the century.[45] Perhaps it is already implied here in Wagner's earlier writings as well.

To ignore the affinities between Wagner's anti-Semitic diatribes, his reformative aesthetic writings, and his music dramas is to close our ears to the reprehensible ideology underlying his overwhelmingly seductive music. How easy and tempting it is to forget the message and to revel in the song! But we should keep the ideological message in mind when assessing the importance of such a figure for the 19th century, as well as the ironic implications of his enthusiastic following today. What a quandary it is, when listening to Wagner, to find oneself eavesdropping on his song for Germans, even as one hears the agony behind Beckmesser's shrill and foreign *Koloratur.*

Notes

1 Richard Wagner, *The Mastersingers of Nuremberg/Die Meistersinger von Nürnberg.* English National Opera Guide Series, no. 19 (London, 1983), 66.

2 On the applicability of the "culture industry" thesis to the Paris of this period, see Peter Bürger, "Literarischer Markt und autonomer Kunstbegriff: Zur Dichotomisierung der Literatur im 19. Jahrhundert," in *Zur Dichotomisierung von hoher und niederer Literar,* ed. Christa Bürger, Peter Bürger, and Jochen Schulte-Sasse (Frankfurt, 1982), 241–65. I am indebted to Peter Uwe Hohendahl for this reference.

3 Nietzsche was one 19th-century reader who did not miss the point, as a passage from "Richard Wagner in Bayreuth" makes clear: "Wagner himself seeks to interpret the promotion of music by the Germans by supposing among other things that, denied the seductive stimulus of a naturally melodious voice, they were compelled to take the art of music with something of the same degree of seriousness as their religious reformers took Christianity. . . ." Friedrich Nietzsche, *Untimely Meditations,* trans. R. J. Hollingdale (Cambridge, 1989), 223.

4 Moritz Adolf (also referred to as Maurice Adolphe) Schlesinger's true name was Mora Abraham Schlesinger, see "Schlesinger," *Riemann Musik Lexikon: Ergänzungsband Personenteil L-Z,* ed. Carl Dahlhaus (Mainz, 1975), 580.

5 The firm of Adolf Martin Schlesinger owned the rights to Weber's music and printed the works of Spontini, Mendelssohn, Loewe, Beethoven, Bach, Berlioz, Cornelius, Liszt, and Chopin. By 1836, four years before Wagner began working for his expatriated son, Adolf Martin's firm had published over 2,000 titles. See Rudolf Elvers, "Schlesinger," *The New Grove Dictionary of Music and Musicians,* ed. Stanley Sadie (London, 1980) 16:660.

6 Ibid., 660–61.

7 See Richard Wagner, *Sämtliche Briefe,* ed. Gertrud Strobel and Werner Wolf (Leipzig 1967) 1:478–80 (letter to Schlesinger of 27 April 1841); Richard Wagner, *My Life,* trans. Andrew Gray (Cambridge, 1983), 174.

8 F. J. Fétis had founded the journal in 1827; the joint publication began in November 1835 with vol. 2, no. 44, and was thereafter referred to both as *Gazette musicale de Paris* and *Revue et gazette musicale de Paris;* it ceased publication in 1880. See MacNutt, 661; Louis Eugène Hatin, *Bibliographie historique et critique de la presse périodique française* (Paris, 1866), 591; Léon Guichard, *La Musique et les lettres au temps du romantisme* (Paris, 1955), 172–78. I would like to thank Seymour S. Weiner for sharing with me his invaluable bibliographic expertise in clarifying the publication history of this journal.

9 On this journal and its concerts, see Jacques-Louis Douchin, *La vie erotique de Flaubert* (Paris, 1984), 25; Benjamin F. Bart, *Flaubert* (Syracuse, 1967), 26–28, 81–82, 108, 116, 185. Mention is made in these works of the *Gazette musicale* because Flaubert was infatuated for a time with Schlesinger's wife.

10 Wagner, *My Life,* 185–86, 192–93.

11 Wagner's first published essay was "Die deutsche Oper," which appeared on 10 June 1834 in the *Zeitung für die elegante Welt,* but "De la musique allemande" was the first essay in which the ideological plan of his future theories emerged in clear form. On "Die deutsche Oper," see John Deathridge, *The New Grove Wagner* (London, 1990), 13. Due to his poor command of French, Wagner had to write his texts in German and pay half his honorarium to a translator, who fashioned a French rendition for his publication in the *Gazette.* See Wagner, *My Life,* 186; Robert L. Jacobs and Geoffrey Skelton, trans. and eds., *Wagner Writes from Paris . . .* (New York, 1973), 12–13; Robert Gutman, *Richard Wagner: The Man, His Mind, and His Music* (New York, 1968), 75. Of the nine texts Wagner wrote between July 1840 and October 1841 ("On German Music," "Pergolesi's 'Stabat Mater'," "The Virtuoso and the Artist," "A Pilgrimage to Beethoven," "On the Overture," "An End in Paris," "The Artist and Publicity," "A Happy Evening," and "Der Freischütz: To the Paris Public"), eight were published in the *Gazette musicale,* and another ("La reine de Chypre d'Halévy") was to follow there in the spring of 1842. See Jacobs and Skelton, 1986–97.

12 Scholarship often mentions the early Parisian texts solely for the comparative clarity of their style and their resemblance to works of E. T. A. Hoffmann and Heine; they have received surprisingly little attention as the first evidence of Wagner's aesthetic-social program. See Hans Mayer, *Richard Wagner in Selbstzeugnissen und Bilddokumenten* (Hamburg, 1974), 12; Dieter Borchmeyer, *Das Theater Richard Wagners* (Stuttgart, 1982), 19, 100; Martin Gregor-Dellin, *Richard Wagner: Sein Leben, sein Werk, sein Jahrhundert* (Munich, 1983), 150–58; L. J. Rather, *Reading Wagner: A Study in the History of Ideas* (Baton Rouge, 1990), 35.

13 After the close of "A Happy Evening" (*Ein glücklicher Abend*) the narrating editor's remarks begin thus: "The following articles I publish from among my dead friend's papers. To me this first one ["On German Music"] *seems to have been intended to win friends among the French for his Parisian undertaking,* where its successors unmistakably betray the deterrent impressions already made on him by Paris life." Richard Wagner, *Richard Wagner's Prose Works,* trans. William Ashton Ellis, 7 (1898; repr. New York, 1966), 83 (my emphasis). Unless otherwise noted, all further references to Wagner's works will be to this eight-volume edition and will be indicated parenthetically by volume and page number, followed by volume and page number of Wagner's German text. Unless otherwise noted, references to Wagner's German will be to Richard Wagner, *Dichtungen und Schriften,* ed. Dieter Borchmeyer, 10 vols. (Frankfurt, 1983). This reference, for example, would appear thus: (7:83 / 5:151–52). I have used Ellis's translation merely as the basis for my own and have made numerous alterations throughout.

14 It can scarcely have been coincidental that Wagner envisioned the paradigmatic male German musician as "klein"!

15 See Wagner, 4:179 / 3:72.

16 Wagner's anti-Italian remarks antedated his first visit to that country in 1852, which he came to love. See Paul Gerhardt Dippel, *Richard Wagner und Italien* (Emsdetten, 1966), 14.

17 See 7:118–22 / 5:31–32.

18 See 8:92–93 / 5:50–51.

19 Two examples highlight the distorted view critics have held of Wagner's Parisian writings from the early 1840s. The following, amazingly one-sided, assessment stems from Jacobs and Skelton: "[Wagner] writes . . . with an open mind. . . . How very human he is . . . and yet how impressive and endearing: an impassioned idealist, a penetrating thinker, a shrewd observer, warm-hearted, courageous and brimming over with high spirits, poetry and humour" (14); Ernest Newman was equally generous when he described "On German Music" as "very touching in its wistful little vision of tiny, cozy German towns" (*Wagner as Man and Artist* [New York, 1924], 193).

20 See *Richard Wagner's Prose Works* 3:79–122. All references to Wagner's German text will be to Richard Wagner, *Gesammelte Schriften,* ed. Julius Kapp, 13 (Leipzig, 1911), 7–29, and will be indicated parenthetically by "JM" (for "Das Judentum in der Musik") and page number. Borchmeyer omits Wagner's anti-Semitic essay from his ten-volume edition of Wagner's works.

21 See also Leon Stein, *The Racial Thinking of Richard Wagner* (New York, 1950), 24; for a more apologetic discussion of Wagner's anti-Semitism, and one that disavows affinities between his Judaeophobic prose writings and his music dramas, see Jacob Katz, *The Darker Side of Genius: Richard Wagner's Anti-Semitism* (Hanover, New Hampshire, 1986).

22 Like many before him, Bryan Magee assumes that "Judaism in Music" was written because of Wagner's antipathy to Meyerbeer and Halévy, and does not mention Schlesinger in this context. See Bryan Magee, *Aspects of Wagner* (New York, 1969), 50–51.

23 See Willi Apel, *Harvard Dictionary of Music,* 2d ed. (Cambridge, 1977): "Melisma," 516; "Coloratura," 184.

24 Apel, 184.

25 Wagner, *The Mastersingers of Nuremberg,* 93.

26 See Dietrich Fischer-Dieskau, *Wagner and Nietzsche,* trans. Joachim Neugroschel (New York, 1976), 44.

27 Richard Wagner, "Know Thyself," *Richard Wagner's Prose Works* 6:264–74, here 269–72; Wagner, *Gesammelte Schriften* 14:182–93, here 187–91. Borchmeyer omits this anti-Semitic essay as well from his edition of Wagner's writings.

28 Marc A. Weiner, "Wagner's Nose and the Ideology of Perception," *Monatshefte* 81 (1989): 62–78; here 72–76.

29 Adolf Martin Schlesinger published the first edition of Bach's *St. Matthew Passion,* a fact Wagner undoubtedly knew, and the irony of which, given his desire to monopolize Bach as uniquely German, he no doubt resented. See Elvers, 600.

30 Richard Wagner, *The Ring of the Nibelung,* trans. Andrew Porter (New York, 1976), 91–92.

31 See, for example, the following passages from *Opera and Drama:* "Art . . . is nothing other than the fulfillment of a longing *to know* [or recognize] *oneself* [*sich selbst zu erkennen*] in a represented, admired, or beloved object, *to find oneself again* in the phenomena of the outer world through their representation. . . . Myth is the poem of a *common* [or shared] view of life [*das Gedicht einer gemeinsamen Lebensanschauung*]" (my emphasis). See 2:155–56 / 7:153–55.

32 The story appeared in the *Gazette musicale* on 19, 22, and 29 November and 3 December 1840; the original German text was published on 30/31 July and 2–10 August 1841 in the *Dresdner Abendzeitung.* Wagner writes in *My Life* (198): "The 1841 volume of this publication, then published by Arnold in Dresden but long since defunct, contains the only printed version of this manuscript." See also letter of 1 June 1841 to Theodor Winkler, in *Sämtliche Briefe* 1:493–95. For its republication in vol. 1 of his *Gesammelte Schriften und Dichtungen,* the text had to be retranslated from the French. See Borchmeyer, "Nachwort zu Band V," *Dichtungen und Schriften* 10:297.

33 Elvers, 660; MacNutt, 660–61.

34 See Donald Jay Grout, *A History of Western Music,* 2d ed. (New York, 1973), 535; Maynard Solomon, *Beethoven* (New York, 1977), 278.

35 Jules Janin, "Le diner de Beethoven: Conte fantastique," *Gazette musicale de Paris* no. 1 (5 January 1834): 1–3; *Gazette musicale de Paris* no. 2 (12 January 1834): 9–11. All further references will be indicated parenthetically. On this text, see Hermann Hofer, "Expérience musicale et empire romanesque: Hoffmann musicien chez Jules Janin, Champfleury et Alexandre Dumas," in *E. T. A. Hoffmann et la Musique,* ed. Alain Montandon (Bern, 1987), 303–14, here 306. Wagner's work actually refers to, or at least joins, a minor French literary tradition of texts treating the motif of Beethoven which had appeared in Schlesinger's journal. Honoré de Balzac's "Gambara" had appeared in the *Gazette musicale* between 23 July and 20 August 1837, only three years after the publication of Janin's work and three years prior to the appearance there of Wagner's story. See Honoré de Balzac, "Gambara," *La comédie humaine* (Paris, 1979) 459–516; on this text, see also Guichard 180–86. Thus, beginning with his first issue, Schlesinger's journal published a text every three years that alluded to his own visit to Beethoven.

36 Wagner mentioned Janin twice after his "Pilgerfahrt" had appeared, the first time in a "Bericht für die *Dresdner Abendzeitung*" of 23 February 1841, and again in an article on a Parisian performance of *Der Freischütz* published in the *Gazette musicale* on 23 and 30 May of the same year; see Wagner, *Dichtungen und Schriften* 5:71; see also Jacobs and Skelton, 152. It has often been argued that Wagner based his fictitious account of an aspiring musician's visit to Beethoven on Johann Friedrich Reichardt's *Vertraute Briefe, geschrieben auf einer Reise nach Wien und den österreichischen Staaten zu Ende des Jahres 1808 und zu Anfang 1809,* but the year of the "Pilgrimage" (1824) is much closer to Janin's 1819 than to the year of Reichardt's text. It was Wagner who informed Cosima, and Cosima who noted in her diary, that the "Pilgrimage" was based on the German text and, given its ideological implications, it is hardly likely that either would have readily emphasized its relation to a French source. On Wagner's indebtedness to

Reichardt, see Cosima Wagner, *Die Tagebücher,* ed. Martin Gregor-Dellin and Dietrich Mack (Munich, 1976) 1:806; Gregor-Dellin, *Richard Wagner,* 153; Borchmeyer, "Nachwort zu Band V," 198.

37 See Shirlee Emmons, *Tristanissimo: The Authorized Biography of Heroic Tenor Lauritz Melchior* (New York, 1990), 411.

38 Ibid., 7, 14; in the foreword to the book (x), the Wagnerian soprano Birgit Nilsson describes Melchior's voice as having "a darkness that there should be in a Wagnerian tenor."

39 Richard Wagner, *Die Meistersinger* (Leipzig, n.d.) (piano-vocal score), 393.

40 See Richard Wagner, *Siegfried* (Leipzig, n.d.) (piano-vocal score), 225–37.

41 *Opera News* (1 April 1990): 46.

42 John Culshaw, *Ring Resounding* (New York, 1976), 218.

43 On Alberich, Beckmesser, and Mime as caricatures of Jews, see Theodor W. Adorno, *In Search of Wagner,* trans. Rodney Livingstone (Manchester, 1981), 20–26; on Klingsor as a Jew, see Gutman, 428–30.

44 Melchior never sang Walther on stage, but he did make several recordings of excerpts from the role. See Emmons, 411–51. One could argue that Walther's vocal music requires a sound reminiscent of Lohengrin and Erik, a lighter, higher, brighter sound not heard in the *Ring, Tristan und Isolde,* or in *Parsifal.* Some singers believe that Wagner wrote his heroic tenor roles with two kinds of tenor in mind, one reminiscent of the dramatic Italian tenor, the other demanding a different, more baritonal kind of voice.

45 Friedrich Nietzsche, *The Birth of Tragedy* and *The Case of Wagner,* trans. Walter Kaufmann (New York, 1967), 71. On the conflation of the Jew and the feminine at the turn of the century, see George L. Mosse, *Nationalism and Sexuality: Middle-Class Morality and Sexual Norms in Modern Europe* (Madison, 1985), 143–46; Sander L. Gilman, "Strauss, the Pervert, and Avant-Garde Opera of the Fin de Siècle," *New German Critique* 43 (Winter 1988): 35–68.

Wagner's Last Supper:
The Vegetarian Gospel of His *Parsifal*

Jost Hermand

More than most other composers of the 19th century, Wagner was capable of sweeping along his listeners not just by the seductive power of his music, but also by the appeal of his programs and ideologies. In contrast to the representatives of so-called absolute music such as Johannes Brahms and his followers, whose emphasis on the formal element in music struck him as academic, artisan-like, and, thereby, near anachronistic, Wagner included in almost each of his works a message in which he, as the propagandist of "the music of the future," tried to express his own worldview. The confusing thing about these messages is that they tended to change almost constantly over the course of his artistically active life, between 1835 and 1882, and that they contradicted each other or, at least, overlapped each other unevenly. In the face of this frequent change, the following questions arise for anyone who aims at critiquing Wagner's ideology: Was Wagner—despite his militant stance on the most diverse issues of his era—only one of the epoch's many fellow travellers, someone who simply tried to conform ideologically over the span of time from Young Germany and the 1848 Revolution up to the Second Empire; or was he a highly principled artist who always maintained a critical stance amid the wide-ranging forms of his commitment?

At first glance, i.e., in regard to the contents of his various music dramas, we gain less the impression of a rebel than of a fellow traveller, if not an outright renegade, who after 1848 increasingly sacrificed his originally critical spirit to the resigned outlook of the post-1848 era and then to the national-mythicizing tendencies of the early years of the Second Reich. For, within his oeuvre, *The Ban on Love* (1836), an erotic emancipation opera in keeping with the Young German movement, was followed by *Cola di Rienzi* (1841), a pre-March revolutionary opera, *The Flying Dutchman* (1844), an opera of salvation through sacrifice, *Tannhäuser* (1845), an opera of scandalous licentiousness and penance, *Lohengrin* (1846-48), a late-romantic legend opera, the first plan for the *Ring* (1848), a romantic-anticapitalist work in the spirit of the Forty-Eighters, *Tristan and Isolde* (1865), a post-March opera of resignation indebted to the widespread Schopenhauer cult, *The Mastersingers of Nuremberg* (1868), an opera celebrating the ideas of class reconciliation and Germany's cultural mission, *The Ring of the Nibelung* (1876), a music drama that hearkens back to the Germanic roots of the new Empire in the form of a mythologically exalted tetralogy, and, finally, *Parsifal* (1882), a "sacred dramatic festival" conceived for the Bayreuth stage, closely linked with the religious debates, the vegetarian movement, and the anti-Semitic struggle of the 1870s.[1]

But despite the frequent shift of perspective and program, which corresponds to the many dramatic ruptures in the German history of this era, all of these works are simultaneously manifestations of a constancy in change that lends the Wagnerian oeuvre an undeniable continuity despite all its ideological disconti-nuities. To simplify, this coherence is primarily attributable to the following factors: firstly, to the unmistakably unique character of his music, which from *Rienzi* to *Parsifal* constantly employs the same surging, yearning, lush sound tending to the bombastic which, to be sure, transfers from the melodic ever more strongly into the declamatory, but in the process never loses its tendency toward the overwrought and intoxicating; secondly, to the thoroughgoing poeticization of the chosen plot lines, through which Wagner's philosophical messages—beyond all critical or affirmative tendencies—are elevated to the allegedly universal, the spiritually sublime, or the eternally German; and, thirdly, to his enormously over-blown heroics, his histrionic individuality, even egomania, which give all Wag-nerian writings and music dramas their unmistakable imprint.

Seen in this light, Wagner's works always reveal a peculiar disparity between a sociopolitical commitment, on the one hand, whose critical, emancipatory, anti-capitalist, even revolutionary tendencies cannot be denied, and, on the other hand, an aggressively social-climbing mentality that seeks to exploit, in a bourgeois-liberal sense, all these noble intentions by relating them only to himself and his art. With this highly ambivalent orientation, Wagner is part of the general develop-ment of the German bourgeoisie in the second half of the 19th century, which explains his enormous success within this class after the founding of the Second Reich in 1871; but at the same time, he goes beyond this parvenue stance by virtue of his emphatic artistry, not just by means of theatrically enhanced costumes and feelings of aristocratic grandeur, but even by assuming the pose of the royal, if not the superhuman. Therefore, it was precisely in the young Nietzsche, who also sympathized with an almost Caesarean usurper mentality, that Wagner found a devoted disciple and prophet, at least until Nietzsche—in the course of a rapidly rising feeling of self-importance—exposed him as a charlatan, gifted but operating with counterfeit currency, and began to brand him as a quintessential representative of all the contemptible traits of the socially advancing bourgeoisie.

The interesting twist is the fact that, although Wagner was regarded by many of his adherents as the most important artist of the new Reich, and his *Ring of the Nibelung* was considered the crowning achievement of all the wishes cherished throughout the 19th century for the rebirth of a truly German art,[2] he, as a former Forty-Eighter in whom a spark of the old democratic fervor was still glowing, did not identify with the new Reich in as one-sided a manner as some of his contemporaries believed. Especially since the publication of Cosima Wag-ner's *Diaries,* we know just how dissatisfied with Bismarck, Wilhelminian militarism, and the Germans in general Wagner actually was during his last years, even after the great Bayreuth triumph of 1876, and that he actually considered emigrating to the United States (to Minneapolis, to be precise).[3] Earlier on at the time of the German military victories in France, Wagner, as often before in his life, saw a chance for a new political involvement. At that time, he had hoped that the Germans would bombard Paris and then set it aflame in order to liberate "the world from the pressure of all evil," and had spoken out publicly against a premature armistice.[4] The depth of his feeling for the national cause is documented by, among other things, a poem he sent to Bismarck in January 1871, that read: "The German host / is standing firm on France's faithless heart; from fight to fight / its blood pours out with anguished heat: / with silent strength / and pious force / it carries out unheard-of deeds." In March 1871, Wagner even composed a "Kaiser March" for the former Prussian king, whom he had called "that demented monarch" as recently as 1866. Thanks to its blatant topicality, this work was immediately performed all over Germany. In May of 1871, Wagner conducted this march, together with Beethoven's Fifth Symphony and excerpts from *The Valkyrie* and *Lohengrin,* before the imperial couple in Berlin and was enchanted by the stormy applause that greeted the work. And even in 1876, when the imperial couple came to Bayreuth for the opening of the festival opera house and the premiere of the *Ring,* his belief in the new Reich, in which he played such a prominent role, was still relatively unbroken. But shortly afterward, when Bayreuth became quiet again and he found no one to finance another festival summer season, Wagner felt ignominiously rejected by the Germans and their princes and lapsed into a protracted pout.

And it was during the following years of withdrawal that his *Parsifal* came into being. Not a trace of his former national enthusiasm is to be found in this work. What predominates instead is a highly complex mixture of Buddhistic asceticism, patriarchal-Christian concepts of purity, and messianic-Caesarean will to power, which in part can be traced back to substantially older layers of Wagner's thought, as expressed in *Lohengrin* and *Tristan.* But alongside this, *Parsifal* also contains ideological concepts, partly of a progressive, partly of a reactionary type, which can only be understood in light of events contemporaneous with the 1870s, and which in part overlap with his earlier ideologemes or stand in open contradiction to them.

Among the progressive elements are, generally speaking, Wagner's concepts of social regeneration, which again took on sharper contours in the years after 1876. Because he felt abandoned in his Bayreuth festival idea by the Kaiser, the aristocracy, and the Reichstag, and was on the brink of declaring bankruptcy, he suddenly saw in the new Reich, which he had heretofore viewed primarily in terms of victory and glory, a purely materialistic construct dominated solely by "gold," i.e., a crude materialism. And due to his wretched financial situation during this period, Wagner returned to his earlier anarchic populist or socialist concepts, which gave him hope for a transvaluation of all values. He repeatedly charged the new Reich with standing by idly while hundreds of thousands of Germans were emigrating to the United States, and with maintaining an enormous and staggeringly expensive army for "the protection of the propertied classes against the nonpropertied."[5] Altogether, the very concept of private property appeared increasingly problematical to him during this time, and he felt increasingly drawn to socialism. When in 1878 the Bismarckian laws were promulgated to protect the body politic against the "clear and present danger" posed by the Social Democrats, Wagner was outraged: "The future belongs to this movement, and all the more so because the only measures being taken against it are stupidly repressive."[6] In particularly dark moments, society as a whole appeared corrupt to him. The new Reich "turns my stomach," he wrote to Ludwig II on 10 February 1878, since its constitution seemed to him to rest on a materialistic outlook that was downright "barbaric."[7] Not the men of letters, the artists, but the industrialists and the officers were accorded the highest respect in this Reich, he complained. Instead of supporting art, this state no longer set itself any higher goals, but simply yielded power—in the sense of a shabby liberalism—to the economically stronger who were interested only in profit.

On the basis of such resentments, Wagner reacted to "modernity" in general with a deep hatred which—like many exalted ideologies of this era—frequently took on a nationalistic and racist coloring. Instead of blaming the industrialists or the system of profit and competition that they represented for the growing "degeneracy," Wagner saw the major representatives of the un-German, i.e., uncultural, Western civilization in the French and the Jews, just as Wolfgang Menzel had done in his polemics against the "Israelites" among the Young Germans.[8] While Wagner's Francophobia, because of his growing resentment against the new Reich, diminished slowly after 1876, his anti-Semitism became ever stronger in the following years. As we know, Wagner had already attacked such Jewish competitors as Felix Mendelssohn-Bartholdy and Giacomo Meyerbeer in his tract *Jewry in Music* (1850), in which he had defamed them as representatives of a liberal wheeler-dealer mentality who had been granted far too much freedom. Already at that time, Wagner had stated that the only "redemption" for Jews would be their "demise," as foreshadowed by the figure of Ahasuerus.[9] In the broad wave of anti-Semitism of the 1870s that culminated in the writings of Adolf Stoecker, Eugen Dühring, Heinrich von Treitschke, and Paul de Lagarde, Wagner took up such topics once again and branded the Jews—in contrast to the German "artistic geniuses"—as materialists, even "predatory animals" devoid of any idealism and interested only in profit.[10] Especially Wagner's essays "Modern" (1878), "What Is German?" (1878), "Know Thyself" (1881), and "Heroism and Christianity" (1881) are studded with anti-Semitic slogans. In these pieces, "modernity" is simply equated with "Jewishness," and the argument is made that, while every German always feels committed to an "idea," the Jews are always "looking out for their own advantage."[11] At other points, Wagner even advocated the "complete deportation" of the Jews from Germany, or he expressed the wish, when he heard of the fire that destroyed the Vienna Burgtheater in 1881, that "all Jews be burned in a performance of *Nathan.*"[12]

Many of his private utterances from this period are equally anti-Semitic, as is documented by the *Diaries* of Cosima Wagner. Here, too, slurs abound concerning the "growing influence of Jews" within the German leadership elite, which he denounced as "ruinous" for the new Reich.[13] He maintained that the Jews had gained this influence primarily by means of their commercial adroitness, their striving for gold. Within the arts, too, one increasingly encountered these "alien elements."[14] Wagner even complained that in his nightmares he was totally "surrounded by Jews."[15] If he had more clout, he asserted, he would ban all "Jewish holidays" and "opulent synagogues."[16] Eclectic and inconsistent as he was, Wagner did make certain exceptions. One of them was his star conductor, Hermann Levi, whom he regarded highly. Wagner nonetheless informed him during a conversation that "he had thought of having him baptized and taking him to communion."[17] Wagner declared that by remaining "unbaptized," Levi had disqualified himself from conducting the premiere of such a work as *Parsifal.*[18]

But as vehement as Wagner's anticapitalist and racist hatred was for the Jews, his anticivilizationist hatred for the beast in man was even stronger, and partially superseded his anti-Semitism. Especially in the second half of the 1870s, Wagner stated again and again that humankind had been depraved, degenerate, and rotten since ancient times. He pinpointed the time of "original sin" as the transition of man from a gatherer of fruits and berries and a tiller of the soil to the carnivorous beast of prey. Wagner had long been fascinated by a "green utopia," as documented by his *Ring of the Nibelung* in which his belief in the purifying power of nature, especially in the form of water, had already played a central role. This is revealed not just by individual sections, such as the well-known "Forest Murmurs," "Siegfried's Rhine Journey," or the scene in which Siegfried, natural man par excellence, suddenly understands the language of the birds, but also by the central idea of *The Ring,* according to which nature only finds peace again after the hybrid race of gods and men has disappeared. The inspiration for this worldview can undoubtedly be traced back to Wagner's intensive reading of Schopenhauer in the 1850s and 1860s. In his work *Parerga* (1851), Schopenhauer had already lashed out against the heedless disregard for nature and, especially, the "ruthless treatment of animals," which he blamed on the Judaeo-Christian tradition that regards animals as soulless creatures over which man has absolute dominion. In order to point to an alternative, Schopenhauer — and, later on, Wagner — praised the Buddhists who had always believed in a close "kinship" between man and animal. Schopenhauer was especially outraged by "vivisection," through which "poor helpless animals" were needlessly "martyred to death." Even dogs, "the most noble of all animals," were subjected to such tortures. Only if such creatures were no longer treated as "mere objects," Schopenhauer declared, but instead were granted an unconditional "right" to life, would man finally prove himself to be a creature capable of true compassion.[19]

A further impulse that led Wagner to embrace a new view of nature was surely the German "vegetarian" movement of the 1850s and 1860s. Active in it was the former Forty-Eighter Gustav Struve, who advocated an ethic respectful of all living creatures and in 1869 published the book *Vegetable Diet: Foundation of a New Worldview*. In the same year, the various German vegetarian groups met—at the suggestion of Eduard Baltzer—for their first general gathering in Nordhausen.[20] In his book *Ideas toward Social Reform* of 1873, the same Baltzer maintained that man is not by nature a "carnivore" but instead a "fruit-eater," as proved by the absence of carnassial teeth in the human jaw. Moreover, he claimed, only a "natural," i.e., blood-free, diet would lead to purity, happiness, social harmony, and, therefore, to eternal peace.[21] Wagner, the easily swayable, was so taken by all these maxims that he not only paid lip service to the idea of vegetarianism, but also, in 1871, actively participated in the founding of Germany's first vegetarian restaurant located in Bayreuth.[22]

But let us finally turn to *Parsifal* and the impact that Wagner's new views on vegetarianism and purity had on its text. His first prose draft for this work, which seemed to hold the promise of a masterwork to the young King Ludwig II, was put to paper in 1865,[23] that is, at the high point of Wagner's preoccupation with Schopenhauer. The ethos of compassion expressed in it was connected ever more strongly in the following years with Wagner's aversion to meat-eating and to vivisection, indeed to the use of violence and militarism in general. When he wrote the definitive text of *Parsifal* in the spring of 1877, Wagner therefore emphasized not just the specifically medieval elements of the source but also—as in the sketch for the opera *The Victors*—Buddhist-vegetarian elements, according to which only Parsifal's compassion with the animal enables him to achieve the requisite compassion with his fellow man. It is strikingly evident to what extent Wagner included in this text notions of purification based on a clear commitment to a natural, vegetarian way of life. Already the first scene, in which Amfortas is seeking "relief" from his pains with cold baths containing a medicinal herb, derives not from Wolfram but is instead clearly influenced by contemporary concepts of natural healing.[24] Shortly afterwards, we hear that in the realm of the Grail Castle all animals are "sacred," i.e., inviolable, and may not be hunted. Thus, when the young Parsifal makes his first appearance, shortly after slaying a swan with one of his arrows, Gurnemanz declares indignantly: "You could murder? Here in the holy forest, / Whose quiet peace encircled you? / Where animals approached you tamely, / Welcomed you warmly and piously? / What did the birds sing to you from the treetops? / What harm did the faithful swan do to you? / To search for his mate, he flew up / To circle with her above the lake, / Splendidly consecrating it to a healing bath: / Were you not awed by it,

were you only tempted / To a wildly childish shot with the bow? / He was dear
to us: What is he to you? / Look! Here you pierced him: / The blood still glares,
the wings hang limp; / The snowy plumage all spotted dark, — / Blinded his
sight, do you see his blank stare? / Are you aware of your sinful deed?"[25]
Whereupon Parsifal, horrified, breaks his bow and casts away the remaining
arrows. And this scene, too, is not derived from Wolfram, but is one of Wagner's
addenda.

A similar concept is expressed in the following Holy Communion scene at
the Grail Castle, where the repeated emphasis on the transubstantiation of "flesh
and blood" into "bread and wine" is of course derived from the Bible, but is meant
by Wagner in a specifically vegetarian sense, as his later writings make evident.
In the third act, when Parsifal has finally purified himself from all earthly dross,
Gurnemanz lovingly initiates him into the lore of the "herbs and roots" which
he had learned "from the animals" of the forest.[26] Thus, Parsifal finally becomes
capable of regarding nature (which had previously meant little to him) with "quiet
rapture." "How beautiful the vale seems to me today!" he exclaims. "Although I
encountered miraculous flowers, / Which lasciviously entwined me up to my head,"
we hear in reference to Klingsor's garden, "I never saw so mild and gentle / The
blades, the blossoms, and the flowers, / Nor did this all have such a heady
fragrance / And speak so sweetly dear to me."[27] Nature no longer holds anything
demonically alluring for him, but is spread out before him — in another transformation of Christian into pantheistic elements — in the splendor of "Good Friday
magic," which covers hill and dale "with holy dew."[28] And it is through this
religious transformation that Parsifal finally becomes capable of closing the
bleeding wound of the suffering Amfortas, is crowned king of the Holy Grail,
and rules over a realm of bloodless, gentle "purity."

This constellation of ideas so strongly preoccupied Wagner that during the
following years, while working on the composition of *Parsifal,* he returned to
it repeatedly and sought to elaborate on it in a number of essays. Wagner advocated
vegetarianism perhaps most emphatically in his "Open Letter to Mr. Ernst von
Weber" of 1879. Here he declared that the present day, "from the vivisectionist's
operating table to the gun factory," was totally "stripped of idealism" and worshiped
only "utilitarianism." Even the societies for the prevention of cruelty to animals
rested largely on this principle, he argued, instead of being founded on the true
morality of "compassion." The only hope for a change under these circumstances,
according to Wagner's letter, lay in a new religion of "mercy" of the kind the
Brahmans had shown towards animals. Although "meat-eating" could not be
entirely dispensed with in the "rougher climates" of the north, Wagner wrote, bor-
rowing from Schopenhauer, at least vivisection and the excessive consumption
of meat ought to be eliminated. Only thus could humankind achieve a higher stage
of consciousness. How awful to live in a society, we read at the end of this letter,
in which a nocturnal break-in to the "torture chambers" of vivisection to liberate

certain animals destined for martyrdom was equated by the state with "a crude outburst of socialist actions against property rights," placing the opponents of vivisection on a par with the Social Democrats as an equal "danger to the public."[29]

Similar thoughts occupied Wagner in the year 1880, as we can read in Cosima Wagner's *Diaries*. The book that impressed him most strongly at the beginning of this year was the vegetarian utopia *Thalysia or the New Life* (1840-42) by Jean Antoine Gleizès, published in German in 1873. Regarding the conversations she had with her husband at their house Wahnfried between January 1880 and March 1881, Cosima mentions this book no fewer than nineteen times. In it, Wagner found a confirmation of his view that "world history begins at the very moment when man becomes a predator and kills the first animal."[30] The views of Gleizès "fit beautifully with my current project," he declared on 9 January 1880.[31] A short time later, Cosima Wagner noted: "He's tending ever more strongly toward vegetarianism," and trying to combine the gloomy "views of Schopenhauer" with the "optimism of Gleizès."[32] Besides the love of animals in the writings of Gleizès and Schopenhauer, Wagner emphasized during the same months the strong "sympathy for animals" in the writings of Rousseau and Voltaire, praised Saint Francis of Assisi, and sharply criticized his world of today, which not only tolerated "vivisection" but "slaughtered" all of nature step by step.[33] "What's the point of my art in such an age!" he exclaimed in light of these conditions.[34] When he was visited in December of 1880 by Hans von Wolzogen, one of his chief advocates, Wagner admonished him in a "fatherly tone" finally to become a "vegetarian."[35] Wagner even traced his own digestive problems at that time back to the negative consequences of "eating meat," and recommended a diet based principally on "milk and vegetables."[36]

Wagner's last testimonial in this regard is his essay "Religion and Art," which he published in 1880, two years before the premiere of *Parsifal*. In it, he summarized once again what seemed to him so despicable about the human race since it had turned to the murderous consumption of meat. The carnivores among the human race, he maintained, had in the course of history subordinated all the "fruit-eating tribes" and had then founded "huge empires, states, and civilizations" in order to "enjoy their booty in peace."[37] "Offense and defense, hardship and struggle, victory and defeat, mastery and slavery, all sealed with blood," we read in the second paragraph of this essay, which continues: "after that point in time, the history of the human race shows us nothing else; as a consequence of the triumph of the stronger, an immediate weakening by way of a culture based on the serfdom of subordinates; followed by the elimination of the degenerates by new, coarser forces of still unsatiated blood lust."[38] Only Pythagoras and Jesus, he claimed, had dared to challenge this course of history in the early phase of the Occident. The "mysterium" of Pythagoras had consisted of a thorough-going limitation to "eating vegetables," in which he and his disciples had seen a "religious means of purification from the sin and misery" of this world.[39] In the same vein, Jesus had given his "own flesh and blood," instead of the traditional paschal lamb, as the "final, highest offering of penance for all the sinfully shed blood and butchered meat," and had simultaneously tried to offer his disciples a lasting example in the form of a vegetarian last supper, at which flesh and blood had been transformed into bread and wine.[40] The "most salient cause for the early decline of the Christian religion as the Christian church" was seen by Wagner in this essay primarily in the fact that the most important "doctrine of the Savior," namely "refraining from meat eating," had not been followed.[41] Contemporary civilization was, therefore, by no means as Christian as it pretended to be. On the contrary, it was bloodier than ever. Not only did it organize huge wars of conquest that cost the lives of tens of thousands of people, but it also arranged "a daily bloodbath of hygienic slaughterhouses flushed clean by waters" for countless animals, only to serve up to hard-hearted carnivores the "corpse parts carved beyond recognition" in cooked or fried form.[42] And for such cruel acts high military officers and scientists were decorated with honors, he wrote indignantly.

To escape from this morass, Wagner, according to the third paragraph of "Religion and Art," placed his hope especially in the vegetarian movement, the animal protection leagues, and the temperance unions, which he emphatically challenged to abandon their previous pragmatic utilitarianism and to embrace the concept of a thorough-going "regeneration" of mankind. Even the Social Democratic Party, although he sympathized with it, seemed too co-opted to him. He appealed to its members to take up contacts with the "vegetarians, animal protectionists, and temperance adherents"—thus envisioning a form of ecosocialism, as we might put it today.[43] Only in this way could a "religious," i.e., all-encompassing renewal of the human race come about, he writes, and only thus might it put an end to the ongoing trend toward a purely instrumentalized approach to life. In the same context, Wagner pointed again to *Thalysia* by Gleizès, which he so admired, for "without a detailed knowledge of it, the possibility of a regeneration of the human race" would necessarily remain illusory.[44] Only by means of a "prudently observed vegetable diet," he emphasized again and again, could bloodthirsty, violent predators be transformed into "gentle and just human beings."[45]

Against the background of such theoretical constructs, among which vegetarianism plays not an exclusive but a central role, the text of *Parsifal* takes on a much more concrete meaning than has heretofore been accorded it. Obviously, these ideas appear in it in a highly "poeticized" form, making it easy for listeners or interpreters to abstract them into the realm of the universally human. Upon closer examination, however, we are dealing here with a libretto that stakes out a position which clearly opposes the dominant materialism, the so-called Jewish liberalism, the imperialist blood lust, as well as the cold-heartedness towards animals—and aspires to a redemption from all these mistaken dogmas by means of a spiritual, almost religious regeneration based on the ideology of a pacifistic vegetariansim. This sacred dramatic festival is concerned not with nationalism, but with the salvation of the entire human race from all imaginable evils of the impure, base, bloody, predatory, and meat-eating. This is portrayed in a sublimation into the spiritual, immaterial, radiant, and Grail-like, in order to elevate the true goal and aim into the sphere of the religious.

Parsifal is thus a work in which art assumes the sacred function of religion; here, the artist replaces the priest by celebrating a new cult and giving humankind a new utopia, based on the promise of a purified, bloodless, and nonviolent peaceable kingdom. Accordingly, love appears here for the first time in Wagner's oeuvre not as *eros,* but as *agape.* Seen in this light, his Parsifal is a savior of even greater purity than his Lohengrin. Already after the first kiss, he repudiates contemptuously anything yearning, lubricious, or sexual, and anything connected with blood, and he decides to dedicate his life from that point onwards solely to purity, love of nature, and compassionate understanding.

The key term of this text and of all ancillary writings is therefore always "purity." Its central figure is first a "Fal parsi," a "foolish innocent," before he becomes Parsifal, the "pure fool," who can "absolve and redeem" everyone who comes into contact with him, even Amfortas and Kundry, who had succumbed to the snares of sexuality.[46] In this work he alone, Parsifal, remains completely pure, resisting even the seductive flower girls in Klingsor's garden and thereby becoming one who knows "by compassion,"[47] who can transform even the realm of the impure, dirty, diseased, and bloody back into the pure. Once he has succeeded at this, a "miraculous radiance" pours over everything, and the Grail itself begins to "glow" as the "miracle of the highest salvation," causing everyone present to experience a sacred shudder.[48]

In spite of this dramatically enhanced poeticization, which seems to transcend the world of mere reality, many features of Wagner's *Parsifal* are meant quite literally. Proof is again offered in his last writings, in particular in the essay "Religion and Art" of 1880, in which Wagner states that whenever the older religions were in decline—because man had become impure and therefore "sinful" by the transition to rule of force and meat-eating—art had to "teach a new language" to a "mankind in need of redemption."[49] The most appropriate art form for this task appeared to him to be music, because it was the youngest of the Western arts and with its harmonies could give the most convincing expression to the demands for "renunciation and peacefulness."[50] Instead of pursuing this goal by joining any of the existing parties, Wagner in his final years envisioned the possibility of a universal regeneration of humankind almost exclusively in the "awakening of man to his simple-holy dignity."[51] And in a manner totally atypical of the Bismarck era, he pinned his hopes not on a powerful ruler or authority figure, but instead on one of those "divine heroes" to be encountered only among the "saints," as he wrote in his essay "Heroism and Christianity" of 1881.[52] This saint, this savior king he called Parsifal, in whom he saw not so much a new Christ as a saint of the pure, the natural, and the bloodless, who seemed more like an allegorical figuration of optimism à la Gleizès that has survived the pessimism of Schopenhauer. To be sure, this savior is devoid of any democratic qualities, but he is also free of brutal or militant traits. He is a king of nonviolence who wins others over by his "simple-holy dignity." In conceptualizing him, Wagner was thinking more in Buddhist than in Christian terms. When, on the 20th of October 1878, Hans von Wolzogen showed him the essay "Sacred Dramatic Festival" based on *Parsifal,* and asked him whether the central figure of this work was "patterned on our Savior," Wagner said on the same evening to his wife: "I wasn't at all thinking of the Savior."[53]

But of whom *was* he thinking? Paging through the correspondence between Wagner and Ludwig II, one could almost imagine that the figure of Parsifal represents a homage to the young king, whom Wagner addresses in his letter again and again as "Parzival." "O Parzival! How I must love you, my cherished hero!" he exclaims repeatedly. And the king gladly assumed this role and wrote back magnanimously to Wagner when he was once again financially embarrassed: "Parzival will not forsake his own."[54] But who, then, is Amfortas, if one is seeking so directly for personal references? Probably he is Wagner himself, who was given to histrionics and gladly assumed the most exalted personae, among them that of the aging, suffering King of the Grail. For, ultimately, Wagner was not just a militant idealist who rose to the defense of whatever happened to be the latest weltanschauung that seemed to him at a given moment the only significant, sublime, redemptive one; he was also an egregious egomaniac and a cleverly calculating man of the theater, who knew only too well that every great work of art requires a great ideology capable of moving the people, if that work is to have a broad-based success.

Seen from this perspective, Wagner was an idealist who constantly strove for the highest; at the same time, however, he was a typical representative of everything that he so bitterly repudiated in his writings. Let me offer just a few examples.

First, he was constantly thundering against the overwrought theatricality of such competitors as Meyerbeer, and condemned all works of art that "were calculated from the outset to win over the public."[55] Yet in Parsifal he does exactly this, pulling out all the stops, using an abundance of rituals, i.e., a dazzling display of religious ceremonies, in order to heighten the theatricality of this work to the utmost. Second, he reproached many of his contemporaries with salacious lustfulness, demanding purity, even renunciation from them; yet he himself delightedly yielded, while working on *Parsifal,* to the allures of a Kundry-like femme fatale named Judith Gautier and, at the time of *Parsifal*'s premiere, was still planning a dalliance with a certain Miss Pringle, whom he had engaged as one of the Flower Maidens. Third, he was constantly preaching the beneficent effects of vegetarianism and tried to persuade many of his friends to take up a "bloodfree food"; yet he himself succumbed to the temptation of meat-eating in his own dietary habits. And finally, he saw mankind's future salvation in the return to a "holy-simple dignity," yet could not bring himself to forego wasteful luxury in his own life-style, frequently appearing in a "black velvet waistcoat, black satin knee-pants, black silk stockings, a pale blue satin necktie, a shirt of genuine lace, and an artist's beret," and pleased to see Cosima Wagner wearing a "pink cashmere gown with a wide collar of Belgian lace and a large Florentine hat with a wreath of pink roses."[56]

Examined more closely, Wagner embodied in his person everything that he so bitterly condemned in his operas and writings. Perhaps that is why he was so sensitive toward the seductive charms of all these things. Thus on September 20, 1879, he said to his wife with an undertone of scarcely concealed smugness, as if he were actually that "Cagliostro of modernity," that "magician, mime, and mummer," as Nietzsche liked to portray him: "I know, I am dashing, I drive people crazy."[57] But Wagner was all too conscious—not just of his own seductiveness, but also of his obvious double life, striving for the moral, sacred, and prophetic while remaining an egomaniac, poseur, and sinner. This is expressed perhaps most clearly in the one entry in Cosima Wagner's *Diaries* written in his own hand: "He complained about the tribulations of his destiny as an artist, about having to leave his moral potential uncultivated because of it. He can't do anything offhandedly, or it would turn out badly; to be a completely moral person would mean sacrificing himself completely."[58] It is therefore not incorrect to characterize Wagner as an "expansive personality" who was compelled by his social isolation to relate to his own person and his own work.[59] And Wagner ultimately wanted to be both: an Amfortas enjoying and yet suffering from his egomania and his unquenchable desire for love, and a new Lohengrin—or, better still, a new savior king named Parsifal. Martin Gregor-Dellin has summarized Wagner's ambivalence during the years after 1876 in these terms: "The anarchist and federalist Wagner, who had long since passed judgment on political power in his *Ring of the Nibelung,* the herald of the North German League and the bard of the Bavarian king, the revolutionary and the author of staunchly patriotic verses—this man was in reality neither a political taskmaster nor an opportunist, but a would-be savior: Lohengrin the Second, who wanted to be linked with that to which he did not belong."[60] That is putting it mildly. One could also say: as a typical social climber, Wagner wanted everything—the favor of the powerful and the adoration of the masses, the fame of the prophet and the luxury of the haute bourgeoisie, the following of the committed ones and the support of the wealthy patrons.

All these contradictions are mirrored in the reports about the premiere of his *Parsifal* in the year 1882. At first glance, they seem to voice unanimous approval. In almost all newspapers and journals, this sacred dramatic festival was lauded as a work of the century, if not the millennium, representing one of the most important achievements of German art.[61] Upon closer examination, though, there are also clear distinctions and even critical voices among these reports. The bulk of the unabashedly positive reviews came from the camp of the liberals and nationalists. As might be expected, the liberals especially praised the highly artistic character of this work and defended it against possible misreadings from a religious point of view. Apart from the artistic quality of its music, they therefore emphasized the universally humanitarian tenor of its text, based on a belief in human progress toward ever greater heights, thereby completely overlooking the pseudo-religious and misogynistic dimensions of the work. The nationalists, on the other hand, placed their principal emphasis upon the specifically medieval German element of Wolfram's text and of Wagner's adaptation, but, in the following years, increasingly accentuated the Germanic and, finally, the Aryan in Wagner's outlook. As early as the 1890s, the "folkish"-minded commentators saw in *Parsifal* a "truly inspired rebirth of one of the most important primal Aryan mysteries," namely "salvation" by a national redeemer, by virtue of which this work could be clearly differentiated from the "materialism" of the "Semitic religion."[62] Many of the Christian reviews expressed equally positive views; first and foremost was the anti-Semite Adolf Stoecker, who praised *Parsifal* not only as a "masterpiece of German art," but also as a masterpiece of deep religiosity which could only be compared with the Oberammergau passion play.[63] Other Christian reviewers, however, both Protestant and Catholic, while unanimously applauding the singular "greatness" of this work, expressed certain reservations about the open "profaning" of Holy Communion and redemption on the stage.[64] A few of them found this opera "awesome" in its intention, but criticized its "presumptuous" theatricality with which Wagner did not move his audience to soul-searching, but merely "intoxicated" it.[65]

Some Social Democrats were equally critical in their outlook on *Parsifal.* While they found nothing to criticize about Wagner as a barricade fighter in the revolution of 1848 and as a proponent of a deeply democratic concept of a popular opera, their "freethinker" perspective led them to see his last work only as a "reactionary assassination attempt against common sense and the aspirations of the German people for freedom of ideas and conscience."[66] Although Wagner had advocated socialism in his article "Know Thyself" of 1881, and had written in a clear allusion to his Amfortas figure that state protection of "private property" had driven a "stake into the body of humankind" causing it to "die slowly in painful suffering," the sole SPD editor who attended the premiere saw in *Parsifal* only "mysticism" and "the most rotten 'religious' sentimentality."[67]

The members of the vegetarian leagues reacted all the more positively to *Parsifal.* The husband of Elisabeth Förster-Nietzsche, Bernhard Förster, who advocated German nationalism as well as life reform ideas, wrote: "The core of the *Parsifal* by Richard Wagner is completely accessible and intelligible only to vegetarians!"[68] And Henri Lichtenberger, too, when he published his book *Richard Wagner as Poet and Thinker* in the 1890s, was still fully aware of the vegetarian message of this work and characterized the "vegetarian leagues, animal protection societies, and temperance unions" in regard to *Parsifal* as "useful and beneficial institutions," which were redolent of "weak, contemptible, and somewhat silly associations," but which because of their universal "teachings of regeneration" could become "effective tools of a redemption of the modern world."[69] But as early as 1900, these ideas were pulled into the wake of various folkish and ariosophic delusions and were increasingly narrowed to the salvation of the Nordic race. This is documented by the "Loyal League for Rising Life," which Richard Ungewitter built up in 1910 as an Aryan "sun-worship movement based on pure vegetarianism"; by the vegetarian "League of St. George" founded by Fidus in 1912; by Hermann Popert's novel *Helmut Harringa* of 1910 and his journal *The Vanguard* founded in 1912, in which he propagated a "Germanic racial league based on vegetarianism and temperance"; and by the publications of the "Orchard Colony Eden," which had begun in the 1890s as a vegetarian project and had by 1910 become the cradle of a Germanic racial cult. An equally ambitious undertaking was the journal for practical occultism entitled *Prana,* founded in 1910 by Johannes Balzli, whose vegetarianism was immediately taken up by such guardians of the Nordic grail as Jörg Lanz von Liebenfels and finally led to an Aryan cult which, despite all its excursions into the rosicrucian and theosophical realm, ultimately supported naked imperialism.[70]

Thus the German vegetarian movement degenerated into the swamp of pre-fascism, from which such a petit bourgeois and resentful race fanatic as Adolf Hitler was to emerge, who not only constantly bragged about his love of animals and his preference for a "bloodfree diet," but who also described Wagner's *Parsifal* as his favorite opera. It was Hitler, therefore, who as early as November 1933 promulgated a comprehensive animal protection law for Germany, and in 1934 convened an international animal protection conference in Berlin. It was the same Hitler who liked to term the SS a "brotherhood of Templars around the Grail of the pure blood,"[71] and who compared himself to the accursed Amfortas, who suffered from that fateful blood mixture which was still standing in the way of a victory of the German spirit in the world.

Because of all these political ramifications and depravities, all liberals after 1945 considered the vegetarian ideas in Wagner's *Parsifal* and its accompanying essays as simply preposterous. In his Rowohlt biography of Wagner, Hans Mayer pointed ironically to the "unintended humor" contained in any such linkage of socialism and vegetarianism.[72] Ludwig Marcuse mocked vegetarianism in his book on Wagner under the chapter heading "Humanity for Butterflies."[73] Robert W. Gutman spoke in regard to Wagner's vegetarianism of a "foolishness," in which a "mental unbalance" or even "general degeneration of the ability to think" has become manifest.[74] And even Martin Gregor-Dellin called such notions simply "sectarian."[75] But at least since the 1960s and 1970s, in light of a growing ecological awareness, it is apparent that such judgments fail to do justice to vegetarianism. Nowadays, one is almost tempted to say that Wagner's advocacy of vegetarianism is virtually the best thing about his *Parsifal.*

Translated by James Steakley and the author

Notes

1 Cf. on this general topic Hans Mayer, *Richard Wagner* (Reinbek, 1959), 7ff.
2 Cf. Richard Hamann and Jost Hermand, *Gründerzeit* (Berlin, 1965), 216ff.
3 Cf. Martin Gregor-Dellin, *Richard Wagner: Sein Leben, Sein Werk, Sein Jahrhundert* (Munich, 1983), 788.
4 Ibid., 637.
5 Quoted ibid., 764.
6 Ibid., 772.
7 Richard Wagner, *Gesammelte Schriften und Dichtungen,* 4th ed. (Leipzig, 1907), 10:128.
8 Cf. Jost Hermand, " 'Was ist des Deutschen Vaterland?' Börne contra Menzel," in *Ludwig Börne,* ed. Alfred Estermann (Frankfurt, 1986), 199ff.
9 Wagner, *Gesammelte Schriften,* 5:85.
10 Henri Lichtenberger, *Richard Wagner als Dichter und Denker* (Dresden, 1899), 451f.
11 Wagner, *Gesammelte Schriften,* 5:55.
12 Cf. Gregor-Dellin, 767.
13 Cosima Wagner, *Die Tagebücher,* vol. 2 (1878–1883), ed. Martin Gregor-Dellin and Dietrich Mack (Munich, 1977), 520.
14 Ibid., 273.
15 Ibid., 766.
16 Ibid., 627.
17 Ibid., 755.
18 Ibid., 526.
19 Arthur Schopenhauer, Großherzog Wilhelm Ernst Ausgabe (Leipzig, n.d.) 3:637f. and 5:403ff. Cf. also the chapter "Wagner on the Human Use of Animal Beings," in L. J. Rather, *Reading Wagner: A Study in the History of Ideas* (Baton Rouge, 1990), 78–113.
20 Cf. Jost Hermand, "Gehätschelt und gefressen: Das Tier in den Händen der Menschen," in *Natur und Natürlichkeit: Stationen des Grünen in der deutschen Literatur,* ed. Reinhold Grimm and Jost Hermand (Königstein, 1981), 67f.
21 Eduard Baltzer, *Ideen zur sozialen Reform* (Nordhausen, 1873), 68.
22 Janos Frecot, Johann Friedrich Geist, and Diethart Kerbs, *Fidus. 1868–1948* (Munich, 1972), 34.
23 On the genesis of *Parsifal* generally, cf. *Richard-Wagner-Handbuch,* ed. Ulrich Müller and Peter Wapnewski (Stuttgart, 1986), 331ff.
24 Wagner, *Gesammelte Schriften,* 10:325.
25 Ibid., 335.
26 Ibid., 365.
27 Ibid., 371.
28 Ibid., 371. On the thesis that Wagner regarded vivisection as something typically "Jewish," cf. Rather, *Reading Wagner,* 90ff.
29 Ibid., 209.

30 C. Wagner, *Tagebücher*, 2:472.
31 Ibid., 473.
32 Ibid., 501.
33 Ibid., 679.
34 Ibid., 502.
35 Ibid., 499.
36 Ibid., 542.
37 Wagner, *Gesammelte Schriften* 10:225.
38 Ibid., 227.
39 Ibid., 230.
40 Ibid., 230.Wilhelm Winsch also attempted at the time to prove that Jesus was a vegetarian. Cf.
   Georg Herrmann, *100 Jahre deutsche Vegetarierbewegung* (Obersontheim, 1967), 21.
41 Ibid., 231.
42 Ibid., 233.
43 Ibid., 240.
44 Ibid., 238.
45 Ibid., 242.
46 Ibid., 361.
47 Ibid., 333.
48 Ibid., 375.
49 Ibid., 250.
50 Ibid., 212.
51 Ibid., 274.
52 Ibid., 279.
53 Cf. C. Wagner, *Tagebücher*, 2:205.
54 Cf. Gregor-Dellin, 576, 566.
55 Cf. Wagner, *Gesammelte Schriften* 10:63.
56 Cited in Gregor-Dellin, 645.
57 Ibid., 758.
58 Ibid., 813ff.
59 Ibid., 811.
60 Ibid., 640.
61 Cf. *Bayreuth in der deutschen Presse: Beiträge zur Rezeptionsgeschichte Richard Wagners und
   seiner Festspiele*, ed. Susanna Großmann-Vendrey (Regensburg 1977ff.).
62 Ibid., vol. 3 (part 1): 61.
63 Ibid., 132ff.
64 Ibid., 2:52ff.
65 Ibid., 24.
66 Ibid., 67.
67 Ibid.
68 Quoted in Ludwig Marcuse, *Das denkwürdige Leben des Richard Wagner* (Munich, 1963), 286.
   Bernhard Förster brought out the book *Der Vegetarismus als Teil der sozialen Frage* in 1882.
   One year later, he published the volume *Parsifal-Nachklänge*, in the fifth chapter of which he
   again advocated "vegetarianism" and condemned "vivisection." Cf. Hartmut Zelinsky, *Richard
   Wagner. 1876–1976: Ein deutsches Thema* (Frankfurt, 1976), 56f.
69 Lichtenberger, 29.
70 Cf. Hermand, "Gehätschelt und gefressen," 68f.
71 Hermann Rauschning, *Gespräche mit Hitler* (New York, 1940), 216. Cf. also my "Gralsmotive
   um die Jahrhundertwende," in Jost Hermand, *Von Mainz nach Weimar. 1793–1919: Studien zur
   deutschen Literatur* (Stuttgart, 1969), 269–97.
72 Mayer, 164.
74 Marcuse, 280.
73 Robert W. Gutman, *Richard Wagner: Der Mensch, sein Werk, seine Zeit* (Munich, 1970), 450.
75 M. Gregor-Dellin, 773.

The Social Politics of Musical Redemption

FRANK TROMMLER

I. Wagner as a Writer for Socialists

The surprisingly strong interest which socialists have taken in Richard Wagner has often been explained by the fact that, in the 19th century, reading Wagner preceded listening to Wagner. Reading Wagner meant indulging in his pamphlets, essays, and books, most notably his essays about a cultural revolution through art — *Art and Revolution* (1849), *The Artwork of the Future* (1849), and *Opera and Drama* (1851) — which "made his name all over Europe with a breadth and an intensity that his music had not effected."[1] The ultimate success of Wagner's operas in London was preceded by the initial and rather disappointing reception of *Lohengrin* in the 1850s. The British audience saw in it a fairly conventional opera, not in compliance with the popular image of Wagner as a revolutionary composer. Similarly, the failure of *Tannhäuser* in Paris in 1861 was blamed in part on the audience's exaggerated expectations. This emerging pattern changed with *Tristan und Isolde,* the *Ring* Tetralogy, and *Parsifal,* but in general it can be said that the expectations which Wagner raised as the propagator of a sociopolitical view of the musical drama transformed the experience of his operas into a form that was morally, if not spiritually, uplifting. It was one of Wagner's great talents to be able to stimulate the intellectual anticipation of his contemporaries over several decades to such a degree that his operas became metaphors for the cultural rejuvenation preoccupying artists, intellectuals, and politicians, including numerous socialists.

While the sequence of reading (and explaining) Wagner prior to hearing his music may not have been the case in musical circles and in middle-class homes where daughters played his music, that sequence of reception seems to have been fully assumed whenever he was linked to the cause of the Left. The appreciation of Wagner's revolutionary leanings was motivated by the assumption that, after the defeat of the Dresden upheaval of 1849 in which he participated, Wagner collected his revolutionary fervor into the body of programmatic writings between 1849 and 1851. Moreover, it was assumed that, as a writer, he carried the revolution into the realm of art, from where it would rise like the Phoenix from the ashes, initiating a new communal era free from the constraints of commercialization and exploitation. Finally, it was assumed that Wagner was derailed from this course through the encounter with Schopenhauer's philosophy, but that, nevertheless, the revolutionary spirit remained the source of his incredible inventiveness in opening up the aesthetic realm to a new moral and social mission. Obviously, the argument concerning the continued reverberations of his revolutionary writings became a powerful tool for claiming Wagner for the aspirations of the Left at a time when he became the favored composer of Ludwig II of Bavaria, and when his newly founded festival in Bayreuth attracted aristocrats, wealthy businessmen, and reactionary nationalists as his dominant audience.

It has been argued that the broad success of Wagner's writing on the revolutionary aspects of art and culture was helped by the fact that the socialist movement—or, more precisely, socialist organizations with Marxist leanings, i.e., the German Social Democratic Party—did not produce or encourage programmatic texts on socialism in the arts. This seems to hold true to the extent that published texts are the most reliable indicators of actual convictions, debates, and policies, but evidence of this sort cannot be expected of a period of press censorship and of police action against socialist propaganda, especially of the kind active in Bismarck's Germany between 1879 and 1890. One should not, therefore, overlook the fact that in such a period of political censorship debates on art and culture can contain subliminal political messages. In other words, certain essential texts could have been produced at that time in Germany *if* it had been in the party's interest. Clearly, not many were. The refusal to employ art in the cause of the socialist struggle, a policy which prominent German socialists such as August Bebel, Karl Marx, Friedrich Engels, and Karl Kautsky upheld as part of their political agenda, was known throughout the organization, even if it was not due to the Lassallean influence shared by everybody. This refusal received appropriate attention when Wagner's writings, most prominently his *Art and Revolution,* were discussed in the party press. The reprinting of Wagner's articles in workers' papers in the 1870s was accompanied by critical reviews and warnings regarding his operas.[2]

In *Art and Revolution,* Wagner had attempted to develop a historical-philosophical thesis for his revolutionary aesthetics. Drawing on the romantic notion of a future communion of artist and the people (*Volk*), after the alienating effects of commercialism had been overcome, he represented the glory of art in classical Greece as an expression of the common life of a race of free men, and contrasted this with its degenerate form in the present. Wagner wrote:

> This is art, as it now fills the entire civilized world! Its true essence is industry; its moral goal, the acquisition of money, its aesthetic claim, the entertainment of the bored. From the heart of our modern society, from the golden calf of wholesale speculation, stalled at the meeting of its crossroads, our art sucks forth its life-juice, borrows a hollow grace from the lifeless relics of the chivalric conventions of medieval times, and—blushing not to fleece the poor, for all its professions of Christianity—descends to the depths of the proletariat, debilitating, demoralizing, and dehumanizing everything on which it sheds its venom.[3]

By interconnecting the dismal state of the proletariat with the degeneration of art, Wagner could claim that a revolution inspired by art was the only guarantor of the true liberation of mankind:

It is for art above all to teach this social impulse its noblest meaning and guide it toward its true direction. Only on the shoulders of this great social movement can true art lift itself from its present state of barbarism, and take its place of honor. Each has a common goal, and both can reach it only when they recognize it jointly. This goal is the strong individual, the beautiful individual; the revolution may give him the strength, the art, the beauty![4]

With this forceful image, Wagner established himself as the great visionary within the world of socialist thinking, while maintaining his prerogatives as an artist who searched for that all-encompassing communion with the people. In *The Artwork of the Future,* he defined the revolution of humanity as a liberation of the alienating forms of existing bourgeois culture. The art of the future would emerge as a union of dance, poetry, and music by means of rhythm, harmony, and melody, producing the *Gesamtkunstwerk.* Again, the social revolution — as the formation of a classless community of actors and spectators who made this union possible — was closely tied to his own goal of overcoming the stagnation of commercial theater.

The longest and most ambitious essay of that period, *Opera and Drama,* presented the most elaborate junction of political and aesthetic claims. After a long discussion of the history of the opera, Wagner illuminates the crucial function of myth in musical drama as an inexhaustible source of truth. Myth can be rejuvenated through music. While in the dramatic play it remains a reconstruction of the archaic constellation, in musical drama it opens the future and, through the medium of music, inspires a utopian consciousness. Generally, this essay was considered a rich source for a better understanding of Wagner's place as a revolutionary artist; however, it was too voluminous to compete with *Art and Revolution,* the quintessential prophecy of a great human upheaval. Reading the latter text already provided an exercise in revolutionary emotion.

It is hardly surprising that important arguments which the rebellious group of young Social Democrats, known as *Die Jungen,* directed against the party's unimaginative agitation and organization in 1890/91, were inspired by Wagnerian concepts of a democratization of art in support of the social struggle. In 1888, Bruno Wille, a naturalist writer and socialist maverick, published a summary of *Art and Revolution* in the influential left weekly, *Berliner Volks-Tribüne,* in an attempt to counter the anti-socialist polemic against the culturelessness of the working class. Referring to Wagner's maxim of bringing about an "art for the common people" ("die Kunst dem Volke"), Wille, in turn, accused the existing capitalist system of thwarting the creation of great art and prohibiting popular participation in aesthetic endeavors. By paraphrasing Wagner's pamphlet, he promoted the importance of artists for the socialist movement (which represented the intention of the Naturalists as long as Bismarck's anti-socialist legislation lasted) and quoted Wagner's commitment to an art which would "gain its dignity on the shoulders of our great social movement."[5] Correspondingly, at the founding in 1890 of the theater society Freie Volksbühne, which catered to party members and the workers of Berlin, Wille invoked the Wagnerian notion of generating the feeling of a true folk community in the common experience of art.

Evidently Wagner, the revolutionary writer, served a peculiar function within the orbit of the German socialist party: while some saw him as threatening its scientific and organizational foundation, others viewed him as a valuable counterpoint to its neglect of the aesthetic realm. While Marx dismissed Wagner as "that state musician" of the "Bayreuth fool's festival" in 1876, August Bebel, the popular party leader who repulsed the attack of *Die Jungen* in 1891, argued that Wagner's *Art and Revolution* had a role to play in the socialist vision of the future. He argued this in the most widely read socialist treatise on the future society, *Die Frau und der Sozialismus* (1879). Bebel called Wagner's projection of the free and creative life in the society of the future "entirely socialist" in its conception.[6] Passionate endorsements of Wagner's projection of life and art after the successful revolution came from Clara Zetkin, the most prominent female leader in the SDP next to Rosa Luxemburg, with whom she shared the sense of radicalism. Zetkin, who once belonged to the circle of Bruno Wille, was outspoken in her praise of Wagner's great ability to forge a vision which the proletariat could use in its struggle. As late as 1924, she ended her speech at the Fifth Congress of the Communist International with the following reference to his *Art and Revolution:*

> The fast-moving developments will implement what Richard Wagner delineated as the goal of history. He said: The goal of revolution may give him the strength, the art, and the beauty. This future individual will grow and will carry neither the traces of an intellectual caste nor the traces of the proletarian class, and . . . will be molded only by physically and spiritually perfected humanism. We should speed up the coming of this stage of development by turning into action what Wagner at one moment turned into an insight: that the strength of the revolution goes before the beauty of art and is its pioneer.[7]

Even the acknowledged father of Russian Marxism, Georgi Plekhanov, who rejected the use of art in the revolutionary process, pointed to Wagner's optimism concerning the social as well as aesthetic liberation of the proletariat through revolution. In his famous essay of 1912, *Art and Social Life,* Plekhanov quoted Wagner's critique of the bourgeois aesthetes who accused the working-class movement of philistinism: "As Wagner rightly says, if one pays attention to the facts, it is evident that the working-class movement is not heading towards philistinism but away from it to a free life, toward 'artistic humanism.' "[8]

In most cases, Wagner's essay *Art and Revolution* was read in two ways: as a source for the critique of bourgeois commercialism in the realm of art, which could only be overcome by a revolution, and as a source for the conceptualization of socialist society as the fulfillment of the highest moral and aesthetic aspirations of mankind. Wagner presented arguments for socialism which were not to be found in the theoretical writings of Marx, Engels, or Kautsky, arguments which responded to popular perceptions of greatness and its redemptive power that had become part of public culture in the 19th-century. As the Austrian socialist Engelbert Pernerstorfer asserted in the 1880s, a broad and receptive audience existed for Wagner since his writings had become available in (somewhat) affordable editions, whereas his operas were too expensive for the masses to attend. Reading his works, Pernerstorfer insisted, represented the best approach to Wagner; even the educated classes came to him through the written word, he held, claiming: "The more the state neglects the education of the people and the more the will of the people shapes itself as a determining factor of the spiritual and economic life, the more it is the duty to present Wagner to the people as one of them."[9] Pernerstorfer put Wagner's *Art and Revolution* on a par with Marx' and Engels' historical-philosophical writings, something that could not have happened in the German party press. At the party congress in Erfurt in 1891, Marxism became the official basis for the program of the German Social Democrats.

It is telling that George Bernard Shaw, in 1907, used the *Preface to the First German Edition* of his successful volume on Wagner's *Ring, The Perfect Wagnerite* (1898), for an ironic attack on the dogmatism of the German Marxists. In a book that both praises and criticizes Wagner's stance toward modern capitalism as that of a great socialist, remarks such as the following are not particularly flattering:

> Even the Social-Democrats in Germany differ from the rest only in carrying academic orthodoxy beyond human endurance—beyond even German endurance. . . . They do not care a rap whether I am a Socialist or not. All they want to know is this: Am I orthodox? Am I correct in my revolutionary views? Am I reverent to the revolutionary authorities?[10]

Shaw portrayed Wagner's *Ring* as a grandiose allegory for the decline of humanity in modern capitalist society. He used Marxist arguments when he criticized Wagner for his failure to envision the necessity for a change in Alberich within an evolving capitalism. Alberich the dwarf would have to develop into Alberich the industrialist. Siegfried, in contrast, is the "perfectly naive hero upsetting religion, law and order in all directions, and establishing in their place the unfettered action of Humanity doing exactly what it likes."[11] Siegfried would have to learn Alberich's trade and shoulder Alberich's burden if he were to succeed in his new role. Shaw insists on comparing Marx and Wagner, giving Wagner credit for being a practical man compared with the theoretician in the British Museum, but no less naive when projecting social processes as dramas. He wrote:

> Although the Ring may, like the famous Communist Manifesto of Marx and Engels, be an inspired guess at the historic laws and predestined end of our capitalistic-theocratic epoch, yet Wagner, like Marx, was too inexperienced in technical government and administration and too melodramatic in his hero-contra-villain conception of the class struggle, to foresee the actual process by which his generalization would work out, or the part to be played in it by the classes involved.[12]

Shaw uses the image of Wagner, the socialist who strayed from his revolutionary course after reading Schopenhauer, for promoting his own Fabian socialist ideology vis-à-vis Marxist orthodoxy. Yet even Shaw presents *The Perfect Wagnerite* as an invitation to *read* Wagner. Despite frequent references to the function and beauty of the music in *Der Ring des Nibelungen,* Shaw's focus is on a reading of Wagner's work that makes its revolutionary spirit accessible to the English public. In the *Preface to the First Edition,* Shaw takes issue with the fact that earlier attempts at translating Wagner's numerous pamphlets and essays into English "resulted in ludicrous mixtures of pure nonsense with the absurdest distortions of his ideas into the ideas of the translators."[13] Shaw takes great pains to explain to his British audience why Wagner's work, despite its convoluted style, is worth the effort of reading and listening. He has to prove its accessibility to "the people" to whom Wagner's socialist message is directed. Thus he joins other socialists such as Pernerstorfer in the attempt at redeeming Wagner from being appropriated solely by the luxuriating few. "I write this pamphlet for the assistance of those who wish to be introduced to the work on equal terms with that inner circle of adepts."[14]

According to Shaw's concept of facilitating textual understanding, Wagner's music becomes part of the sociopolitical text. Shaw wants to make sure that "reading" the *Ring* expands the horizon much beyond reading Wagner's essays. By stressing the musical aspect, Shaw responds to the fact that at the end of the 19th century Wagner's operas became — often in excerpts — more affordable to the broader public.

The enthusiasm for Wagner in New York in the 1890s, for instance, was based on a democratization of his image coupled with an astounding expansion of his audience into less privileged classes, and peaked with the American premiere of *Parsifal* in New York in 1903. The Metropolitan Opera became a metaphor for the new populist art form: a socially diverse audience glowing with pride in American culture sat in an opera hall in the best Old World operatic tradition.[15] It is obvious that the motivation for the various groups involved in the event was not exactly the pursuit of revolutionizing capitalist society, but rather the ambition to participate in the higher forms of culture. The difficulty in claiming that America had become the leading home for Wagner's works because of the democratization of his audience, is expressed in the publicity surrounding the performance, which included popular lectures and advertising. As the critic James C. Huneker noted, "hosts of pamphlets, tons of tomes and eternal gabble about the Wagner idea" were made available to interested Americans. This was true to the extent that, as one Wagner commentator confessed, "the unfortunate novice is plied with information about the leading motives and musical characterization till he goes to the opera like a nervous schoolboy trying to remember his lesson."[16] Shortly thereafter, such investments in reading high culture ceased to appeal to a populist audience. With the ready accessibility of mostly musical mass culture, high art and the mass audience again drifted apart.

In the German workers' movement, where the positive reaction to *Art and Revolution* was always accompanied by the criticism of Wagner as a pseudo-revolutionary,[17] the echo of his writings faded into background accompaniment to increasingly frequent performances of his overtures, arias, and orchestral arrangements with which workers' singing societies filled their popular programs. Pieces from *Tannhäuser* and *Lohengrin* were particularly favored. The choice followed the canon which middle-class musical societies had established in the preceding decades. At the singers' festivals in Hamburg in 1904 and 1905, selections from *Rienzi, The Flying Dutchman, Tannhäuser,* and *Lohengrin* were performed. Ultimately, Wagner was used in Nuremberg in 1908 for the opening of the annual culmination of party activities, the congress of the SDP. Nine hundred singers sang the "Einzug der Gäste auf der Wartburg" from his *Tannhäuser* to the enthusiastic applause of the assembled socialist delegates.[18]

Whenever the question was raised whether Wagner was adopted by the working-class movement, or the working-class movement by Wagner, the answer always contained a reference to Wagner's credentials as a revolutionary. To some extent, this debate was itself his democratization, according to the maxim promoted around 1890 by Bruno Wille: "Die Kunst dem Volke."[19] Radical socialists such as Clara Zetkin and Hermann Duncker understood it as part of an encompassing strategy of claiming great cultural heroes and achievements in the name of socialism, as Franz Mehring had done with his book *Die Lessing-Legende* in 1893. In his provocative literary study, Mehring ventured to disinherit the Prussian bourgeoisie of the great enlightener. Mehring's subtitle for this undertaking, "Eine Rettung" ("A Reclamation"), carried a forceful message equally applicable to Wagner: the revolutionary composer had to be redeemed from the abuse of the nationalist and reactionary bourgeoisie.

II. Adorno's Critique and the Sociology of Musical Utopianism

If reading Wagner has made him appear a champion of the Left in the 19th century, 20th-century rereading has stripped him of much of his revolutionary aura. Most important, of course, is the fact that this rereading occurred while his musical works were fully accessible to a broad audience, and routinely referred to in studies of his sociopolitical objectives. Yet there was an even more poignant difference in the approach to Wagner the revolutionary. Twentieth-century critics, aware of the course which "Bayreuth," Wagner's heritage, had taken, could no longer invoke the purity of his programmatic ideas against commercialized music practices and negative philosophical influences on his music which earlier socialists had invoked. Even worse, Hitler's use of Wagner's vision of the artist's union with the "community of the people" (*Volksgemeinschaft*) and of other programmatic issues raised in *Art and Revolution*[20] nullified the political value of these and other Wagnerian texts.

The rancor with which Theodor W. Adorno treated Wagner's involvement in the Revolution of 1848/49 in one of the most insightful and influential studies on the Left in the 20th century, *Versuch über Wagner* (*In Search of Wagner,*

1937/38), clearly reflects the reaction against the requisition of Wagner as a prophet of Nazi art. It is precisely Wagner's striving for a communion between the artist and the people which Adorno exposes as the point of betrayal where Wagner undermines his self-proclamation as a revolutionary, even his engagement in the Dresden uprising of 1849. Adorno does not go along with the labeling of Wagner's musical retraction of the rebellion in the following decades as a derailment; he sees it rather as a confirmation of a weak revolutionary commitment to begin with. "The betrayal is implicit in the rebellion," Adorno asserts:

> No late conversion to a conformist posture was required of the later Wagner; there was no need to repudiate his earlier insurrectionary values: his belief in the peasantry and in nothingness, in the void. . . . It is illuminating enough that Wagner reneged on his part in the revolution almost before the revolutionary events were at an end; no less illuminating is the fact that official Wagner scholarship consciously and painstakingly falsified the account of this involvement. The conflict between rebellion and society is decided in advance in favour of society. In the *Ring,* the victory of society over the opposition and the recruitment of the latter for bourgeois purposes is idealized into a transcendental fate.[21]

This is not just a new reading of a complicated narrative, as Shaw suggested in *The Perfect Wagnerite.* Rather, it is a verdict on Wagner's revolutionary commitment both as a pamphleteer and a musical artist, a verdict which draws heavily on criteria of musical inventiveness and compositional strategies. By tracing Wagner's sociopolitical message in his music and its mythmaking character, Adorno resumes the critique in which Nietzsche at once praises and condemns Wagner's music as a peculiar medium of overcoming dilettantism as an artist (especially as a writer). Thus, in Nietzsche's reading, Wagner's work is exposed as the triumph of appearance over essence. The results are ever more devastating as the Frankfurt sociologist sets out to define Wagner's "social character" as the embodiment of the regressive ideology of the German bourgeoisie after 1849 where the complicity of art and ideology is sealed in the emulation of the existing disorder as fate. Pessimism here is the philosophy of the apostate rebel, the bourgeois revolutionary who nevertheless desperately identifies with the class he betrayed.

Yet in his impressive analysis of Wagner's handling of musical sonority, harmony, and orchestration—where he locates the creation of that famous mystical "mirage of eternity"—Adorno nevertheless reverts to his preconceived notion of the inauthenticity of Wagner's "social character." Thus, Adorno's deterministic view casts a shadow not only on his reading of Wagner's revolutionary involvement, but also on his denying the composer socially progressive impulses in his musical drama. To be sure, Adorno does distinguish between Wagner as composer and as writer, granting the former progressive aspects of compositional modernism. Yet there is little analysis of the political implications of aesthetic innovation. For instance, Wagner's concept of myth as a bearer of an eternal truth is a far cry from the 20th-century fragmented refractions of myth in Kafka or Joyce: he deals in the public material world of dramatic events and confrontations in which things *are* (also) what they seem; his gold is gold, and Amfortas's wound hurts just as does Oedipus's blinding. Without the refractions, this myth appears naked in the mirror of negative aesthetics, thereby easing the rise of regressive dreams. Is that all there is to it? Though a sociologist, Adorno does not engage in scholarly analysis of the 19th-century listening and reading audiences. While he is able to revoke what has been understood as the transformation of the revolution into the musical drama, Adorno overlooks the part of 19th-century audiences in the Wagner phenomenon. He ignores their horizon of expectation; he does not note their eccentric ways of transforming the musical drama into a listener's revolution.

It was not just the progress-minded optimism of Germany's *Gründerzeit* after the unification of 1871 that caused the audience of the premiere of 1876 to understand the *Ring* "almost exclusively not as a hopeless, fatal tale but as a liberating outlook on a future realm of love."[22] Eager to target the emotions of overcoming the present world of materialism which Wagner's music inspired, the audience rallied to experience utopian tendencies in the *Ring,* as had been its practice in the case of *The Flying Dutchman* and *Tannhäuser*. Socialists credited Wagner with breaking the spell of capitalist materialism and providing, beyond the mythical tale of Siegfried and Brünnhilde, an uplifting experience of true socialism. The social implications of the projected redemption gained shape not despite, but rather because of, the inconclusiveness of Wagner's work. They found expression not despite, but rather because of, his disengagement from the realm of treaties and politics.[23] Had the Revolution of 1848/49 not failed in the sphere of liberal politics? Wagner's musical drama bore witness that a new form of revolution had to be forged in order to lift the soul out of the disappointment of liberal idealism.

This development did not go unnoticed in France where the anti-Wagner sentiment carried much of the resentment against the neighbor to the east who had in 1870/71 won an unexpected victory. Meyerbeer's long reign as an opera composer had rested on the general perception that the grand social vision suggested by his music idealized the cultural status quo as an outgrowth of the great French national tradition. After the political debacle of 1870, however, further accommodation of this status quo became impossible. "Many critics, still affirming that a style can be social, now turned to the Wagnerian model," Jane Fulcher noted in her exploration of Meyerbeer's reign. "A new vision of society that coincided with a transformation in the preponderant view of the stage and concomitant theories concerning how the arts communicate drained Meyerbeer's music of the meaning it had."[24] Illuminating the importance of the intellectual context for the transformation of musical taste, Fulcher points at the diversities in the ascription of meaning to musical forms and makes a case for a differentiated study of audiences and their frame of reference. This enhanced perspective explains Wagner's phenomenal ascent within a narrow elite in Paris which in the 1880s, eschewing national stereotyping, constructed a concept of the modern on a particular understanding of his music. Much of this understanding had already been formulated by Baudelaire after the unsuccessful presentation of *Tannhäuser* in Paris in 1861. In its obsession with different stages of otherness and aesthetic negation of bourgeois normality, it resonated not only with certain expressions of *décadence* but also with those of anarchistic, utopian, and socialist projections. Most important was the fascination with Wagner's new construct of a theatrical whole in which these projections assumed larger-than-life proportions; no less intriguing was his grasp of the collective unconscious – as it came to be called – and his ability to express and induce rapture.

While Adorno showed interest in the progressive implications of the reaction to Wagner's modernism, he restricted his view of the specifically political realm of Wagner's work to Wagner's followers, in Germany, among the national and *völkisch* Right, and among the anti-Semites. Focusing on their presence as part of the National Socialist threat to the world in 1937, Adorno later stated that he had not written a "verdict" on Wagner. Rather, he insisted, he had attempted a redemption (*Rettung*) "by extracting the truth of a phenomenon from its sinister dimensions."[25] Calling his endeavor a "Rettung," Adorno ironically placed this essay, which so strongly refutes earlier socialist readings of Wagner as a revolutionary, squarely back into their camp.

Is Adorno's essay, therefore, yet another – though musicologically highly informed – example of the leftist condemnation-cum-salvation of Wagner? Adorno does indeed fit into this matrix, as do other representatives of the exiled Left in the 1930s and 1940s.[26] Georg Lukács, for instance, whose condemnation of Nietzsche as the great guru of modern German irrationalism in *Die Zerstörung der Vernunft* became a mainstay of communist historiography, mentions Wagner only rarely during that period.[27] It seems that the tendency to spare Wagner from the condemnation of Fascism is deeply rooted in the realization that Socialism needs anticipation, and anticipation needs powerful catalysts. Not surprisingly, in his earlier works on modern German drama, Lukács was an outspoken follower of Wagner, when he assigned to the theater the task of anticipating a better future.[28] His great friend of that time in Heidelberg, Ernst Bloch, was engaged in developing a whole philosophy of anticipation in which music, and the music of Wagner in particular, plays a central, catalytic role. In his political definition of this anticipation, Bloch developed and refined many arguments against the charge that Socialism cannot avoid decline and retrogression. He holds against Nietzsche that he failed to acknowledge the anticipatory power of music:

> Even Nietzsche, while grasping music's lack of historical simultaneity, makes it seem all too much of a mere revenant. He relates music itself in too historical a way to past events instead of illuminating it from the perspective of the future, as a spirit of *utopian rank* which, accordingly, is simply constructing a dwelling of its own amid history and sociology, constructing the framework of its own discoveries and inward planes of existence, though with countless elective affinities and free assimilations.[29]

When, in the 1930s, Bloch and the composer Hanns Eisler embarked on a rescue mission for those elements of modern art that were to be spared the Stalinists' verdict of decadence, Wagner represented a case worth pursuing even in the face of his requisition on the part of the Nazis. Adorno joined in this mission at least with his assertion, at the end of *In Search of Wagner,* that Nietzsche, so often right about Wagner, errs in his determinist critique of Wagner's decadence:

> If a decadent society develops the seeds of the society that will perhaps one day take its place, then Nietzsche, like the Russian despotism of the twentieth century which followed him, failed to recognize the forces that were released in the early stages of bourgeois decline. There is not one decadent element in Wagner's work from which a productive mind could not extract the forces of the future.[30]

III. Wagner as a Composer for Socialists

Although in the 19th century reading Wagner preceded listening to Wagner, it did not supersede it. There are enthralling, amusing, and perplexing descriptions of audiences' reactions to Wagner's operas. Some descriptions are in themselves manifestations of the operatic philistinism which Wagner tried to overcome with his *Musikdrama.* Others respond to Wagner's central objective of uniting all aesthetic elements of the musical drama in the performance itself; thus, they become virtual interpretations of his work, the most famous being Charles Baudelaire's *Richard Wagner et Tannhäuser à Paris.* Baudelaire's article gives intriguing insights into the emotional effects of Wagner's music exercised on artistic minds and thus allows some conclusions concerning the changes of musical understanding in the 19th century. It lays open the sensibilities awakened by Wagner's music and the new tendency of listeners to place the musical experience within ideological structures and aesthetic contexts.

The increasing willingness, expressed by Baudelaire in 1861, to consider musical structures both in their aesthetic autonomy and their significance for the dialectic of progress characterized audiences of operas and concerts at the end of the century. The anticipation preceding Wagner's operas, though furthered by his unusual promotional skills, was embedded in a growing trend of redefining the understanding of music according to its associative values. Although accompanying the phenomenal ascent of music to cultural predominance, this trend was not significantly defined with regard to its various stages and social representations[31] except in studies on Schopenhauer's influence on music appreciation. Music critics were usually too absorbed in the formal issues of their trade—as in the long-winded debates concerning Eduard Hanslick's formalist misapprehension of Wagner's music—to address the unique repositioning of music in the public culture of industrializing societies. The fact that the critics spoke of a betrayal of the structural character in the new musical developments confirms the intensity of the change. The growing use of the "musical model" in the public discourse substantiates the amazing preponderance of the associative understanding of music.

Thus, the "seemingly shapeless, purely thematic-associative ways of hearing Wagner's music"[32] are part of a broader pattern. Wagner's challenge to established compositional structures corresponded with the new willingness of listeners to reposition their musical experience. "He is intent on frustrating the fulfillment of the fixed, conventional, closed schemata and on forcing us to relocate ourselves, to find our center anew, in a procedure whose meaning we are constantly asked to reassess."[33] It is this kind of listeners' revolution that made Wagner's musical drama such an inspiration for those who looked for an aesthetic equivalent to their hopes for a social renewal.

This experience—whose political potential also has received surprisingly little scholarly attention[34]—represents a reaction to Wagner's rebellious tendencies which is different from the mainly textual comprehension. It focuses on the effectiveness of the musical drama. Operas are not understood as transpositions of socialist ideas; rather, certain parts of Wagner's musical-mythical drama are experienced as expressive equivalents of socialist projections. The predisposition towards such analogies is itself an outgrowth of a cultural habitus which allows the definition of socialism to be articulated through aesthetic experiences, something which obviously was more frequent among French, Austrian, and Russian than among German socialists. Whereas German socialists tended to pursue a scientific grounding of socialism, turning the science-based discourse into a legitimizing ritual of the party activities, socialists in other countries tended to capitalize more on the drawing power of aesthetic and political emotions.

Engelbert Pernerstorfer's commitment to Wagner in the 1880s clearly shifted the terms of assessment to ones fore-fronting the political potential of the Wagnerian constitution of an emotional community. In his Viennese circle, which included such personalities as the composer Gustav Mahler and the socialist leader Victor Adler, the Wagner-Nietzsche idea of the cultural community—the Nietzsche, that is, of *The Birth of Tragedy from the Spirit of Music*—fostered the vision of a "mighty unity of life," with social cohesion nullifying class barriers, and agitation countering the cooler practices of liberalism. Nationalist and socialist elements overlapped until Adler, appalled by Georg von Schönerer's mounting anti-Semitism, transferred his full allegiance to socialism. Until 1907, Austrian socialists had no direct access to parliament through election. In order to reach their following and to practice politics they had to resort to the means of public demonstrations. Adler's mastery of political symbolism was based on a sensitivity to crowd dynamics which was born of Wagnerian theater practices. Audience and chorus, drawn together by the theme of renewal and regeneration, became a unified entity expressing the community of the celebrants.[35]

Another thorough exploration of Wagner as a composer occurred in France. Wagner in his revolutionary essays had built on the French discussion of the role of art in accomplishing the revolution,[36] and this had helped sensitize radical elites into pursuing musical experience as a bridge to an all-encompassing concept of socialism, as Jean Jaurès argued in *L'Art et le socialisme*. Jaurès pointed to Wagner's idea of the *Gesamtkunstwerk* as a model for the synthesizing energies of socialism, and he rejected mechanical materialism and philistine working-class utilitarianism. Claude-Henri de Saint-Simon had expanded romantic ideas concerning redemption through art to include social regeneration as well as individual renewal as the ultimate goal, and Wagner had become an exemplary practitioner of this synthesis.[37] Jaurès' refusal of the reductionist tendencies in the syndicalist movement and, particularly, in Georges Sorel's social myth of the general strike is based on this synthetic approach. In turn, Sorel, too, drew heavily on Wagner and Nietzsche, concentrating, however, more on their revitalization of myth as both a discursive category and an aesthetic experience. Not incidentally, Sorel advanced the most incisive critique of Marx as the creator of an effective myth of the revolution, adding that Marx's attempt at making socialism scientific would turn out to be the most transitory element in his work.

Related to this critique of the "scientification" (*Verwissenschaftlichung*) of socialism, an even stronger impact of Wagner (and Nietzsche) can be discerned in regard to Russian socialists after the turn of the century, especially after the Revolution of 1905. It was often referred to as the Dionysian element in a movement whose leaders were intensely affected by the symbolist "myth creation" on the basis of a new centrality of theater and music, and whose ultimate goal, the redemption of Russia from its misery, reached deeply into the realm of mystical beliefs that abounded in the Russian society. Erased from the history of Bolshevism by Leninist and Stalinist historians, this Dionysian element can hardly be overestimated in the gestation of the most far-reaching 20th-century revolutionary movement and its cultural orientation. Whereas Wagner's *Art and Revolution* became a crucial text for the reorientation toward a cultural revolution after 1905, and was published again, in a new translation, in 1918,[38] Wagner's music attained the aura of demonstrating the emotional intensity of the revolutionary will. The symbolist writers Vyacheslav Ivanov and Aleksandr Blok and the socialist revolutionary Anatoly Lunacharsky concurred in using their ecstatic-mystical experiences of music as a paradigm for the soon-to-be-practiced collective creativity. Ivanov even used Nietzsche's dichotomy of the Apollonian and the Dionysian in his characterization of the duality between those revolutionaries who pursued a total control of reality (among whom he included Lenin and Stalin) and those who strove for a total reconstitution of social reality under aesthetic auspices (among whom were figures such as Bogdanov and Lunacharsky, who were later either forced underground or eliminated).

Referring to Wagner's goal of fusing art and politics, Lunacharsky put the author of *Art and Revolution* on the same level as the authors of the *Communist Manifesto,* "our brilliant teachers Marx and Engels."[39] Placing Wagner vis-à-vis Marx was not uncommon among socialists at the end of the century, although it was rarely done as effectively as in the case of Lunacharsky, Shaw, or Sorel. It was more common outside of Germany, at a certain distance from the particularities of these luminaries, their work and immediate audiences. This perspective often reduced the comparison of the two men to that of two revolutionary principles, juxtaposing the myth of science and the myth of cultural rejuvenation, and pursuing arguments that, beyond reading and listening, followed their own dynamics within the mythmaking of ideological confrontations. With his presentation of musical-literary-theatrical myths, Wagner held his own in this comparison, especially in the 1880s when religious and mythical tendencies came to be features in definitions of socialism.

None other than Ferdinand Lassalle, the friend and competitor of Marx and the founder of the first German social democratic party, the Allgemeiner Deutscher Arbeiterverein, had attested to Wagner's mythmaking ability in the early 1860s. Lassalle, who formulated his own literary response to the failure of the Revolution of 1848/49 in his drama *Franz von Sickingen* (1859), found himself overwhelmed by Wagner's bold creation of a mythology. In 1862, in a letter to Hans von Bülow, he confessed that reading Wagner's *Ring* had reinvigorated his belief in the heroic grandeur of the Teutons (*Germanen*) and in the powerful *Volksgeist* which had waned after his own unsuccessful attempts at mastering the Nordic myth.[40] Lassalle's admiration for Wagner is mixed with jealousy; after completing his theoretical work *Das System der erworbenen Rechte* in 1861, he found the need of a new mythology for the social movement most compelling.[41]

Lassalle's far-reaching contributions to the German workers' movement reflect these considerations. He shared with Wagner the feeling of triumph and defeat of the revolutionary of 1848/49. He also tried to compensate for his lack of success by embarking on a different revolutionary program. He articulated the need for new forms of organization and propaganda and developed them. He felt that socialism would only sustain the imagination of the workers if it carried the aura of the great aspirations of mankind which had sparked the events of 1848. In response to the defeat of the bourgeoisie in the revolution, Lassalle concluded, the working class had to take up these aspirations. Its growing commitment to scientific socialism needed to be enhanced and balanced with the most spirited expression which Schiller and German idealism had given these aspirations. In lieu of a new social mythology which would carry the torch of the revolution, Schiller's optimistic plays and poems of liberation would convey the poetic inspiration. Lassalle, envious of Wagner for creating myths that pointed beyond the material and psychological reality of the bourgeoisie, found in Schiller the most appropriate and popular inspiration: Schiller had formulated the idealistic norms against which the capitalist reality of the bourgeoisie should be measured.[42] The German Social Democracy adopted Schiller's *Wilhelm Tell,* not Wagner's *Ring.*

Nietzsche's condescension regarding the social democrats as a revolutionary force might have much to do with his inability to envisage the utopian dream in other than Dionysian configurations. Social democrats such as Lassalle or Bebel did just this: they evoked the millenarian dream for the masses as based on rational steps and, therefore, within reach. Once the obstacles to progress erected by the inherent irrationality of capitalism had been overcome, there was virtually no limit to what could be accomplished with the help of modern science and rational planning. The socialist *Zukunftsstaat* was not an echo of Wagner's *Zukunftsmusik,* but rather the fulfillment of rationality in its course through history.[43] It resonated with Schiller's traumatic rejection of the French Revolution which inspired the idyllic version of popular liberation in *Wilhelm Tell.* The emulation of Schiller's optimism and idealism in the German socialist party thus signaled a conscious diversion from the Dionysian elements of collective excess and revolutionary fervor.

Socialists in other countries were less sure whether this diversion was necessary or even desirable. Victor Adler criticized Bebel and the German party leadership for their naiveté toward the psychology of the masses.[44] Adler's definition of psychological strategies derived important conclusions from Wagnerian music. He claimed that reading Wagner's text *Art and Revolution* helped in articulating the millenarian dream, but he also pointed to the continuous need for emotional inspiration which Wagner, in an exemplary way, had awakened and fulfilled in his operas.

Seen in the context of their astounding, though often only temporary, engagement with socialism in late 19th-century Europe, the vibrant response of artistic and political elites to Wagner's music represents a phenomenon which reached beyond the emulation of his revolutionary writings. It originated where Wagner had situated the authenticity of his musical mythmaking: in the performance itself. Geared toward an emotional-associative practice of hearing music, Wagner had focused on the participation of the audience in the performance with a theatrical strategy so sophisticated and effective that it fostered a new era of theater developments. While this strategy has received much attention in its impact on modern theater aesthetics, its political-ideological orientation is usually buried under the rigorous claims of the Right. It is worthwhile — and follows a well-established tradition — to unearth its utopian potential in the context of the emotional-associative understanding of 19th-century audiences as well as in the light of the inspiration which such socialists as Adler, Lunacharsky, and Jaurès ascribed to Wagner's music. Under these auspices, the political potential correlates with the musical emotions, whereas rationality appears as counterproductive to the spark of rebellion and utopia.

When, decades later, Bertolt Brecht argued against the kind of passive acquiescence found in the operas and plays of the 19th century, he probably did not reflect this productive constellation. Brecht was not too far from Wagner in his thoughts concerning the need for an active imvolvement of the spectator. Yet he had little in common with Wagner's musical manipulation of the emotions when he focused on using the theater to induce a critical attitude in the audience. Obviously, Brecht's rating of thinking and feeling as political criteria is based on a different notion of theater, reality, and rationality. It cannot be used without historical qualifications. The response to science, for instance, which Brecht pursued in his concept of a theater for a scientific age, had already been an important impulse in Wagner's reformulation of the musical drama, though in 19th-century terms. In keeping with these terms, Wagner found a surprisingly strong response among socialists who were skeptical toward the ubiquity of theory and science when he credited reason with the maintenance of the status quo, feeling with its rupture. In *Opera and Drama* Wagner said: "The mind will tell us *So it is!* but only when the feeling has told us *So it must be!*"[45]

Notes

1 William Weber, "Wagner, Wagnerism, and Musical Idealism," in *Wagnerism in European Culture and Politics*, ed. David C. Large and William Weber (Ithaca/London, 1984), 45. See also Martin Gregor-Dellin, *Richard Wagner—die Revolution als Oper* (Munich, 1973); and Rüdiger Krohn, "Richard Wagner und die Revolution von 1848/49," in *Richard-Wagner-Handbuch*, ed. Ulrich Müller and Peter Wapnewski (Stuttgart, 1986), 86–100.

2 Wolfgang Friedrich, "Die sozialistische deutsche Literatur in der Zeit des Aufschwungs der Arbeiterbewegung während der sechziger Jahre des 19. Jahrhunderts bis zum Erlaß des Sozialistengesetzes" (Habil.-schrift Halle-Wittenberg, 1964), 87.

3 *Richard Wagner's Prose Works* (London, 1895), 1:42.

4 Ibid., 56.

5 B. W., "Kunst und Revolution," *Berliner Volks-Tribüne* no. 43 (27 October 1888).

6 August Bebel, *Die Frau und der Sozialismus*, 9th ed. (Stuttgart, 1891), 327.

7 Clara Zetkin, "Die Intellektuellenfrage," in her *Ausgewählte Reden und Schriften* (Berlin, 1960), 3:55.

8 G. V. Plekhanov, *Art and Social Life* (London, 1953), 219.

9 Engelbert Pernerstorfer, "Richard Wagner und der Sozialismus," *Deutsche Worte: Monatshefte*, repr. in Hartmut Zielinsky, *Richard Wagner—ein deutsches Thema: Eine Dokumentation zur Wirkungsgeschichte Richard Wagners 1876–1976* (Frankfurt, 1976), 72.

10 Bernard Shaw, *The Perfect Wagnerite: A Commentary on the Niblung's Ring* (New York, 1926), viiif.

11 Ibid., 69.

12 Ibid., 103.

13 Ibid., xviif.

14 Ibid., 2.

15 Burton W. Peretti, "Democratic Leitmotivs in the American Reception of Wagner," *Nineteenth-Century Music* 13 (1989): 32.

16 Ibid.

17 For a good summary of the critical views, see Rudolf Franz, "Wagner der Erlöser," *Neue Zeit* 30.1 (1911/12): 782–91, 804–16.

18 Vernon Lidtke, *The Alternative Culture: Socialist Labor in Imperial Germany* (New York/Oxford, 1985), 98.

19 There are numerous positive references to Wagner's music in texts by working-class writers. See, for instance, Ernst Schuchardt, quoted in Robert H. Lowie, *Toward Understanding Germany* (Chicago, 1954), 141. Cf. also the homage to Wagner by the Austrian socialist Wilhelm Ellenbogen, "Richard Wagner und das Proletariat," *Der Kampf* 6 (1912/13): 376–84.

20 Arne Fryksén, "Hitlers Reden zur Kultur: Kunstpolitische Taktik oder Ideologie?" in *Probleme deutscher Zeitgeschichte* (Lund, 1970), 235–66.

21 Theodor W. Adorno, *In Search of Wagner* (London, 1981), 138f.

22 Susanna Großmann-Vendrey, "Zum hundertjährigen Bayreuth," *Melos/Neue Zeitschrift für Musik* 2 (1976): 265.

23 Herfried Münkler, "Mythos und Politik—Aischylos' 'Orestie' und Wagners 'Ring,'" *Leviathan* 15 (1987): 562–80.

24 Jane Fulcher, "Meyerbeer and the Music of the Society," *Musical Quarterly* 67 (1981): 229.

25 Theodor W. Adorno, "Nachschrift zur Wagner-Diskussion," in *Richard Wagner: Das Betroffensein der Nachwelt. Beiträge zur Wirkungsgeschichte,* ed. Dietrich Mack (Darmstadt, 1984), 272. See also John Bokina, "Wagner and Marxist Aesthetics," in *Wagner in Retrospect: A Centennial Reappraisal,* ed. Leroy R. Shaw et al. (Amsterdam, 1987), 138–51.

26 Joachim Radkau, "Richard Wagners Erlösung vom Faschismus durch die Emigration," *Exilforschung* 3 (1985): 71–105.

27 Ibid., 86f.

28 Udo Bermbach, "Wagner und Lukács: Über die Ästhetisierung von Politik und die Politisierung von Ästhetik," *Politische Vierteljahresschrift* 31 (1990): 449.

29 Ernst Bloch, "The Philosophy of Music," in *Essays on the Philosophy of Music* (Cambridge/London, 1985), 9.

30 Adorno, *In Search of Wagner,* 153.

31 See Leon Botstein, "Between Aesthetics and History," *Nineteenth-Century Music* 13 (1989): 168–78.

32 Anthony Newcomb, "Those Images That Yet Fresh Images Beget," *Journal of Musicology* 2 (1983): 233.

33 Ibid., 237.

34 Cf. Thomas Koebner, "Der 'Ring' und die Revolution," in *Theaterarbeit an Wagners Ring,* ed. Dietrich Mack (Munich/Zurich, 1978), 218.

35 William J. McGrath, *Dionysian Art and Populist Politics in Austria* (New Haven/London, 1974), 208–37.

36 Jane Fulcher, "Wagner, Comte, and Proudhon: The Aesthetics of Positivism in France," *Symposium* 33 (1979): 142–52.

37 *Pages choisies de Jean Jaurès,* ed. Paul Desanges and Luc Meriga (Paris, 1928), 66 et passim.

38 Bernice Glatzer Rosenthal, "Wagner and Wagnerian Ideas in Russia," in *Wagnerism,* 227.

39 Ibid., 234; see also Rosenthal, "Wagner and the Russian Left," in *Wagner in Retrospect* 152–63.

40 Ferdinand Lassalle, *Nachgelassene Briefe und Schriften,* ed. Gustav Mayer (1925; repr. Osnabrück, 1967), 5:26.

41 On Wagner and the search for a new mythology, see Manfred Frank, *Der kommende Gott: Vorlesungen über die Neue Mythologie* (Frankfurt, 1982), 217–30.

42 C. Korn, "Proletariat und Klassik," *Neue Zeit* 26.2 (1907/08): 409–18. Cf. Frank Trommler, *Sozialistische Literatur in Deutschland: Ein historischer Überblick* (Stuttgart, 1976), 40–46.

43 Kenneth R. Calkins, "The Uses of Utopianism: The Millenarian Dream in Central European Social Democracy Before 1914," *Central European History* 15 (1982): 127f.

44 McGrath, *Dionysian Art,* 220.

45 Richard Wagner, *Opera and Drama* (London, n.d.), 367 (chapter 4, "Intellect and Feeling," no. 342).

The Rivalry for Wagner's Mantle: Strauss, Pfitzner, Mann

HANS RUDOLF VAGET

> Mein Erbe nun
> nehm ich zu eigen.
> (*Götterdämmerung* III, 3)

> Dein Erbe aber nehmen wir zu eigen,
> Um es als hohes Gut uns zu bewahren.
> (Hans Pfitzner, *Richard Wagner*)

I

Much has been written recently about the impact of Richard Wagner on European culture and politics.[1] Given the magnitude and the problematical nature of the Wagner legacy, the growing interest especially of literary and cultural historians in Wagner is well justified. I propose to continue this line of investigation, examining the cases of Richard Strauss, Hans Pfitzner, and Thomas Mann, three prominent and highly self-conscious Wagnerians who, each in his own emphatic way, laid claim to being the true heir to Wagner. In making that claim, they played out one of Wagner's own obsessive themes: Who shall inherit? Who is fit to be the rightful heir? What constitutes the heritage? The history of their relationship is still little known and needs to be reconstructed here. It is marked by a series of shifts in the way they perceived each other. I am especially interested in the dynamics that produced those shifts, since understanding them should go a long way in illuminating the aesthetic and ideological issues as well as the political fortunes of Wagnerianism in Germany.

It is central to my purpose to look at Strauss, Pfitzner, and Mann as parts of a larger configuration: that is to say, not individually, but in relation to each other and to the whole cultural landscape of which they are such distinctive features. It can hardly be accidental that this configuration was drastically redefined at two critical historical junctures. This occurred first around 1910, that watershed of modern culture when the Wagnerian paradigm, which Nietzsche had proclaimed to be the dominant one, was gradually replaced by various new modernisms. It occurred again, more drastically, in 1933 when the political system was subjected to a radical "Ästhetisierung," to borrow Walter Benjamin's term, under the aegis of that most fateful of Wagnerians — Adolf Hitler.

The Strauss-Pfitzner-Mann constellation has its origins in Wilhelminian culture, when the musical and, especially, the extramusical influence of Wagner reached its zenith. Born during Wagner's lifetime, the three artists began their careers in that first decade after the death of Wagner when the enthusiasm for his work grew to epidemic proportions. What Nietzsche had predicted for the post-Wagnerian generation—"Wagner sums up modernity. There is no way out, one must first become a Wagnerian"[2]—applied to a great number of young artists in Germany and Europe,[3] and it applied with particular force to Strauss, Pfitzner, and Mann, all fervent Wagnerians.

Strauss, the oldest of the three, did not begin as a Wagnerian.[4] His father—a hornist who had played under Wagner in the Munich court orchestra and at Bayreuth—was in fact an unabashed anti-Wagnerian. Richard Strauss first looked to other, cosmopolitan models, notably Liszt and Berlioz. He soon became a Wagnerian, however, as the sensational success of his early work carried him to a position of preeminence on the German musical scene. Although there always remained some doubts in certain quarters concerning the German character of Strauss's music, he was widely perceived to be heir apparent to Wagner. His early work, especially that remarkable series of compositions beginning with *Don Juan* (1888) and culminating in *Salome* (1905) and *Elektra* (1908), brought about a refinement and modernization of the Wagnerian idiom that put him at the head of musical "progress." Strauss was modern *and* successful, which set him somewhat apart from the other post-Wagnerian figures such as Mahler, Pfitzner, Reger, Humperdinck, and, somewhat later, the young Schönberg. Although he produced lieder and chamber music, he made his mark in the large-scale symphonic form of the so-called tone poem and in opera, the two genres with which the fate of post-Wagnerian music seemed to be tied up most intimately. We may not want to attach too much weight to the title "Richard II" that Hans von Bülow bestowed upon him,[5] but it does seem indicative of the way in which he positioned himself that in 1889 Strauss sought and then maintained close ties with Bayreuth, especially to Cosima Wagner.[6] As soon as he had taken over his new position as "Hofkapellmeister" in Weimar in the fall of 1889, he informed Wagner's widow that he was planning to hold readings from the master's works for the benefit of the local Wagner-Verein.[7] The "Herrin" of Bayreuth was very much taken by the young musician and described him as "our rising star," fanatically devoted to "our cause."[8] Strauss's development during that crucial period, in musical as well as ideological terms, can indeed be described as a progression from "Wagnerianer zum Erben Wagners."[9] Thus, when Mann referred to Strauss as the "king" of the Wagnerians,[10] he merely expressed a view that was widely, though not universally, held in Wilhelminian Germany.

Pfitzner's devotion to the Wagnerian cause was, if anything, more fanatical.[11] In contrast to Strauss, he was a strict nationalist in both his political outlook and his music. Aside from Wagner, he traced his musical lineage to Weber, Marschner, and Schumann. An influential segment of the musical establishment was, therefore, to proclaim him the only guardian of German musical tradition and the only reliable bastion against cosmopolitans such as Busoni, and against the "Neue Musik" of Arnold Schönberg and his disciples. In that anti-modernist camp of musical nationalism, Pfitzner was regarded as the "heimliche Kaiser" of German music.[12] Pfitzner, who, unlike Strauss, was an effective writer, did everything to reinforce this view. In this regard, too, he presented himself as Wagner's successor. Like Wagner, he declared he had no choice but to sing *and* to lecture; to hold a pen in one hand and a hoe in the other.[13] And indeed, it was an essayist and polemicist that Pfitzner declared himself most forcefully as the keeper of the Wagnerian flame—flickering though it may have appeared to him. His early essays were published under the title *Vom musikalischen Drama;*[14] they are Wagnerian in letter and in spirit, and they mark, at the date they appeared (1915), an unabashedly reactionary position.[15] In an aesthetic climate in which reaction was defiantly equated with progress—"Reaktion als Fortschritt"[16]—Pfitzner was able to present himself as the savior of German music. As such, he launched two vigorous attacks in 1917 and 1920: first, against Ferruccio Busoni and his neoclassical program, in which he sensed a "Futuri-stengefahr";[17] and second, against the musicologist Paul Bekker and modernism in principle, which he ridiculed as the manifestation of musical impotence.[18]

At the center of Pfitzner's musical thought, we find the idea of inspiration, or "Einfall." This strikingly old-fashioned and romantic notion is the key to Pfitzner's definition of form and creativity: inspiration is metaphysical in its origin, and it determines musical form. Given this traditional and popular notion of art and creativity, it does seem surprising that Pfitzner was not more successful as a musician. The great, noisy, and lasting success that his rival Strauss enjoyed kept eluding him, and Pfitzner did not take it lightly. All his life, he suffered, as he himself admitted, from being Number Two.[19] He is, however, the creator of *Palestrina,* which put him at least briefly in the limelight of musical life in Germany. It is, arguably, the most ambitious Wagnerian opera we have—as no one argued more eloquently than Thomas Mann. But despite *Palestrina* and despite the great respect Pfitzner commanded as the spirited though quarrelsome head of the musical conservatives, he never succeeded where he wanted to succeed most—in the Wagnerian genre of music drama. With the exception of *Palestrina,* his other four operas have disappeared from the repertory. Even his sole master-piece is virtually unknown outside Germany. It would seem that Pfitzner was indeed, as Carl Dahlhaus observed, essentially a *lied* composer who was never really at home in the theater.[20]

Thomas Mann's Wagnerianism was of a different kind and spirit. Fascinated by Nietzsche's critique of Wagner, he carried the fashionable Wagnerianism of the time further than any of his contemporaries, who merely flirted with it. Starting with *Little Herr Friedemann,* he began to emulate in his writing certain Wagnerian devices, notably the leitmotif. Henceforth, it was his ambition until the end to produce good scores,[21] by which he meant Wagnerian scores. Already in his first novel, *Buddenbrooks,* he took *The Ring of the Nibelung* as one of his models. His Wagnerian manner, he confessed shortly thereafter, had become something completely instinctive with him.[22] Around 1910, his relationship to Wagner underwent a crisis that seems only to have strengthened his passionate engagement with the creator of *The Ring* and of *Tristan and Isolde*. In contrast to Strauss, however, he always maintained a critical distance from Wagner; and, unlike Pfitzner, he always regarded Wagner not as an exclusively German but as a European phenomenon. Perhaps the most balanced view of his passion for Wagner can be found in a letter of 1942 to Agnes Meyer: "The way I talk about Wagner has no chronology or logical progression. It is and will always remain ambivalent, and I am capable of writing one thing about him today, and quite a different thing tomorrow."[23] It is this ambivalent enthusiasm — or, rather, enthusiastic ambivalence — that accounts for his success in employing Wagnerian devices in the service of psychological analysis and narrative organization. More clearly than anyone else, he understood that Wagner's method of composition, starting with *Das Rheingold,* represented a challenge to the narrative conventions of the 19th-century novel and an opportunity for its modernization. He seized that opportunity and thus deftly sidestepped the trap of naturalism. The Wagnerianism of Mann's writing is indeed pervasive. It marks both the extent and the limit of his modernity. Soon after the Wagnerian model lost its luster around 1910, Mann's literary production ceased to be part of the modernist project in the strict sense.[24]

II

Strauss, Pfitzner, and Mann differed greatly with respect to their background, temperament, and outlook. The difference is especially marked between the two composers. Strauss was born to a well-to-do family, his mother being a Pschorr from one of the great brewing families in Munich. His childhood was sheltered and carefree, and he was endowed with a balanced and sunny disposition. Moreover, he was a child prodigy who at age 17 had his first large-scale work, a symphony, performed by Hermann Levi, the first conductor of *Parsifal.* Henceforth, success and fame and ever-increasing royalty from compositions accompanied him. Pfitzner's road was more arduous in every respect. Born in Moscow, where his father held a temporary position as a violinist, he grew up in Frankfurt under deplorable, thoroughly petit bourgeois conditions. Although born outside Germany, or perhaps because of it, Pfitzner grew up to be an ardent, even fanatical nationalist in contrast to Strauss, whose Bavarian stock was comfortably wed to an easy cosmopolitanism. Add to this Pfitzner's notoriously irascible temper and a certain misanthropic bent with suicidal tendencies, and you begin to appreciate Thomas Mann's euphemistic characterization of the composer of *Palestrina:* "I suppose he was not born to feel at ease; he is a difficult, sore, ambivalent person."[25] What sustained Pfitzner, though, and made him feel superior, was his unshakable conviction that he was a genius destined to be the recipient of difficult but genuine inspiration from a metaphysical source. It is this lofty, romantic conception of the artist that lies at the core of *Palestrina,* and that is affirmed by it.

Despite such obvious differences, our three Wagnerians share a number of basic characteristics that mark them as belonging to the same general topography of the Wilhelminian cultural landscape. At least four such common elements can be singled out, the first of which was the belief in the privileged status of music. Strauss, Pfitzner, and Mann inherited and fully embraced the philosophy of music articulated in German Romanticism. In the case of the two musicians, this is hardly surprising, but it is remarkable for a storyteller. Put simply, all three were Schopenhauerians. It was Schopenhauer who had provided the philosophical underpinnings for the new valorization of music in romanticism when he argued that the will, the ultimate metaphysical essence of the world, found its most direct and powerful expression in music, and only in music. This meant, among other things, that music was elevated to the highest position in the hierarchy of the arts. Schopenhauer's redefinition of music remained a fundamental axiom in their view of art and life—as it had been for Wagner, of course.

Second, all three worked under the shadow of Wagner. In a letter of 1920, Thomas Mann stated: "Wagner is still the artist I understand best, and in whose shadow I continue to live."[26] This observation holds just as true for Strauss and Pfitzner. All three habitually compared themselves to Wagner and never ceased to measure their accomplishments with his. Considering this fixation on Wagner, it does not seem unfair to attribute to all three a certain dependency, a sort of aesthetic addiction that may have affected the free development of their own style and voice, although one must add at once that this does not apply in equal measure to each. Pfitzner's development, it seems to me, was more harmfully affected by the shadow of Wagner than was Strauss's or Mann's.

Third, in the work of each is present a strong sense of the end. Strauss as well as Pfitzner and Mann were keenly aware of their status as latecomers—as heirs of a unique, music-dominated culture that would not survive them. One of Strauss's most haunting compositions bear the title "Vier letzte Lieder" (1948); in a sense, all their works were "last songs." Mann conceived *Doctor Faustus* as an allegory of the end—the catastrophic end—of the culture he knew and represented. The awareness of this state of affairs is inscribed in this book wherever one looks, most clearly at the beginning of chapter 43: "Meine Erzählung eilt ihrem Ende zu—das tut alles. Alles drängt und stürzt dem Ende entgegen, in Endes Zeichen steht die Welt. . . ."[27] Quite fittingly, this melancholy outcry is couched in Wagnerian (*Das Rheingold,* scene 4) words and sentiments. Perhaps the most succinct expression of this sense of the end can be found in Act I of *Palestrina,* written just before and during World War I:

> Ich bin ein alter, todesmüder Mann
> Am Ende einer großen Zeit
> Und vor mir seh' ich nichts als Traurigkeit—.[28]

And fourth, a feature prominent in each is the representation of the artist as a nonpolitical man. When Thomas Mann wrote his *Reflections of a Nonpolitical*

Man (1918), he spoke not only for himself but for the type of German culture whose survival he thought was at stake in the war of 1914–18. That "Kultur" was defined as nonpolitical, which is to say, as independent vis-à-vis any political agenda, ideological creed, or aesthetic program. At that time, Mann believed with Schopenhauer that intellectual life, and culture in general, hovered above the real life of economic needs and political interests like an exquisite fragrance, and that the history of the arts unfolded alongside but independently of world history, innocently and free of bloodstains – "schuldlos und nicht blutbefleckt."[29] Mann could have cited this sentence in his *Reflections* as a motto, since it accurately expresses one of his fundamental convictions at that time. Instead, it was Pfitzner who used this key passage from Schopenhauer[30] as a motto for *Palestrina.*

Mann's nonpolitical stance was shared by the vast majority of German intellectuals and artists, including Pfitzner, who figures prominently in the *Reflections,* and Strauss, who, for reasons yet to be discussed, is barely mentioned. As he was in the habit of doing, Mann would cite Goethe, Schopenhauer, Nietzsche, and Wagner as the great examples of Germany's nonpolitical culture. In one of his more unconscionable manipulations of the historical evidence, Mann argued: "A nation's taste for democracy is in inverse proportion to its distaste for politics. If Wagner was in any sense an expression of this notion . . . it was in his hatred of politics."[31] Of the three prominent Wagnerians, it was undoubtedly Mann who produced the shrillest noises when the war broke out. In a series of articles,[32] he welcomed the war; the self-proclaimed nonpolitical artist completely identified with the German cause, justifying German aggression as legitimate defense. Strauss, on the other hand, showed remarkable restraint. Although a patriot and nationalist at heart, he refused to sign the anti-Western proclamation of German artists and intellectuals of October 14.[33] His music had triumphed in London and Paris, and he was not going to turn England and France against him.

Pfitzner, however, did not need to take such concerns into consideration; he had no foreign audience. He lived and worked in Straßburg, which then was German. He was in charge of musical life in the city from 1907 to 1918, conducting, teaching, and composing; it was in Straßburg that he wrote *Palestrina.* He, too, thought of himself as a nonpolitical artist; in fact, he represented the nothing-but-a-musician type of artist in the purest and most striking form. In a characteristic comment, he referred to himself as "der ich von eigentlicher Politik nicht das geringste verstehe, sondern nur die gefühlsmäßig nationale Einstellung hatte."[34] This dates from 1947 and strikes one as a little self-serving. There can be no doubt, however, as to where Pfitzner stood when we learn that in 1916 he dedicated two compositions to Admiral von Tirpitz, the commander of the German Navy.

As was the case with many Germans, Pfitzner's political awakening was triggered by the Treaty of Versailles, which he passionately rejected. He also rejected the Weimar Republic and with it the new democratic order of Germany.

Add to this his coarse anti-Semitism, which he seems to have cultivated as part of his Wagnerianism,[35] and one would be hard pressed to make a distinction between Pfitzner and an ordinary Nazi. Given these leanings, it is hardly surprising that in 1924 he allowed Adolf Hitler (then still virtually an unknown outside Munich) to visit him in the hospital.[36] They found that they shared many hopes concerning the future of Germany, and this encounter, it seems, led in due course to Pfitzner's support of the Nazis. After 1933, however, Pfitzner was not courted by the Nazis so eagerly as was Strauss, nor as he had expected.[37] In 1934—too early, he thought[38]—he was unceremoniously retired from his professorship at the Munich "Akademie der Tonkunst." Two years later, as a conciliatory gesture, he was awarded the title "Reichskultursenator."[39] Pfitzner was too testy and difficult to serve the Nazi regime as a figurehead as Strauss had agreed to do; so he continued to be an unhappy, grumbling man even in the Third Reich. None of this, however, can detract from the sad fact that Pfitzner was in basic ideological agreement with the Nazi regime. There is no record of any significant criticism or any gesture of resistance or opposition.

Nor is there from Strauss. It is tempting to brand him a Nazi simply on account of his notoriously obsequious role as President of the "Reichsmusikkammer."[40] But his case is not quite so clear-cut as Pfitzner's. It is true that he did not decline when he was offered a position in November 1933. The Nazis did not bother actually to ask him whether he would accept because apparently they were sure of his ideological sympathies. He had given clear enough signals when in 1933 he took over a Berlin Philharmonic concert from Bruno Walter,[41] who was pressured to bow out, and when he agreed to conduct *Parsifal* in Bayreuth for Toscanini, who had protested the racial discrimination of the new regime.[42] Strauss, however, did not completely fit the Nazi mold. He soon proved to be too elitist and cosmopolitan in his tastes; in addition, he lacked the right anti-Semitic fervor. Not only did he have a Jewish daughter-in-law, he also held on to his Jewish librettist Stefan Zweig, which soon led to the termination of his role as the head of the Reich's revamped musical organization. He was forced to resign in June of 1935 when a letter to Zweig, in which he claimed merely to feign cooperation with the Nazis,[43] was intercepted by the secret police and brought to Hitler's attention. Whereupon Strauss wrote, on 13 July 1935, an abjectly servile letter to Hitler, begging for an interview in order to justify himself; mercifully, the letter was ignored.[44] Nonetheless, Strauss was able to live and to work freely, and to enjoy the privileges accorded the Reich's most honored musician.

Was it opportunism or naiveté that led to Strauss's collaboration? Or even ideological sympathies? He was probably too old and too much the product of the Wilhelminian era to become a proper Nazi. But there is no denying that Strauss shared with most of his compatriots a certain general fascist outlook[45] that had its roots in the nationalism, authoritarianism, and racism of the era in which he had grown up. To what extent the Nazis' ostentatious appropriation of Wagner played a role is difficult to judge. What is obvious, however, is Strauss's self-deception in believing that he could remain a nonpolitical artist while serving in such a visible and politically sensitive position. His is perhaps the most egregious and saddest example of the "I am nothing but a musician" syndrome. Thomas Mann was in a rather forgiving mood when he spoke of Strauss's "monumentale Wurschtigkeit" with respect to his role in the Third Reich.[46] To Mann, both Strauss and Pfitzner represented two prominent examples of the type of nonpolitical artist that he now implicated in the crisis of modern culture and, specifically, the "German catastrophe." This is precisely the subject of *Doctor Faustus,* a novel that would be unthinkable without Mann's own conversion from a nonpolitical to a politically committed writer. That conversion was the result of the most dramatic and decisive lesson of his life. He learned it slowly and reluctantly, but still in time to oppose those forces which his fellow Wagnerians Strauss and Pfitzner were ready to embrace.

III

Considering their growing ideological divergence, it seems inevitable that Strauss, Pfitzner, and Mann clashed. That they clashed in 1933, immediately after the Nazis came to power, also seems logical — at least in retrospect. What at first appears less inevitable is the fact that they clashed over the question of Wagner. On 16 April 1933, the *Münchner Neueste Nachrichten* published an open letter under the headline "A Protest From Richard Wagner's Own City of Munich."[47] It was signed by 45 prominent citizens of Munich, among them Strauss and Pfitzner. Their "Protest" was directed against their fellow citizen Thomas Mann, specifically against a lecture on Wagner delivered at Munich University on 10 February, less than two weeks after Hitler had come to power. Mann had spoken on the invitation of the local Goethe Society in commemoration of the 50th anniversary of Wagner's death. The address was culled from a much longer essay written for that occasion, entitled "The Sorrows and Grandeur of Richard Wagner,"[48] and considered by Mann as one of his most inspired pieces of writing.

It is not quite clear whether the signers of the letter wanted to protest primarily the content of Mann's speech, which they found objectionable, or whether they were offended by the fact that he had repeated it in Amsterdam, Brussels, and Paris, thereby committing the sin of "defaming" Germany abroad. In any case, they objected to three specific points. Mann, they said, had presented Wagner's work as a "fertile field for Freudian psychoanalysis"; he had arrogantly disparaged, they felt, Wagner's work as merely a "case of dilettantism monumentalized by a supreme effort of the will"; and he had tried to make Wagner a modernist when, instead, he should have recognized in him the "embodiment of the deepest German sensibilities." Needless to say, these allegations grossly misrepresent Mann's argument, which is subtle, complex, and sustained by a deep though not uncritical admiration.

It was not immediately clear who had initiated the "Protest." Strauss was not directly involved; he simply went along. Suspicions centered on Hans Knapperts-busch, the great Wagnerian conductor,[49] on Siegmund von Hausegger,[50] the President of the Munich Academy of Music, and on Pfitzner,[51] who was an in-veterate polemicist and apparently belonged to the inner circle of the protestors. In the meantime, however, new archival evidence has become available that points to Knappertsbusch, General Director of the Bavarian State Opera, as the originator of the campaign against Mann.[52]

Thomas Mann first saw the "Protest" in Lugano, Switzerland, where he was vacationing after his lecture tour. His diary records the shock: "stricken with disgust and horror."[53] He realized at once that the term "protest" was a euphemism and that this action was a murderous denunciation. It meant excom-munication from Germany—a Germany newly risen, as the protestors pointed out in the first sentence of their letter. And indeed, the "Protest" of the Munich Wagnerians led to Mann's exile. He would not return to Germany until 1949, and then only for a brief visit. Mann's instinct was right. Had he returned to Munich he would have been arrested at the border, as we now know from a so-called "Schutzhaftbefehl" found in the Nazi archives.[54] Even without being fully aware of what the Nazis intended to do with him, Mann felt that the Munich "Protest" and its consequences constituted the most traumatic experience of his life. He never forgot it, and he pointedly reminded the Germans of this "illiterate and murderous campaign against my Wagner essay"[55] when he was asked, imme-diately after the war, to return home to "heal the wounds."

As might be expected, Strauss and Pfitzner scholarship tends to downplay this whole ignominious episode. Any attempt at clarifying the circumstances of the campaign against Mann must go beyond the immediate context of Munich and the year 1933. Long before, Mann had begun to warn his contemporaries against National Socialism. And so the Nazi regime signaled open season on Mann from the start. As early as 17 February, a week after Mann's Wagner speech, the *Völkischer Beobachter,* the party paper, pointed out how very inappropriate it was ("äußerst unangebracht") that he was holding forth on Wagner in Brussels when the only appropriate and dignified commemoration of Wagner was being held in Germany in the presence of Chancellor Adolf Hitler. In that note, Mann is labeled as a "Halbbolschewik"—a clear enough indication of the new regime's intentions with respect to him.[56] It appears, then, that those who initiated the "Protest from Richard Wagner's Own City of Munich" took their cue directly from the *Völkischer Beobachter.*

There are other antecedents also, and these, too, have to do with Wagner. In 1931, Mann had permitted his "Wälsungenblut," written in 1905, to be published in French. That story, a parodistic treatment of *Die Walküre,* had to be withdrawn at the time and was known in Germany only through a private, limited edition of 1921.[57] When this most notorious of Mann's Wagner stories appeared in France, the recent Nobel laureate was charged with shameless profiteering, dishonesty towards his German public, and—this the most ominous accusation—the representation of "Blutschande."[58] These accusations appeared throughout Germany in a syndicated article by Friedrich Hussong, a hack for the pro-Nazi Hugenberg papers. Clearly, the Nazis deemed any and all of Mann's dealings with Wagner extremely inappropriate, a profanation of the Wagnerian heritage, the sacred national treasure.

We now begin to realize that the Munich "Protest" of 1933 was merely the tip of an iceberg. It marks the culmination of a struggle over the Wagnerian heritage that dates back as far as Wagner and Nietzsche. It is my contention that an adequate understanding of the Strauss-Pfitzner-Mann configuration is predicated on the realization that their rivalry is but a part of a larger ideological struggle over the highly ambiguous and explosive heritage of Wagner.

IV

Mann's fascination with Strauss began at an early stage. In 1894, he had moved from his native Lübeck to Munich where, as we know from his letters and notebooks, he began to frequent the opera and the concert halls. He must have already heard some Strauss compositions, because as early as 1895 he declared that Richard Strauss was his favorite composer—after Wagner, of course.[59] At that time Strauss's work only up to *Till Eulenspiegel* had appeared, i.e., none of the operatic masterpieces. It was his encounter with the first of these, with *Salome,* that left the most lasting impression. We have to assume that by that time Mann knew the composer personally, since Strauss regularly visited the house of Professor Alfred Pringsheim, a leading Wagnerian in Munich and since 1905 Mann's father-in-law. Writing about that period, Katia Mann confirmed that they knew Strauss quite well.[60] There exists, however, no correspondence between Strauss and Mann; apparently no personal rapport was established.

Salome had its world premiere on 9 December 1905, in Dresden. Mann was in the city on a reading tour and made a point of seeing one of the repeat performances a few days later. He was impressed.[61] Here was a work that seemed to sum up "decadence" and to open new doors to a modern type of music drama. *Salome* was daring *and* successful—a succès de scandale, to be sure, but indisputably a success. Strauss had scored a triumph in a territory that Mann himself was hoping to conquer with "Wälsungenblut," ill-starred though the story was. As late as *Doctor Faustus,* after Mann had become quite disenchanted with Strauss, we can sense behind the sarcasm directed at the "begabter Kegelbruder" how deep an impression *Salome* had made; it is described as a "powerful and striking opera."[62] More revealingly, the encounter with this opera is linked to a decisive biographical event in the life of Mann's hero, the composer Adrian Leverkühn: his infection with the deadly agent of genius.

It was in the light of the *Salome* experience that Mann came to view Strauss as the "king" of Wagnerians. This characterization can be found in his notes for "Geist und Kunst,"[63] an ambitious essay for which he began to collect material in March of 1909. After two years, however, he abandoned the project, bequeathing it to his fictional alter ego Gustav von Aschenbach in *Death in Venice*. "Geist und Kunst" was intended as a comprehensive stock-taking of contemporary culture and of Mann's own position. Wagnerianism and its prospects in a rapidly changing intellectual climate was to be a central focus of the essay. Surprisingly, it is already here that Pfitzner makes his first appearance in Mann's work. He did have three operas to his credit—*Der arme Heinrich* (1893), *Die Rose vom Liebesgarten* (1900), and *Das Christelflein* (1906)—but his fame was nowhere near that of the creator of *Salome* and *Elektra*. Mann notes that Pfitzner, the author of an essay on the eminently Wagnerian topic of "Grundlagen der Opern-dichtung,"[64] is the stronger of the two composers, both intellectually and as a writer. He is even inclined to view Pfitzner as the greater natural talent, as more inspired and profound than Strauss, who is seen here, as he often was at that time, as a brilliant but cold technician.[65] In the end, however, Mann judges Strauss to be the greater artist—more compelling and more effective. Pfitzner appears as an alternative and antidote to Strauss, but not yet on a par. All things considered, Strauss strikes Mann as the more contemporary and interesting type of artist[66]—but just barely.

A quite different picture begins to emerge from Mann's letters of that period. While in "Geist und Kunst" he intended to put Strauss above Pfitzner, in his correspondence he begins to dismantle the pedestal on which he had placed the creator of *Salome*. This disparity confirms the suspicion that Mann built up Strauss as the "king" of Wagnerians merely in order to challenge that title. It was *Elektra* that caused him to have different thoughts on Strauss's relationship to Wagner. Mann saw the Munich premiere of *Elektra* under Felix Mottl.[67] Shortly there-after, he commented: "Strauss's so-called 'progress' is all twaddle. Everyone of them continues to feed and draw on Parsifal."[68] Mann, who had just been to Bayreuth, seemed surer than ever that Wagner's last work was "the ultimate in modernism. Nobody has ever gone beyond it."[69] In a similar vein, and echoing Nietzsche, a note for "Geist und Kunst" makes the point: "Wagner is still a burn-ingly topical issue, a problem, the problem of modernism itself—and everything that has followed, including *Elektra,* seems uninteresting by comparison."[70]

Reserved and skeptical as this sounds, it does not really prepare us for Mann's sharply negative reaction to *Der Rosenkavalier*. He again saw the Munich premiere of Strauss's latest triumph, under Mottl, on 1 February 1911. Grudgingly, he acknowledged that here, too, the opera had been a "colossal" success, and that the composer received a 15-minute ovation and a dozen curtain calls. About the work itself, he had this to say: "Four hours of dinning noise about a charming jest." He goes on to castigate the composer for stylistic incongruities in trying to combine Wagnerian music drama with Viennese operetta; for the anachronism of the famous waltzes; and for the crude orchestration which, he feels, drowns out the countless linguistic subtleties of the text. Strauss knows nothing, Mann asserts, about Wagner's great art of *not* blanketing the voice with the orchestra. "In short," the letter concludes, "I was rather irritated; in my opinion Strauss has not acted like an artist towards your work."[71] Perhaps the most intriguing aspect of this remarkable letter is that it is addressed to Hugo von Hofmannsthal, Strauss's librettist. One cannot help thinking that Mann attempted to drive a wedge between the poet and the composer. Most importantly, however, with this harsh critique of *Der Rosenkavalier,* Mann apparently wrote off Strauss; he no longer counted him among the guardians of the Wagnerian heritage. With *Der Rosenkavalier,* Strauss had deviated from the direction Mann thought Wagnerianism should go. Strauss had opted for nostalgia and mass appeal, and Mann did not approve. He was, of course, right in realizing at once that this work signaled a change of direction. It stands as a highly visible landmark of a divergence that occurs around 1910, in which, as Carl Dahlhaus described it, the older Wagnerian tradition split into two competing camps: Neoclassicism and "Neue Musik."[72]

Mann later came to view the *Rosenkavalier* more favorably and to appreciate its charms, but at the time it caused him to turn away from Strauss. *Elektra* was not so progressive as it purported to be, and *Der Rosenkavalier* was blatantly regressive. The upshot of these developments could only be this: Strauss was no longer the most interesting modern composer.

We may now begin to see why in the *Reflections of a Nonpolitical Man* Strauss was replaced, as it were, by Pfitzner, who, ironically, was the more old-fashioned and regressive of the two. It is tempting to speculate that Gustav Mahler might have been the contemporary composer to be championed by Mann. A letter to Mahler, written after the first performance of the Eighth Symphony in Munich, suggests that Mann was ready to espouse Mahler—a "man who embodies, as I believe, the most serious and sacred artistic will of our time."[73] This budding relationship was cut short, however, by Mahler's untimely death in 1911.

Strauss is mentioned only twice in Mann's *Reflections,* which in itself speaks volumes when compared to the eloquent twenty-page essay devoted to *Palestrina.*[74] It seems highly unlikely that such a shift could have been caused by aesthetic considerations alone, especially in light of the revisions of Mann's own position. Soon after his letter to Hugo von Hofmannsthal, he felt prompted to rethink the whole issue of Wagner and modernism once again. As a result of this "crisis" vis-à-vis Wagner, he began to sympathize with what he had just condemned.

In a brief essay written in Venice and published under the title "Auseinandersetzung mit Richard Wagner," Mann admits to himself: "I have the impression that Wagner's star is in the descendant in the skies of the German mind."[75] Once again, he turns to Nietzsche and calls specifically for a "new classicism." Trying to imagine the "artistic masterpiece of the 20th century," Mann avers: "I see something that differs radically—and favorably, it seems to me—from that of Wagner: something conspicuously logical, well formed and clear. . . ."[76] In light of this, one would excpect Mann to side with the composer of *Der Rosenkavalier* and the very neoclassicist *Ariadne auf Naxos,* especially since he always maintained a certain sympathy for Strauss's European and cosmopolitan orientation. All this came to naught, however, with the outbreak of war. Like Hans Castorp on the Magic Mountain, Mann was stunned by the war—as though a thunderbolt had awakened him. Groping in the dark and uncertain of his direction, Mann instinctively leaned on the position that promised the most support. He donned the role of a patriot and tried to cover his ignorance of history and of political matters by displaying a strident chauvinism. In that situation, *Palestrina* and its author appeared to him to show the greatest affinity to his own position. Mann tells in his *Reflections* how surprised and grateful he was when, in 1917, he discovered that both Pfitzner and he had independently hit upon the formula of "Sympathie mit dem Tode."[77] It seemed to indicate certain fraternal affinities, and Mann indeed speaks of their "Brüderlichkeit." But this matter is considerably more complex, for it involves the central question of the Wagnerian heritage.

Pfitzner and Mann were introduced to each other by Bruno Walter,[78] Mann's neighbor in Munich's Herzogpark and "Royal Bavarian General Musical Director." Walter was planning a week-long Pfitzner festival; its high point was to be the first performance of *Palestrina* on 12 June 1917, in the "Prinzregententheater." Mann's enthusiasm for this work was sparked by the libretto even before he heard Pfitzner's score, to which he was introduced by Bruno Walter on the piano.[79] So devoted was he to Pfitzner's opera that he attended all performances. He also wrote a glowing essay about it, which was published in the *Neue Rundschau* the same year and later incorporated into the *Reflections of a Nonpolitical Man.* Mann's essay is without a doubt the greatest tribute ever paid this opera, but it is not without its internal contradictions. In it, he speaks at length of the infinite sympathy he feels towards the character of Palestrina, especially his ethos as an artist, and he celebrates the work as the perfect expression of "the psychology and moral of all conservatism."[80] To him, it is of the utmost significance that *Palestrina* "completely lacks progressive optimism, political virtue, that is, . . . its sympathy is not for the new but for the old, not for the future but for the past, not life but—death."[81] In other words, Pfitzner's sympathies lie with German Romanticism and with Wagner.

Mann only hints at the similarities with Wagner's *Meistersinger* and *Parsifal.* They are in fact quite obvious and deliberate. To Mann, *Palestrina* was the "grave song" of romantic opera in the grand style of Wagner; he considered it "the 'capstone' of the structure of romantic opera, . . . the wistful end of a *national* artistic movement that finished gloriously with Hans Pfitzner."[82] But whose voice is speaking here? Mann's or Pfitzner's? Should we not expect that Mann's reading of *Palestrina* would reflect his insight of 1911 that Wagner's star is falling and that the "artwork" of the future will be quite un-Wagnerian? When he encountered in *Palestrina*—unexpectedly, it seems—a work that was so extremely conscious of its own Wagnerian lineage, his sympathy welled up and he defiantly declared his love for what he knew was irretrievably lost.

We do not know whether Pfitzner agreed with Mann's assessment of his relationship to Wagner, but it is hard to imagine that he did. Pfitzner admitted that the basic dramatic design of his opera was consciously modeled after *Die Meistersinger*. Both operas are about the birth of a new musical work, a mass in one case, a prize song in the other; Ighino is David, and Palestrina, both Stolzing and Sachs. Stylistically, there is a marked affinity to *Parsifal*, most obviously in the use of the bells that so impressed Mann. Originally, it seems, Pfitzner intended to write a "Bühnenweihfestspiel,"[83] as *Parsifal* is subtitled, before he settled on "Musikalische Legende," which is decidedly a more suitable description. He was, of course, aware that Wagner's vision of the artist's relationship to the people had to be revised. "The difference," Pfitzner pointed out, "is expressed most clearly in the concluding scenic pictures. At the end of *Die Meistersinger,* there is a stage full of light, rejoicing of the people, engagement, brilliance, and glory; in my work, there is, to be sure, Palestrina, who is also celebrated, but in the half-darkness of his room under the picture of the deceased one, dreaming at his organ. *Meistersinger* is the apotheosis of the new, a praise of the future and of life; in *Palestrina,* everything tends toward the past, it is dominated by sympathy with death."[84] Again, we can't help wondering whether Mann, who reports this comment of Pfitzner's, is not here imposing on Pfitzner, ever so subtly, his own diagnosis of the present state of Wagnerianism. The work itself, while rejecting the notion of artistic progress, actually established a much more affirmative perspective. If Pfitzner's Palestrina is indeed the "savior of music," as he is so emphatically characterized, then he must have some future in mind for which music needs to be saved. As much as Pfitzner tried to ward off and to stem the tide of musical progress, he had a very clear notion as to which direction future musical production should take: towards Wagner and German Romanticism. In other words, Pfitzner was convinced that there was a future for Wagnerianism; Mann, on the other hand, had bid a fond farewell to this illusion in 1911.

The Mann-Pfitzner alliance would be quite unthinkable without, and independent of, the outbreak of the war and the accompanying eruption of a most feverish nationalism. It was more an ideological and tactical alliance than the sort of fraternal bond of kindred spirits that Mann wanted, and perhaps needed, to see in it. At its core, which was its reflection on the present state of Wagnerianism, Mann's essay on *Palestrina* harbored a fundamental contradiction, one that was merely papered over in the *Reflections of a Nonpolitical Man*. In the political turmoil of the postwar period, however, the Mann-Pfitzner alliance had no chance of survival. Eventually, it was Pfitzner—forever the blunt polemicist—who terminated the relationship in 1925. That it survived that long was probably due to several gestures of loyalty on the part of Mann at a time when the two wartime allies began to drift apart.

The first of these gestures came in 1918 with Mann's "Call to establish a Hans Pfitzner Society for German Music."[85] This brief text echoes Mann's earlier tribute to Pfitzner in presenting the creator of *Palestrina* as the "most richly tradition-bound" (*überlieferungsvollster*) of living composers. Contrary to all evidence, Mann also asserts Pfitzner's popularity — or, rather, his potential for popularity. His equivocation on this point seems to be indicative of some deeper-seated doubts. They surface elsewhere, as for instance in a letter of 1918, in which Mann remarks about Pfitzner's second opera, *Die Rose vom Liebesgarten* and its libretto by James Grun: "It is a truly German misfortune that this luxurious musical dream is tied forever to this candy store of a text [*Konditorei von Text*]."[86]

The following year, Mann was the speaker at a celebration of Pfitzner's 50th birthday. His brief address takes up and completely reverses the earlier comparison of Pfitzner and Strauss in the notes for "Geist und Kunst." Although Strauss is not mentioned, there could be no doubt in anybody's mind — this being Munich — who was meant when Mann spoke of Pfitzner's competitor. The Wilhelminian era, Mann now argued, was more favorable to Strauss and to the cosmopolitan and intellectual elements of his work than it was to Pfitzner. His time was now, and yet to come. This assertion must have sounded startling to anyone remembering Mann's interpretation of *Palestrina*. The only reason that Pfitzner is now thought to be the man of the hour is his nationalism: he is said to be more familiar with the mystery of the German character than Strauss; his music is at home in the "sacred vale in which the sources of the nation's life flow."[87] Even if we make allowances for the occasion on which it was delivered, Mann's birthday tribute to Pfitzner marks a low point in his critical writing. It tries to combine what for reasons of intellectual hygiene ought to be kept separate. Citing the mighty example of Wagner (and Dostoevsky), Mann now ascribes to Pfitzner's work a combination of reactionary and revolutionary tendencies — a combination whose time was yet to come. He now extols the future potential of a work which, only two years earlier, he celebrated for its lack of belief in any future, its sympathy with death. And he declares Pfitzner's music to be most topical, modern, and alive, although he himself had recognized eight years earlier that Wagnerianism, the basis of Pfitzner's work, had no future. Mann's comments on this occasion strike one as contradictory and confusing, and as such they reflect (more accurately than he would have admitted) his own political confusion in post-Versailles Germany and revolutionary Munich.

Mann included the two texts on Pfitzner in his 1922 collection of essays, *Rede und Antwort,* and thus gave them additional currency at a time when he actually could no longer fully subscribe to his own views of 1918 and 1919. Mann's political conversion from reactionary monarchist to liberal democrat took place in 1921/22.[88] The German public first became aware of it in October 1922 when, on the occasion of Gerhart Hauptmann's 60th birthday, he called upon the German youth to accept and support the new democratic form of government. Henceforth, Mann was regarded as a traitor and a "Judas" in conservative circles, including, of course, Pfitzner and Strauss; the rightist press named him "Saulus Mann"[89] and cried "Mann Overboard." It testifies to Mann's instinctive understanding of the sinister political implications of German Wagnerianism that he soon began to add to his newfound democratic convictions earnest warnings against the nationalist cult of Wagner. He finally admitted publicly that the "popular cult" of Wagner in Germany "grows more vulgar by the day."[90] Wagner, he realized with disgust, had been made the patron saint of "a troglodytic sort of Teutonism" (*eine höhlenbärenmäßige Deutschtümelei*) while the real Wagner—the Wagner of Baudelaire and Nietzsche—was being repressed and misrepresented.[91]

In the last of his "German Letters" to the American magazine *The Dial,* written in the summer of 1925, Mann described his new dilemma most succinctly. Speaking of *Tristan und Isolde,* he admitted that this work meant something ultimate and supreme to him, something he had loved more than anything else. But in the present hour, Mann feels, the Germans should be forbidden, for reasons of conscience, to indulge in their love for the world of Wagner. The spirit of Wagner, Mann argues, is unhealthy and harmful to the "soul of Europe which, if it is to be saved to life and reason, requires some hard work and some of the self-conquest that Nietzsche had practiced in such heroic and exemplary fashion."[92] The voice speaking here is very much that of the author of *The Magic Mountain*—an author, that is, who conquered his own "sympathy with death," and who now prescribes cosmopolitanism and Nietzsche as remedies for his Wagner-sick contemporaries. What Mann urges is a new emphasis on Nietzsche's critique of Wagner and on those aspects of Wagner's work that made him not only a German but a European phenomenon.

It is impossible to imagine that Pfitzner could agree to any of this. Never much given to tactfulness, Pfitzner signaled the end of their relationship in a letter on Mann's 50th birthday. They had not seen each other for some time, but he confessed that he preferred this state of affairs, his respect and gratitude notwithstanding, to a meeting with Mann for the purpose of discussing "your public political . . . manifestations of late which have painfully alienated me from you."[93] Mann acknowledged the alienation, viewing it—generously, and not without a certain vainglory—as merely "a latter-day, journalistic acting out of the case of Nietzsche versus Wagner."[94] Just as Nietzsche's conscience made him free himself from Wagner, so he, Mann, had in the present situation to follow his own "sense of responsibility which may be sharper than that which a musician needs to feel." "We are at liberty," the letter concludes, "to fall out with one another, but we shall not be able to prevent future ages from often mentioning our names in one breath."[95] Mann's prediction turned out to be only partly true. *Palestrina* is not the only link between them. Today, their names appear to be linked more closely through the "Protest of Richard Wagner's Own City of Munich"; this association tends to overshadow their earlier close relationship.

Mann's falling out with Pfitzner did not result in any warmer feelings towards Strauss. To Mann, the creator of *Der Rosenkavalier* remained what he had judged him to be in 1911: an artist whose time had passed. Thomas Mann's fame, on the other hand, reached its zenith in Germany with the publication of *Der Zauberberg* in 1924. Theirs was a peculiarly artificial non-relationship, with both men avoiding and ignoring each other. They met on only two occasions, once in 1918 in the home of Bruno Walter,[96] and again in 1932 at a celebration of

Gerhart Hauptmann's 70th birthday.[97] The first of these encounters occurred too soon after the triumph of *Palestrina* and was, for that reason alone, not very conducive to any rapprochement. The second, because of its formal nature, did not provide a suitable forum, either. Besides, by that time, Mann and Strauss found themselves at opposite ends of the political spectrum. Even so, the encounter of Hauptmann, Strauss, and Mann at that juncture appears to be worth pondering. It brought together three of the most prestigious figures in Germany who then were at different stages of their illustrious careers, and were now heading in opposite directions, politically speaking. Hauptmann had been considered for a long time the leading literary figure, and Mann had been celebrating him as the unofficial king of the Weimar Republic. At the same time, he hardly missed an opportunity to signal to the world that he himself aspired to, and claimed, the position of preeminence and supremacy in German letters[98] — a position he had attained, in the eyes of the German public, with the publication of *The Magic Mountain* and the awarding of the Nobel Prize in 1929. Strauss, the erstwhile "king" of Wagnerians, was deposed already before the war. In December of 1932, at the Hauptmann celebration in Munich, Mann could easily be perceived, on the one hand, as the reigning prince of German letters and, on the other, as the most vigilant guardian of the Wagnerian heritage. Only two months later, however, in a stunning reversal of his fortunes, Mann was driven from that position at the top of the cultural heap into exile from Germany. Ironically, but by no means fortuitously, this fateful turn of events resulted from Mann's noble but, for the time being, unsuccessful attempt at saving Wagner from the claws of his exploiters and falsifiers. In the last analysis, this impulse to save Wagner from the Wagnerians may be regarded as the most urgent agenda Mann's great essay of 1933 sought to address.

V

Strauss never publicly acknowledged his role in the infamous Munich protest. It seems that he considered it a trifling affair. When he came to Zurich in 1934, where Mann had taken residence, he immediately inquired about him and told a mutual acquaintance, of whom he knew she would report it to the Manns, that it was a pity Mann did not want to return to Germany: he could very well live there; nobody had anything against him. Asked about the meaning of the Munich "Protest," the new President of the "Reichsmusikkammer" conceded that this had been "a somewhat hasty affair" (*eine etwas übereilte Sache*).[99] He had signed only because Siegmund von Hausegger had besieged him. Besides, Mann's otherwise brilliant essay did contain a few things that needed to be refuted. Mann recorded this episode in his diary without comment, letting the shallowness of Strauss's excuses speak for itself. It makes one wonder whom Strauss was more ignorant about — Mann, or the Nazis? On other occasions, Mann made no bones about his feelings towards Strauss. On 2 May 1934, he wrote in his diary, speaking of *Salome:* "Has not Richard Strauss, this naive product of the imperial era, become far more old-fashioned than I? As an artist, should he not be far more 'impossible' in the Third Reich than I? He is stupid and wretched enough to place his fame at its disposal, and the Reich makes stupid and wretched use of it."[100] And yet, the author of *Doctor Faustus* eventually judged Strauss more leniently than Pfitzner, sensing in the creator of *Der Rosenkavalier* a monumental case of "je-m'en-fichisme" rather than personal animosity.[101]

Pfitzner's case was quite different. He was a conscientious man of strong convictions, outspoken and articulate; and Mann once was close to him. "What people are ultimately prepared to overlook," Mann observed correctly, in "such a blithe spirit as Richard Strauss . . . they are not prepared to overlook in the artist and writer Hans Pfitzner"[102] — especially not in light of Pfitzner's defiant defense of his action. The manifesto of the Munich Wagnerians had triggered not a flood but, at least, a trickle of protest in some German papers. Mann himself was able to publish, in a Berlin paper, a restrained and politely worded reply. Its point was to state simply and clearly "that this protest proceeds from a gross misunderstanding, and that its content and tone do me a grave and bitter injustice."[103] Pfitzner's reply is rather peculiar and characteristic of his warped sense of everything bearing on Wagner and Germany.[104] Instead of addressing the issue, or responding to Mann, he complains about being unjustly attacked, and abuses his alleged attacker, Willi Schuh, the noted Swiss music critic.[105] Pfitzner was especially incensed about Schuh's charge of ingratitude to Mann; in order to show the world how things really stood between them, he published his exchange with Mann in 1925 — the two letters in which they acknowledged their estrangement. Apparently, the letters were supposed to show that Pfitzner no longer had any compelling reason to be grateful to Mann. They also were meant to document that among men and fellow artists disagreements, even about Wagner, could be discussed respectfully. What Pfitzner would not tolerate, however, was the fact that Mann had carried his controversial views on Wagner abroad to present them to uninitiated foreigners who were bound to misunderstand him, and take it as a slur not only on Wagner but on Germany. It is revealing and depressing to see that with this line of argument Pfitzner echoes rather exactly the official Nazi view of the matter in the *Völkischer Beobachter*. Pfitzner's and the Nazis' position with respect to Wagner here reveal their essential congruence.

Mann prepared a lengthy response[106] in which he pointed out the inadequacy of Pfitzner's article, the self-serving silliness of his arguments, and the chauvinist condescension towards non-German admirers of Wagner, whom Mann calls more sophisticated and tolerant than their German counterparts. Above all, he attempted to open Pfitzner's and the German public's eyes to what was so painfully obvious to him: the Munich "Protest" was no mere disagreement about some esoteric matter, but a "lethal act of denunciation"; under the present conditions in Germany, it meant his "national excommunication."[107] It meant above all that, with regard to Wagner, Mann was no longer to have a voice in Germany; his views on Wagner were in effect banned. Mann's article in response to Pfitzner was intended for the *Neue Rundschau,* formerly Mann's favorite publication outlet. But in the summer of 1933, its publishers felt it was no longer safe to publish a defense by their most important author. Pfitzner and the Munich Wagnerians carried the day.

For the next twelve years, at least in Germany, Wagner's work was bathed and soaked in Nazi ideology—an onus it has been struggling to shed ever since. Today, with critical interest in Wagner again growing, the Pfitzners, Hauseggers, and Knappertsbuschs have relinquished what they had appropriated with such arrogance and narrow-mindedness. Occasionally, however, their brand of Wagnerianism still rears its head, as for instance in 1976, when the Bayreuth centennial *Ring* production by Patrice Chereau was denounced. But such voices ring hollow today and find hardly an echo.

The approach to Wagner which today commands interest and intellectual respect is the sophisticated reading of Wagner, cleansed of its nationalist and provincial odors, that Mann fought for so eloquently. It is a cosmopolitan Wagner, not enshrined in any particular cult or ideology, but open to, and eagerly inviting, analytical inquiry. The question of Wagner's Germanness, his roots in German Romanticism, and his knotted entanglement with German history still remains an issue. It is an issue that may best be explored along the lines suggested by Mann in 1933: "Wagner's art is the most sensational self-portrayal and self-critique of the German character that could possibly be imagined; as such it is calculated to make German culture interesting even to the most doltish foreigner, and a passionate preoccupation with that selfsame Germanness which it glorifies in a manner both critical and decorative. Therein lies its nationalism, but that nationalism is steeped in a European artistry to a degree that renders it profoundly unsusceptible to any simplification."[108]

Notes

1 See David C. Large and William Weber (eds.), *Wagnerism in European Culture and Politics* (Ithaca/London, 1984). Cf. also Dieter Borchmeyer, *Das Theater Richard Wagners: Idee—Dichtung—Wirkung* (Stuttgart, 1982), 303–62; Ulrich Müller (ed.), *Richard Wagner 1883–1983: Die Rezeption im 19. und 20. Jahrhundert. Gesammelte Beiträge des Salzburger Symposiums* (Stuttgart, 1984); Leroy R. Shaw et al. (eds.), *Wagner in Retrospect: A Centennial Reappraisal* (Amsterdam, 1987); and, especially, the section of "Wagner und die Folgen," in Ulrich Müller and Peter Wapnewski (eds.), *Richard-Wagner-Handbuch* (Stuttgart, 1986), 609–830.
2 Friedrich Nietzsche, *The Birth of Tragedy* [and] *The Case of Wagner,* trans. with commentary by Walter Kaufmann (New York, 1967), 156.
3 Cf. Erwin Koppen, *Dekadenter Wagnerismus: Studien zur europäischen Literatur des Fin de Siècle* (Berlin/New York, 1973); and Raymond Furness, *Wagner and Literature* (New York, 1982).
4 On Strauss, cf. especially George R. Marek, *Richard Strauss: The Life of a Non-Hero* (New York, 1968); Norman Del Mar, *Richard Strauss: A Critical Commentary on His Life and Works,* 2d ed. (Ithaca/London, 1986). See also Walter Thomas, *Richard Strauss und seine Zeitgenossen* (Munich, 1964); and Theodor W. Adorno, "Richard Strauss," *Neue Rundschau* 75 (1964): 557–87.

5 See Karl Schumann, *Das kleine Richard Strauss-Buch* 2d ed. (Reinbek, 1981), 22.
6 See *Cosima Wagner–Richard Strauss: Ein Briefwechsel,* ed. Franz Trenner (Tutzing, 1978).
7 Ibid., 11, 13.
8 Ibid., ix.
9 Anna A. Abert, "Richard Strauss und das Erbe Wagners," *Die Musikforschung* 27 (1974): 165–70.
10 See note 63 below.
11 On Pfitzner, cf. Johann Vogel, *Hans Pfitzner in Selbstzeugnissen und Bilddokumenten* (Reinbek, 1989), hereafter cited as Vogel; Joseph Müller-Blattau, *Hans Pfitzner: Lebensweg und Schaffensernte* (Frankfurt, 1969); Bernhard Adamy, *Hans Pfitzner: Literatur, Philosophie und Zeitgeschehen in seinem Weltbild und Werk* (Tutzing, 1980), hereafter cited as B. Adamy; and Ulrik Skouenborg, *Von Wagner zu Pfitzner: Stoff und Form der Musik* (Tutzing, 1983). See also the chapter "Post-Wagnerian Opera," in Carl Dahlhaus, *Nineteenth-Century Music,* trans. J. Bradford Robinson (Berkeley/Los Angeles, 1989), 339–51. On the relationship of Strauss and Pfitzner, see especially Thomas, *Richard Strauss,* 192–221.
12 Cf. Richard Hamann and Jost Hermand, *Stilkunst um 1900* (Berlin, 1967), 491.
13 See the preface to Hans Pfitzner, *Vom musikalischen Drama: Gesammelte Aufsätze* (Munich/Leipzig, 1917), 7.
14 See note 13.
15 Cf. Dahlhaus, 5, 341f.
16 Rudolf Louis, *Die deutsche Musik der Gegenwart* (1909), as quoted by Hamann and Hermand, 129.
17 Hans Pfitzner, *Futuristengefahr* (Munich/Leipzig, 1917).
18 Hans Pfitzner, *Die neue Ästhetik der musikalischen Impotenz, ein Verfallssymptom?* (Munich, 1920).
19 Referring specifically to Strauss, he remarked: "Nun, ich bin der jüngere; ich habe persönlich lange 'die Nummer 2' der öffentlichen Rangliste ertragen müssen. . . ." Quoted by Vogel, 49.
20 Dahlhaus, 341.
21 Cf. Mann's letter to B. Fucik, 15 April 1932, in *Letters of Thomas Mann 1889–1955,* selected and trans. from the German by Richard and Clara Winston (New York, 1971), 186: ". . . I see the novel as a kind of symphony–a tissue of ideas and a musical construction. In these terms *The Magic Mountain* is probably more like a musical score than any of my other books" (henceforth cited as *Letters*).
22 See his 1904 essay "Der französische Einfluß," *Gesammelte Werke* (Frankfurt, 1974) 10:837–39 (henceforth cited as *GW*).
23 Thomas Mann, *Pro and Contra Wagner,* trans. Allan Blunden, with an introduction by Erich Heller (Chicago, 1985), 203 (henceforth cited as *Pro and Contra Wagner*).
24 Cf. my "Thomas Mann and James Joyce: Zur Frage des Modernismus in *Doktor Faustus*," *Thomas Mann Jahrbuch* 2 (1989): 121–50.
25 Letter to Bruno Walter, 24 June 1917, in *Letters,* 86.
26 Letter to Ernst Bertram, 4 June 1920, in *Pro and Contra Wanger,* 67.
27 *GW* 6:599.
28 Hans Pfitzner, *Palestrina: Musikalische Legende in drei Akten* (Mainz/London/New York, 1951), 19.
29 Ibid., 3.
30 Arthur Schopenhauer, *Parerga und Paralipomena,* Paragraph 52; cf. Bernhard Adamy, "Das Palestrina-Textbuch als Dichtung," in *Symposium Hans Pfitzner, Berlin 1981,* ed. Wolfgang Osthoff (Tutzing, 1984), 21–65.
31 *Pro and Contra Wagner,* 63.
32 See especially "Gedanken im Kriege," *GW* 13:527–45; this essay has never been translated into English.
33 Cf. *Richard Strauss and Romain Rolland: Correspondence. Together with fragments from the 'Diary' of Romain Rolland and other essays . . . ,* intro. Gustave Samazenilk (London, 1968), xiif.
34 Hans Pfitzner, *Eindrücke und Bilder meines Lebens* (Hamburg-Bergedorf, 1948), 64.
35 See, for instance, the section "Männerfreundschaft," the subject of which is Pfitzner's friendship with his boyhood companion and benefactor, the publisher and editor Paul Nicolaus Cossmann, who died in Theresienstadt, ibid., 63–71. On Pfitzner's anti-Semitism, cf. Vogel, 81, and the section entitled "Judentum" in Adamy, 304–11.

36 Cf. Adamy, 300f.
37 For a succinct summary, see Fred K. Prieberg, *Musik im NS-Staat* (Frankfurt, 1982), 215–25.
38 Cf. Adamy, 322–29.
39 See Vogel, 111.
40 On Strauss's role in the Third Reich, cf. Marek, *Richard Strauss,* 270–88; Prieberg, *Musik im NS-Staat* 203–15; and especially the new, comprehensive study of Strauss's activities in his post as President of the Reichsmusikkammer, Gerhard Splitt's *Richard Strauss 1933–1935: Ästhetik und Musikpolitik zu Beginn der nationalsozialistischen Herrschaft* (Pfaffenweiler, 1987), henceforth Splitt.
41 Cf. Splitt, 42–59.
42 Cf. ibid., 59–64.
43 The text of this letter is reprinted in Splitt, 219.
44 The letter is reprinted in Marek, *Richard Strauss,* 283, and Splitt, 221.
45 Cf. Splitt, 216.
46 *GW* 13:744.
47 The text of the "Protest" is reprinted in *Pro and Contra Wagner,* 149–151. Cf. Wesley V. Blomster, "Thomas Mann and the Munich Manifesto," *German Life and Letters* 22 (1969): 134–46; Jürgen Kolbe, *Heller Zauber: Thomas Mann in München 1894–1933* (Berlin, 1987), 402–05.
48 *Pro and Contra Wagner,* 91–148.
49 Mann suspected Knappertsbusch to have initiated the action; see *Pro and Contra Wagner,* 159.
50 This seems to be the conclusion of Dieter Borchmeyer, "Thomas Mann und der 'Protest der Richard-Wagner-Stadt München' im Jahre 1933: Eine Dokumentation," *Jahrbuch der Bayerischen Staatsoper* (Munich, 1983), 51–103.
51 Pfitzner must definitely be regarded as one of the decisive figures behind the "Protest," since he – according to a letter published in Adamy (254) – took out a sentence and approved the language of the manifesto.
52 One cannot overlook a certain similarity between the Munich protest of 1933 and Pfitzner's vicious attack, in *Die neue Ästhetik der musikalischen Impotenz* (1920), on Paul Bekker, the distinguished musicologist, for allegedly disparaging remarks about Beethoven's genius in his book *Die Sinfonie von Beethoven bis Mahler* (1920).
   The new evidence is contained in an unpublished letter of 3 April 1933, in which Knappertsbusch asks 42 like-minded Munich personalities to join him in protesting Mann's characterizations of Wagner; they all did. There can be no doubt that this letter (Bayrisches Hauptstaatsarchiv, Akte Staatstheater, Nr. 2014) represents the proverbial smoking gun.
53 Thomas Mann, *Diaries 1918–1939.* Selection and Foreword by Hermann Kesten, trans. Richard and Clara Winston (New York, 1982), 151; henceforth referred to as *Diaries.*
54 See Kolbe, *Heller Zauber,* 407–26, "Die Austreibung."
55 Letter to Walter von Molo, 7 September 1945; *Letters,* 479.
56 For the complete text of the brief article in the *Völkischer Beobachter,* see Peter de Mendelssohn, "Das Jahr Dreiunddreißig," *Neue Rundschau* 86 (1975): 212.
57 Cf. James Northcote-Bade, *Die Wagner-Mythen im Frühwerk Thomas Manns* (Bonn, 1975), 53–70; Hans Rudolf Vaget, *Thomas Mann Kommentar zu sämtlichen Erzählungen* (Munich, 1984) 155–69.
58 Cf. my "'Sang réservé' in Deutschland: Zur Rezeption von Thomas Manns 'Wälsungenblut'," *German Quarterly* 62 (1984): 367–76.
59 See Thomas Mann, *Aufsätze, Reden, Essays,* ed. and with notes by Harry Matter (Berlin/Weimar, 1983), 378f.
60 See Katia Mann, *Meine ungeschriebenen Memoiren,* ed. Elisabeth von Plessen (Frankfurt, 1976), 101.
61 Letter to Heinrich Mann, 17 January 1906; *Thomas Mann, Heinrich Mann: Briefwechsel 1900–1949,* ed. Hans Wysling (new expanded edition: Frankfurt, 1984), 69.
62 Thomas Mann, *Doctor Faustus,* trans. Helen T. Lowe-Porter (New York, 1971), 156.
63 See T. J. Reed, " 'Geist und Kunst': Thomas Mann's Abandoned Essay on Literature," *Oxford German Studies* 1 (1966): 53–101; Hans Wysling, " 'Geist und Kunst': Thomas Manns Notizen zu einem 'Literatur-Essay'," in Paul Scherrer/Hans Wysling, *Quellenkritische Studien zum Werk Thomas Manns* (Bern/Munich, 1967), 123–233, esp. 166; henceforth referred to as "Geist und Kunst."

64 First published in *Süddeutsche Monatshefte* 5 (1908): 1–11; repr. in Pfitzner, *Vom musikalischen Drama.*

65 See "Geist und Kunst," nos. 24 and 53, pp. 166, 178 respectively.

66 Ibid., no. 94, pp. 200f.

67 Letter to Hugo von Hofmannsthal, 23 December 1908; Thomas Mann, *Briefwechsel mit Autoren,* ed. Hans Wysling (Frankfurt 1988), 198; henceforth referred to as *Briefwechsel mit Autoren.*

68 Letter to Walter Opitz, 26 August 1908; *Pro and Contra Wagner,* 45.

69 Ibid.

70 "Geist und Kunst," no. 53, pp. 178; also in *Pro and Contra Wagner,* 41.

71 Letter to Hugo von Hofmannsthal, 5 February 1911; *Briefwechsel mit Autoren,* 202f. (my trans.)

72 Dahlhaus, *Nineteenth-Century Music,* 336.

73 Letter to Gustav Mahler, September 1910; Thomas Mann, *Briefe 1889–1936,* ed. Erika Mann (Frankfurt, 1961), 88 (my trans.).

74 Thomas Mann, *Reflections of a Nonpolitical Man,* trans. and intro. Walter D. Morris (New York, 1982), 297–314; henceforth cited as *Reflections.*

75 *Pro and Contra Wagner,* 47.

76 Ibid., 311f.

77 *Reflections,* 311f.

78 Cf. Adamy, 228f.

79 See Bruno Walter, *Theme and Variations: An Autobiography,* trans. James A. Galston (New York, 1946), 210ff.

80 *Reflections,* 306.

81 Ibid., 310.

82 Ibid., 312.

83 See Vogel, 66,

84 *Reflections,* 311.

85 "Aufruf zur Gründung des Hans Pfitzner-Vereins für deutsche Tonkunst," *GW* 11: 744–45.

86 Letter to Ida Boy-Ed, 19 March 1918; Thomas Mann, *Briefe an Otto Grautoff 1894–1901 und Ida Boy-Ed 1903–1928,* ed. Peter de Mendelssohn (Frankfurt, 1975), 191.

87 Ibid., 421 (my trans.)

88 Cf. T. J. Reed, *Thomas Mann: The Uses of Tradition* (Oxford, 1974), 275–316, and especially Herbert Lehnert and Eva Wessel, *Nihilismus der Menschenfreundlichkeit: Thomas Manns "Wandlung" und sein Essay "Goethe und Tolstoi"* (Frankfurt, 1991), passim.

89 See Vaget, *Thomas Mann Kommentar,* 164.

90 Letter to Joseph Ponten, 21 January 1925; *Pro and Contra Wagner,* 78.

91 "Kosmopolitismus," *GW* 10: 184–91; cf. *Pro and Contra Wagner,* 81.

92 "German Letter VI," *GW* 13: 307–15 (*The Dial,* October 1925); cf. *Pro and Contra Wagner,* 80 (my trans.).

93 Letter to T. Mann, 18 June 1925; Adamy, 245f. (my trans.).

94 Letter to H. Pfitzner, 24 June 1925; *Pro and Contra Wagner,* 79; *Letters,* 145.

95 Ibid., 145f.

96 Letter to Ida Boy-Ed, 21 January 1918; Mann, *Briefe.*

97 In an unpublished letter to Mann, written in June of 1945 but never sent, Strauss reminded Mann of their last and friendly encounter before 1933, on the occasion of Hauptmann's 70th birthday. Permission to quote from this letter, which is extant in the Strauss archive, has been withheld. Cf. Richard Strauss, *Briefwechsel mit Willi Schuh,* ed. W. Schuh (Zurich, 1969), 80. Cf. also Thomas, *Richard Strauss,* 283.

98 Cf. Peter von Matt, "Zur Psychologie des deutschen Nationalschriftstellers: Zur paradigmatischen Bedeutung der Hinrichtung und Verklärung Goethes durch Thomas Mann," in *Perspektiven psychoanalytischer Literaturkritik,* ed. S. Goeppert (Freiburg, 1978), 82–100.

99 Thomas Mann, *Tagebücher 1933–1934,* ed. Peter de Mendelssohn (Frankfurt, 1977), 422 (19 May 1934).

100 *Diaries,* 209.

101 "Deutsche Hörer," 12 December 1945; *GW* 13:744.

102 "Reply to Hans Pfitzner," *Pro and Contra Wagner,* 159.

103 "Reply to the 'Protest from Richard Wagner's Own City of Munich'," *Pro and Contra Wagner,* 153.

104 "Zur Kundgebung gegen die Wagner-Rede Thomas Manns," *Frankfurter Zeitung,* 2 July 1933; repr. in Borchmeyer, "Thomas Mann," 84–86.

105 See Willi Schuh, "Thomas Mann, Richard Wagner und die Münchner Gralshüter," *Neue Zürcher Zeitung,* 21 April 1933; repr. in Borchmeyer, "Thomas Mann," 74–76.

106 "Reply to Hans Pfitzner," *Pro and Contra Wagner,* 154–67.

107 Ibid., 166.

108 "The Sorrows and Grandeur of Richard Wagner," *Pro and Contra Wagner,* 145.

Monatshefte Occasional Volumes

Series Editor
Reinhold Grimm
(University of California, Riverside)

Walter F. W. Lohnes and Valters Nollendorfs, editors
German Studies in the United States: Assessment and Outlook

Reinhold Grimm, Peter Spycher, and Richard A. Zipser, editors
From Dada and Kafka to Brecht and Beyond

Volker Dürr, Kathy Harms, and Peter Hayes, editors
Imperial Germany

Reinhold Grimm and Jost Hermand, editors
Blacks and German Culture

Reinhold Grimm and Jost Hermand, editors
Our Faust? *Roots and Ramifications of a Modern German Myth*

Volker Dürr, Reinhold Grimm, and Kathy Harms, editors
Nietzsche: Literature and Values

David P. Benseler, Walter F. W. Lohnes, and Valters Nollendorfs, editors
Teaching German in America: Prolegomena to a History

Reinhold Grimm and Jost Hermand, editors
From Ode to Anthem: Problems of Lyric Poetry

Reinhold Grimm and Jost Hermand, editors
From the Greeks to the Greens: Images of the Simple Life

Kathy Harms, Lutz R. Reuter, and Volker Dürr, editors
Coping with the Past: Germany and Austria After 1945

Reinhold Grimm and Jost Hermand, editors
Laughter Unlimited: Essays on Humor, Satire, and the Comic

Reinhold Grimm and Jost Hermand, editors
1914/1939: German Reflections of the Two World Wars

Reinhold Grimm and Jost Hermand, editors
Re-Reading Wagner